A
Disturbance
in the Field

D1664971

RELATIONAL PERSPECTIVES BOOK SERIES

Volume 46

RELATIONAL PERSPECTIVES BOOK SERIES

LEWIS ARON & ADRIENNE HARRIS
Series Editors

The Relational Perspectives Book Series (RPBS) publishes books that grow out of or contribute to the relational tradition in contemporary psychoanalysis. The term "relational psychoanalysis" was first used by Greenberg and Mitchell (1983) to bridge the traditions of interpersonal relations, as developed within interpersonal psychoanalysis and object relations, as developed within contemporary British theory. But, under the seminal work of the late Stephen Mitchell, the term "relational psychoanalysis" grew and began to accrue to itself many other influences and developments. Various tributaries—interpersonal psychoanalysis, object relations theory, self psychology, empirical infancy research, and elements of contemporary Freudian and Kleinian thought—flow into this tradition, which understands relational configurations between self and others, both real and fantasied, as the primary subject of psychoanalytic investigation.

We refer to the relational tradition, rather than to a relational school, to highlight that we are identifying a trend, a tendency within contemporary psychoanalysis, not a more formally organized or coherent school or system of beliefs. Our use of the term "relational" signifies a dimension of theory and practice that has become salient across the wide spectrum of contemporary psychoanalysis. Now under the editorial supervision of Lewis Aron and Adrienne Harris, the Relational Perspectives Book Series originated in 1990 under the editorial eye of the late Stephen A. Mitchell. Mitchell was the most prolific and influential of the originators of the relational tradition. He was committed to dialogue among psychoanalysts and he abhorred the authoritarianism that dictated adherence to a rigid set of beliefs or technical restrictions. He championed open discussion, comparative and integrative approaches, and he promoted new voices across the generations.

Included in the Relational Perspectives Book Series are authors and works that come from within the relational tradition, extend and develop the tradition, as well as works that critique relational approaches or compare and contrast them with alternative points of view. The series includes our most distinguished senior psychoanalysts along with younger contributors who bring fresh vision.

RELATIONAL PERSPECTIVES BOOK SERIES
LEWIS ARON & ADRIENNE HARRIS
Series Editors

RELATIONAL PERSPECTIVES BOOK SERIES

LEWIS ARON & ADRIENNE HARRIS
Series Editors

A Disturbance in the Field

Essays in
Transference-Countertransference
Engagement

STEVEN H. COOPER

Routledge
Taylor & Francis Group
New York   London

Routledge
Taylor & Francis Group
270 Madison Avenue
New York, NY 10016

Routledge
Taylor & Francis Group
27 Church Road
Hove, East Sussex BN3 2FA

© 2010 by Taylor and Francis Group, LLC
Routledge is an imprint of Taylor & Francis Group, an Informa business

Printed in the United States of America on acid-free paper
10 9 8 7 6 5 4 3 2 1

International Standard Book Number: 978-0-415-80628-2 (Hardback) 978-0-415-80629-9 (Paperback)

Library of Congress Cataloging-in-Publication Data

Cooper, Steven H., 1951-
 A disturbance in the field : essays in transference-countertransference engagement / Steven H. Cooper.
  p. cm. -- (Relational perspectives book series ; v. 46)
 Includes bibliographical references and index.
 ISBN 978-0-415-80628-2 (hardcover) -- ISBN 978-0-415-80629-9 (pbk.) -- ISBN 978-0-203-87178-2 (e-book)
 1. Transference (Psychology) 2. Psychoanalysis. I. Title.

 RC489.T73C66 2010
 616.89'17--dc22   2009052611

Visit the Taylor & Francis Web site at
http://www.taylorandfrancis.com

and the Routledge Web site at
http://www.routledgementalhealth.com

To Jennifer Ellwood and Ruth Eleanor Mayer

Contents

Acknowledgments

Adrienne Harris encouraged me to write this book. As I went along, she critiqued it and helped me to shape my ideas. I appreciate her friendship and generosity of spirit in helping me to find out more about how I currently think about psychoanalysis. She was an exceptional editor in somehow managing to be both direct and light of hand.

Kristopher Spring, my assistant editor from Taylor & Francis, provided a sense of possibility and encouragement about the project from the beginning. I have appreciated his responsiveness and flexibility during the writing process. He was a thoughtful collaborator in every sense.

For the last 4 years, I have had the opportunity to serve as one of the joint chief editors of *Psychoanalytic Dialogues* with Anthony Bass and Stephen Seligman and for the first year and a half with Neil Altman and Jody Messler Davies. Tony, Stephen and Hazel Ipp, the executive editor, and I have spent many hours together discussing psychoanalytic papers and psychoanalytic publishing. *Psychoanalytic Dialogues* has been an important clinical and intellectual community for me for many years, and I appreciate my colleagues who serve on the editorial board of the journal. They all give a great deal of their time to the journal. For me, it has been a challenging and rewarding labor of love. Anthony Bass and Stephen Seligman generously read and helped me develop my ideas for two of the chapters of this book, and I appreciate their input.

My friend and colleague James Frosch read and critiqued two of the chapters in this book and, as has always been his way, gave generously of his time. Henry Smith carefully read and critiqued Chapters 3 and 4 in various stages. His input was invaluable in helping me clarify my thoughts.

Over the last 4 years, I have resumed teaching at the Cambridge Health Alliance (The Cambridge Hospital) at the Harvard Medical School after having taught there from 1980 to 1990. Kimberlyn Leary gives tirelessly of herself to promote the psychodynamic training of young psychologists at the hospital. With her support, I am honored to be able to teach psychology interns and residents. Over the last 30 years at both Cambridge Hospital and Beth Israel Hospital teaching has nourished my thinking about psychoanalysis. These students at the hospital, the Boston Psychoanalytic Institute and Society, and at the Massachusetts Institute for Psychoanalysis have taught me a great deal.

I have been extraordinarily fortunate to be asked by my patients to try to help them. I have had and continue to have much to learn.

This book is dedicated to my wife Jennifer Ellwood and my mother Ruth Eleanor Mayer. Jennifer's read of me, her support, her playfulness, and her depth of friendship I treasure. She adorns the cover of this book.

Chapter 1

Introduction
The romance and melancholia of loving psychoanalysis

The title of this book, *A Disturbance in the Field*, evokes for me the breadth of experience for patient and analyst in relation to transition, disruption, repair, and growth.

This is a book about transitions in clinical work. Some of the transitions are subtle, such as when a patient is able to usefully open new parts of himself in both an old and a new context. Other types of transition relate to points of impasse. Often, the transitions described relate to periods when either or both patient and analyst begin to look at a constellation of experiences or even what are traditionally termed symptoms in a different way. Needs begin to be seen as demands; self-criticism begins to be seen as related to unrealistic or perhaps even grandiose fantasies about the self; patient or analyst begins to see the ways that the analysis itself has been assaulted by unconsciously destructive trends.

I hope that I have been able to paint some pictures of the kind of atmosphere that exists between patient and analyst in relation to these moments of transition. Moreover, I try to talk about the analyst's imagination as he tries to grasp these transitions and to help the patient to expand his imaginative capacity in integrating the meaning of transition. Despite my strong interest in the mind of the analyst and countertransference as a clinical tool, I do not want to overly valorize the countertransference. In recent years I believe that we run the risk of emphasizing too much the place of the analyst's subjectivity in clinical work.

The "field" that I aim to illuminate is an intrapsychic and interpersonal field. I am deeply interested in unconscious conflict, unconscious fantasy, and the interpersonal process in analytic work. I cannot decide that one of these surfaces is more important than another. The analyst tries to hold these dimensions of field in his or her imagination and to make it knowable to the patient just as the patient tries to do so for the analyst.

At this point in the history of psychoanalysis, our thinking, our clinical work, and our journals are filled with the interpenetration of models. The insights offered by one analyst are used and incorporated into the vision of another. It has taken us a while, but fortunately we have been able to begin to grow beyond a kind of institutionalized splitting.

This collection of essays reflects my version of the intrapsychic and interpersonal field. I hope that it captures a sense of how I am learning from my patients and learning about psychoanalysis.

In each chapter, I try to demonstrate my use of these various models since I am incapable of stepping back and in strictly theoretical terms to describe how I have done so. I hope that I demonstrate how the concepts of defense, conflict, state shifts, and compromise formation are essential to understanding people and how, for me, it is impossible to utilize these concepts without a two-person model.

I also try to show how we have stretched psychoanalytic concepts such as transference, countertransference, enactment, and projective identification to a kind of limit. I have no solutions to this problem in this book. I think that this book constitutes my personal stretching of these terms to their limit and my limit. What I continue to feel after 30 years of being a psychoanalyst is that there are two major frontiers that are equally important in understanding analytic process: One is unconscious conflict and fantasy, and the other is interpersonal experience and interaction. I offer this collection of essays as my best effort to illustrate how I integrate the two frontiers in my clinical work and my thinking about theory.

Our language and concepts are indeed too limited. They continually strain under the burdens of categorization and dichotomy. Terms such as negative and positive transference, negative and positive countertransference, good and bad objects, and new and old objects are as limited as the dichotomies intrinsic to drive theory, such as libidinal and aggressive. If there is anything one learns from doing analysis it is that all experience is varied and layered and holds the complexity of many things at once. Our language in psychoanalysis is still primitive and undeveloped. I wish that I could say that I have redressed this problem in this book. What I have done is try to get at and, no doubt, enact some of what Balint (1968) referred to as the "poverty of interpretation."

It is after all rather startling that we have one word for "I" or one word for "self" despite the many meanings that these concepts entail. This speaks to the nature of our ancient and impoverished language for getting at these experiences. I suspect that future generations of analysts, particularly generations who do not grow up on the language of dichotomies, will be productive in generating new ways of thinking about analytic process.

Yet, the problems are complicated partly by the fact that we come by dichotomies quite honestly. While gender and identity are multifaceted, there are some elements of dichotomy that are probably influenced by our anatomical dichotomies. We are also either dead or alive, awake or asleep, hungry or satiated, sexually gratified or frustrated, safe or dangerous no matter how much we claim that these experiences or "facts" exist on a continuum.

In the remainder of this introduction, I would like to talk about some less-emphasized aspects of theory since theory frames and holds our language. I want to discuss less the many differences in the content of theory but rather how we each hold our theory. Perhaps this discussion will serve as a backdrop for the largely clinical chapters that follow. First, however, a note on some elements of my overarching approach to clinical work follows.

It may be useful to briefly mention some crossroads, a few intersections where theory relates to clinical work before exploring the ways that the analyst holds his theory. I want to mention briefly the limitation of the two theories that I find most useful and how other theories may help with these limitations. I value most the contributions of relational theory and contemporary Kleinian approaches, and there are also concerns that I hold toward each.

The risks and perils accompanying analysts who term themselves relational is always the valorization of the analyst's subjectivity to the exclusion of a focus on the patient's subjective experience. Any well disciplined, well trained, and seasoned analyst of this stripe would object to this concern by saying that we cannot know the patient's experience except by attuning ourselves to and honoring the analyst's subjectivity. I agree. Yet it is far too easy to dismiss the problems and hazards in this approach with this statement, just as there are considerable hazards in all approaches to psychoanalysis.

A cartoon that I came across fifteen years ago captured the essence of the problem. A man is dressed in work clothes and is speaking into the phone. The caption reads: "Enough about me, you're the one who called 911". The hazard of valorizing the analyst's subjectivity is remedied by a dedication to the principle that I hold as invaluable—that analysts must devote themselves to thinking about their participation. This self-reflective process about why the analyst is feeling what he is feeling, why he is thinking or not thinking about his patient in particular ways is a way of maintaining a constant check on this hazard. I find invaluable the notion of always considering how I am being recruited to be a particular kind of object by the patient, a mode of disciplined listening that I have learned more about by reading the work of Joseph, Feldman, Steiner, and Britton as well as the work of Mitchell, Bromberg, and Davies. In my view this ability to think about recruitment is the strength, and it is a considerable one, of the contemporary Kleinian and Independent School contributions to psychoanalysis. Self–psychology always provides a useful lens on the matter of how the analyst's use of his own subjective responses may repeat earlier forms of parental neglect or empathic failure toward the patient. Ego psychology provides a way of thinking about the patient's shifts from affect and idea that the analyst can't be aware of if he is too focused on his own subjective reactions, no matter how much they are also informative.

But it is in thinking about the patient's recruitment of us as objects and our responsiveness to the patient; the patient's internalization of our experiences and our internalized object representations; the back and forth of this communication between internalized object worlds and interpersonal interaction; the interplay of unconscious fantasy and "reality" that I find both relational and Kleinian worlds indispensable to my work.

Relational Theory is a kind of meta-theory, an assemblage of overarching principles to approach clinical work. It does not provide a theory of technique that can be entirely separated from elements of other approaches. Instead it provides a set of working guidelines: it values disciplined listening but not necessarily a set of prescribed techniques; it considers constantly the analyst's self-reflective participation (e.g. Mitchell, 1997); it values the dialectic between ritual and spontaneity (Hoffman, 1998), old and new objects (Cooper and Levit, 1998), nuances of interplay of patient experience and analyst's modes of relating within interpretive positions (Benjamim, 2004); and it focuses on the ubiquity of enactment. It is why I think that relational thinking has been to varying degrees integrated and incorporated into all theoretical orientations.

The risks and perils of Kleininan theory are those that relate to the analyst's vulnerability to minimize his own participation in enactment and the impact that his participation has on his patient. I find invaluable the Kleinian consideration that the analyst is complicit in the various ways in which he is being recruited by the patient's internalized object world (e.g. Sandler, 1974; Feldman, 1997). But there is not enough consideration of how the patient is receiving the analyst's participation and the ways in which enactment is constant (e.g. Mitchell, 1997; Cooper, 2008; Smith, 2000; 2008), not intermittent. The Kleinians are correct to have concerns that various elements of analyst-disclosure (ie. disclosure used to make interpretations) may enact collapses of therapeutic space or even violate boundaries in repetitive self and object patterns developed earlier in the patient's life. So too, I agree with Caper (1997) that the analyst must have a mind of his own. But I believe that relational perspective might be very useful to Kleinian analysts in helping them to understand better a subject matter of great interest to them: the patient's access to the analyst's mind. In my view the patient's internalized object relations and unconscious fantasy itself is always being influenced by the interaction with the analyst (e.g. Bonovitz, 2004; Chapter 5 in this book). Elements of relational theory provide ways of understanding a dialogic structure that can help the patient to have access and make use of the analyst's mind, his formulations and experience (e.g. Benjamin, 2004; Davies, 2005).

HOW DO WE HOLD OUR THEORY?

I think that how the analyst holds his or her particular theory is at least as important as the analyst's choice of theory. I have a strong bias toward not letting our love of analysis or love of a particular theory become a "usurping self" (Coleridge, 1834) in the form of fixed ideas about how things are supposed to unfold in analysis. Love involves surrender and a willingness to give up or reconfigure parts of self in the service of an ideal, such as getting closer to another, protecting another, or honoring another. In analysis, surrender is related to the goal of helping someone understand himself more fully. The valorization of a theory or an idea about how analytic work is supposed to go, in contrast to surrender, involves the obliteration of another person or of self, a usurping self. The theory is a success, but the patient dies.

Even more important, I think what helps people in psychoanalysis in large degrees is the experience of knowing oneself and learning about oneself in the presence of another self. If the analyst is absorbed by his or her method and theory, too much in love with those objects, as it were, then the analyst will not have enough left over to engage with and learn from the patient. One chapter in this volume is devoted to the analyst's countertransference to the method of psychoanalysis.

I am interested in how the analyst holds a romantic or melancholic embrace of his or her favored theory. Is the romantic version burdened by idealizations? Is the melancholic version burdened by nihilism? Is the analyst capable of holding a breadth of attitudes toward his or her theory—openness to change or a capacity to stand by this theory in difficult times?

Our relationship to theory is a particular kind of object relation. Some analysts are more monogamous with regard to their theory, while some love many. Some are more devout, while others are more "flexible" in their practice. We have particular responsibilities in relation to what theory we choose and how we practice with that theory.

I suggest two broad categories to distinguish the analyst's relation to theory: the romantic and the melancholic. I do not use the distinction between romantic and melancholic to refer to the content of different psychoanalytic theories. For example, Strenger (1989) beautifully distinguished between romantic and classic aspects of different psychoanalytic theories. Kohut (1969) discussed varying ideological traditions implicit in Freudian theory as "guilty man," while self-psychology was characterized as "tragic man." Many authors, including Hoffman (1998) and Mitchell (1993), have addressed whether there are romantic versus tragic visions of human psychology emphasized in theories such as those proposed by Freud, Ferenczi, Balint, Guntrip, Loewald, and Kohut. But, my focus is much more on the analyst's relationship to his or her own theory, not the romantic or melancholic content of the theory itself.

The romantic version of an analyst's relationship to theory emphasizes how much the theory is helpful to the analyst in his or her understanding of the patient. It refers to the analyst's romance with his or her theory or theories. As a totality, the theory helps the analyst to organize disparate parts of analytic experience. It helps the analyst to explain how he finds himself thinking and working. Thus, it is an explanation that, to some extent, emanates from the sense of a natural fit. The theory also organizes the analyst's identity as an analyst and sustains the analyst through periods of uncertainty and ambiguity intrinsic to the work. This identity for those who wish to identify themselves as a Kleinian, ego psychologist, relational or self-psychologist, also probably involves a mode of presentation to the outside world, a way to be recognized and a way that the analyst wishes not to be recognized. Many analysts prefer not to think of themselves or to be called a this or a that.

Within the more romantic dimension of the analyst's approach to theory, the analyst may or may not idealize his or her theory. I view the idealization of one's theory as a degraded form of relationship to theory. Idealization implies the sacrifice of individuals (patient or analyst) to concepts or principles and is anathema to the notion of disciplined experimentation and growth that are at the heart of productive analytic work. The analyst's idealization of a theory is also fundamentally solipsistic, not "relational." Idealization of theory is dehumanizing since, in Adorno's (1950) terms, the human is degraded and subjugated to fallibility unless it serves to prove the tenets of the theory. Idealization trucks only with humans who fulfill its predictions and descriptions of how things are supposed to go. Rarely does it truck with understanding patients.

A melancholic position emphasizes that every theory is a theory waiting to be rendered limited or problematic by clinical work with a particular patient. Melancholic positions make the analyst lean toward a more pragmatic approach to theory. It may also make the analyst lean toward a pluralistic openness, a willingness to utilize a variety of theories in helping us to understand clinical work. Melancholic positions allow the analyst to make vigorous use of one theory with a particular patient with a sense that it may prove to be limited in its helpfulness in analytic work with another patient.

The melancholic position also provides a vantage point from which to consider or at least acknowledge that to some extent there is a kind of manic phase in the development of each new psychoanalytic theory. Each theory arises in the context of solving a problem or limitation posed by a previous theory—Klein's response to the undeveloped object relations dimension of Freudian theory; Ferenzci's and his descendant's (e.g., Balint, Guntrip, Fairbairn, and American relational theory) response to Freud's more limited focus on the neuroses; the development of ego psychology as an elaboration of the importance of ego functions and the yet-to-be-developed elements of defense analysis in Freudian theory; the failure to take into account a healthy narcissistic developmental line in Freudian theory elaborated by self-psychology; and the failure of much of early psychoanalytic theory to account for the person of the analyst addressed by interpersonal and relational theory. Each of these new theories represents an attempt to redress limitations in previous theories.

The degraded version of the melancholic relation to theory is a kind of theoretical nihilism. This is not a healthy, functional use of pluralism but rather a despairing one. In this version, no theory is really good enough for very long, and we move from theory to theory when we reach the limitations of each theory. In this type of object relation to theory, essentially the analyst is unable to be held and framed by a particular theory. The analyst is theoretically parentless and somewhat privately self-sufficient. The analyst wanders from theoretical home to theoretical home. He or she is lonely.

Martin Cooperman, a beloved teacher for many years at Austen Riggs, had this comment attributed to him: "The patient comes to analysis with symptoms and the analyst comes to analysis with a theory. If things go well they each give up what they initially brought to analysis." I think that a part of what Cooperman meant is that no theory can "understand" a unique person. Each theory is too general, too much a composite of observations gleaned from many patients—a kind of affective and ideational summary or average of working with many patients. And, each theory represents a more distant perch than the way that patient and analyst come to know each other. Cooperman's statement is a good example of the melancholic relationship to theory. It reminds me of the way that Winnicott and Lacan in different ways spoke of the analyst's willingness to be used and discarded by the patient, not unlike the good enough parent.

I view Cooperman's position as distinct from those that claim not to use theory. I do not believe that there is such a thing as not using theory; a more productive way to frame the question involves the degree to which the analyst is aware of his or her theory and the ideals and ideas that direct the analyst's decision making.

I have been strongly influenced and continue to be influenced by strands of Freudian, Kleinian, self-psychological theory, and in the last 20 years relational theory. My relationship to theory is decidedly melancholic. I use a variety of theories to help me understand my patient and the limits of my approach. I like to think about the value in standing outside our theory and trying to think about clinical work in various ways. I use the term *the pluralistic third* to help describe how I work with various theories to investigate some the decisions that I make. Each theory requires of the analyst a level of personal responsibility related to thinking about what the analyst is seeing and not seeing from the analyst's particular vantage point. Put another way, this questioning is a way to "love" and make use of one's theory rather than idealize it.

FALLING IN LOVE AND BEING IN LOVE WITH PSYCHOANALYSIS

I make distinctions between wholesale idealizations of theory and theorists versus ways that analysts, as very specific individuals, make use of theory and parts of theory. Sometimes, falling in love involves varieties of idealization and a wish to more fully embrace another, even at times to sustain the illusion of merger with another. Sometimes analysts, often young analysts, merge with their theory, and it is only over time that they undergo elements of deidealization and disillusionment that yield to their own particular and partial ways of embracing and discarding theory.

When I was introduced to psychoanalysis, I fell in love in some very specific ways. At a personal level, I found psychoanalytic treatment very helpful when I was a young man. I also identified with my analyst, and this was crucial in terms of my decision to become a psychologist and later a psychoanalyst, particularly since I studied philosophy and literature prior to graduate studies. As a late teenager, I read some Freudian texts with much of the same zeal and enthusiasm that I read Nietzsche and Marx. These were "total institutional" (Goffman, 1961) systems that appealed partly because I was looking for comprehensive explanations.

While I was first studying about psychoanalysis before I received "formal analytic training," I also was introduced to several teachers whom I admired greatly. Each introduced me to a new body of ideas, and in his own way, each lived and breathed psychoanalysis. It was also an opportunity to learn psychoanalysis from outside an institution that, in retrospect, I feel fortunate to have learned before receiving formal training.

On balance, I would say that I fell in love with psychoanalysis, "hard." Some people who become analysts come to it slowly, over time, thoughtfully or with caution as they learn more about it. I was smitten from the get-go and found myself idealizing analysis and a variety of analytic theories. My love has been an enduring love as it undergoes change, disillusionment, new appreciation, and new questions—but enough about me.

Our relationship to falling in love with psychoanalysis versus loving psychoanalysis is crucial to understanding the analyst's relationship to his or her work with patients, technical choices, relation to personal theory, and method in general. I suggest that falling in love is often best seen in terms of an idealization that provides blind spots even as it helps the analyst to organize experience and build a psychoanalytic identity. In contrast, loving psychoanalysis includes the degree to which we accept the limitations of psychoanalysis and our own theoretical orientation. It includes the degree to which we are willing to integrate disciplined experimentation into our method versus embracing more wholeheartedly what we have been taught.

For example, when I was first beginning to be interested in psychoanalysis, one of my first teachers was Merton Gill, who had been developing some of his ideas about the early interpretation of transference. I was a true believer in the merit of his arguments and found it helpful with a number of my new patients. Yet over time, I found that in working with some of my patients it was less helpful, at times disruptive to our process of working together. This allowed me also to develop a more nuanced and sophisticated application of Gill's ideas to all of my patients, and I learned about how I disagreed with some of his ideas about the theory of technique. I had gone from falling in love with his methodology and its accompanying idealization to a more functional deidealization, which in turn made it easier to make use of his work in my work.

Our loving feelings toward psychoanalysis provide a new angle on the much-maligned concept of neutrality. Many have elaborated the degree to which neutrality is an abstract ideal more than an absolute, achievable interpretive position. One of the complexities related to the neutrality concept relates to how our investment in our method is a part of our self-interest. Being in love with psychoanalysis may sometimes create difficulty for analysts in deeply integrating the limitations in our method. In fact, for some analysts it probably sounds like therapeutic nihilism even to refer to the concept of limitation (Cooper, 2000b). Our investment or passion in theory always has an impact on the kinds of neutrality that we are able to achieve.

I suppose this takes me full circle to a way to appreciate anew Freud's concept of therapeutic modesty and to integrate it with the notion of a melancholic approach to theory. While Freud was in love with psychoanalysis and his developing ideas that gave birth to psychoanalysis, he struggled repeatedly not to let his being in love influence the development of his theory. (See Parsons, 2006 for an extensive discussion of this matter.)

Freud's treatment of Herr E provides an interesting snapshot into his struggle to manage his feelings of being in love with psychoanalysis while trying to investigate and develop his method. To some degree, Freud seemed to be struggling with being in love with his theory to the point that he was also aware of his wishes for Herr E to be an extension of his theory. Freud was quite happy about the progress that his patient was making and the degree to which Herr E's progress confirmed some of his technical and theoretical principles. He wrote to Fliess as the treatment began:

> You can imagine how important this one continuing patient has become to me. ... Buried deep beneath all his phantasies we found a scene from his primal period before twenty-two months which meets all requirements. ... I can hardly bring myself to believe it yet. It is as if Schliemann had dug up another Troy which had hitherto been believed to be mythical. Also the fellow is feeling shamelessly well. He has demonstrated the truth of my theories in my own person, for with a surprising turn in his analysis he provided me with the solution of my railway phobia. (1954, pp. 305–306)

Only 3 months later, Freud's excitement about Herr E's progress and its implications for his theory development had decidedly changed, giving rise to a major innovation in his theory of technique:

> Prospects seemed most favorable in E's case and it was there that I had the heaviest blow. Just when I thought I had the solution it eluded my grasp, and I was confronted with the necessity of turning everything upside down and putting it together again afresh, losing in the process all the hypotheses that until then had seemed plausible. I could not stand up to the depression of all this. I soon found that it was impossible to continue the really difficult work in the face of depressions and lurking doubts. When I am not cheerful and master of myself every single one of my patients is a tormenting spirit to me. I really thought I should have to give in. I adopted the expedient of renouncing working by conscious thought, so as to grope my way further into the riddles only by blind touch. Since I started this I have been doing my work, perhaps more skillfully than before, but I do not really know what I am doing. (1954, pp. 311–312)

This letter to Fliess shows us much about the origins of Freud's technique related to free-floating attention. But, it also tells us something about his ability, indeed necessity, to modify and change his theory as he learned about doing clinical analysis. In this letter, there is the essence of the capacity for a melancholic position in relation to theory. Freud's despair was intense about the need to reject his theory but not so despairing that he was unable to surrender to a new way of thinking and learning about the nature of his developing understanding of psychoanalytic process. It gave birth to a revolutionary technical discovery to let the analyst be adrift in his associations.

Canestri (2006) and Fonagy (2006) have each usefully emphasized the importance of moving from clinical practice to theory. Innovations in technique do not generally come from theory, they lead to new theory. I regard Canestri's position to theory as decidedly metabolic.

I have previously argued that, for all analysts, "facts all come with a point of view." Freud wanted his patient, Herr E, to demonstrate that his beginning ideas about technique and therapeutic action were correct, and to the extent that they were not, he became distraught at times and hopeless. While Freud was the progenitor of our method, I do not think that any analyst is immune from the problem with which Freud struggled with Herr E. To some extent we love the theories we choose because they are a part of us. I believe that our theoretical choices are embedded in our body experience (e.g., Cooper, 1996), so when our patients disprove our theories, we take it quite personally whether we want to or not.

Loving one's preferred theory in analytic work needs to be tempered with an ability to see the blind spots in one's theory. This is where the analyst's theoretical choice and personal responsibility comes into play. Facts not only come with a point of view, but also each fact has new and original meaning waiting to be discovered (Ferro, 2004) unless it is, as Coleridge put it, "a fixed idea" that tells us who we are rather than letting us be who we are in relation to clinical facts.

I have heard some patients complain that their analyst (sometimes me) loves his or her technique more than the patient. To some extent, of course, this is an epic battle for many a patient as the patient tries to get the analyst to love him or her, while the analyst's job is to understand the patient and show the patient how to understand him- or herself (Freud, 1912). However, there is something to the idea that if the analyst is also in love with his or her method it can become an obstruction for analytic work in at least a few ways. Each theory is vulnerable to the criticism: "The operation was a success, but the patient died." I agree with Slavin and Kriegman (1998) that the analyst needs to change, although I think that this is a concept that has unfortunately been misunderstood and oversimplified. Analysts change with their patients because they are learning more about who the patient is and how they are implicated through the countertransference link. In some way, each analyst must surrender to the patient just as the analyst ana- lyzes the patient's method of self-cure (Chasseguet-Smirgel, 1985; Kahn, 1970) that interferes with the patient giving up old, ineffective solutions to problems, conflict resolution, and the integration of various affective states and experiences. In a sense, the notion of the analyst as a new object also includes the fact that the analyst has to become a new object to himself. Each analyst becomes a new object in a different way with each patient.

Falling in love with an ideology, theory, or method is intrinsically at odds with being a good psychoanalyst in a way that Cooperman's quota- tion in this chapter addressed. In a sense, we use our theory or method to learn enough with our patient to shed our theory in a unique interpersonal context with each patient. This is a love that is based more on who the real person of the patient and the real person of the analyst are, not who they are expected to be in accordance with a theory.

This argument is at odds with those analysts who idealize clinical work in such a way that makes them reject theory or even claim that they do not use theory. I am highly suspicious of such arguments. If we listen to the work of any analyst who claims that he does not have a theory or a theory of therapeutic action, what is revealed are implicit protean forms of unarticulated theoretical influences, theory particles if you will, that are disavowed but still influential. I always listen to the clinical material presented by another analyst with the aim of trying to deconstruct the implicit or explicit model that seems to inform the decisions that the ana- lyst makes whether he or she lays claim to working with theory or not.

This mode of "not using theory" is in fact a form of being in love with psychoanalysis as an idealized idea about analysis more than a practice of self-reflective participation. It is a love that degrades and minimizes the theoretical holding environment that partly influences his decisions.

Many young analysts fall in love with psychoanalysis in ways that relate to the help that they have received in their personal analyses. This love is one that will never disappear, but it will likely change. Over time, they will see the limitations in their own analysis and in analysis in general. They will get to know more fully the illusion intrinsic to any other form of falling in love.

Perhaps psychoanalysis has taken enough of a fall as an institution that it is less likely now than in years past to encounter people in training who are in some ways looking for something to idealize. In days past, some aspects of analytic training would reinforce elements of idealization and mystification about becoming an analyst. Students today are much more sophisticated about the substantial amount of criticism that has been levied against psychoanalysis from various corners, including disaffected analysts and patients. I suggest that the students of today are in a better position than earlier generations were to learn about psychoanalysis. While the position may be more melancholic, it may be more suited to these students becoming talented psychoanalysts.

THE PLURALISTIC THIRD

Different clinical theories valorize particular aspects of clinical understanding. I try to hold myself accountable through thinking about the blind spots consequent to prizing the particular lenses that I trust most. I use a concept that I call the *pluralistic third* (Cooper, 2007b) to think about clinical work from a variety of perspectives. I hope that in the clinical examples in this book I demonstrate how I make use of such a concept.

The pluralistic third means, somewhat counterintuitively, that there is value in thinking critically about our decisions from perspectives other than the one we initially used. While this can be harsh, and often has been in somewhat destructive conversations involving comparative psychoanalysis, I hold a great deal of hope that there can be value in thinking critically about our decisions using the pluralistic third—to provide a third to the dyadic relationship the analyst holds to his or her own theory and its limitation with a particular patient. To some extent, this can be a bit of a rigged experiment because few of us ever use only one model. Thus, I may in fact be using elements of inquiry about what I have done that are already a part of how I work. Furthermore, various psychoanalytic theories have interpenetrated one another in ways that can sometimes make it difficult to tell whether there is more disagreement between analysts within the same orientation versus analysts from different orientations (Cooper, 1996; Smith, 2003; Teicholz, 2006).

My working ideal about clinical information and process is related to what Ronald Britton (1998) refers to as "vulnerable knowledge." It is always the case that we are working with ambiguity about "clinical facts" (Ferro, 2005). Sometimes, the pluralistic third may help us to think about this ambiguity.

The rationale for this approach relates to how, given that we have an unconscious attachment to our theory, it is axiomatic that we have intrinsic blind spots as well. Just as a hologram is created through the interference of light from separate sources, so the pluralistic third can sometimes allow for a different perspective on the blind spots. Bion (1963) referred to these blind spots in the clinical encounter with two terms: "selective fact" and "overvalued idea." Both concepts involve the degree to which we can sometimes be prone to rely too much on our initial formulations to make sense of things. These tendencies to listen with selective focus are also manifested in theory building and the application of theory.

Selected facts stand in contrast to what Britton (1998) calls vulnerable knowledge. Britton is trying to elaborate how our tendency to be influenced by unconscious factors is embedded within our vigorous efforts to claim total rationality in our belief systems.

I am interested in how our countertransference to our own theory or ideology keeps us from benefiting from vulnerable knowledge. Stepping outside our theory is from my point of view more consistent with an *adaptive melancholic position* involving deidealizing our theory and the mourning of the lost idealization. It allows for the idea that our beliefs may sometimes be misapplied, in part defensively determined and thus selectively perceived.

For example, each theory is reliant on a particular valorization of illusory analytic play space—the selfobject function in self-psychology; the drive derivative in close process ego psychology; dyadic/interpersonal reality, the analyst's subjectivity, and the concept of enactment within relational theory; and for the Kleinians, unconscious fantasy, the transition from paranoid to depressive position, as well as a very specifically defined use of countertransference. I wish to develop useful and sympathetic, although external, models of questioning these constructs of illusory space that are specific to each approach. (For example, Freud implicitly addressed the illusory space in drive theory when he defined drive as a mythological/metaphorical frontier between psyche and soma.)

Developing ways of questioning our work neither requires nor recommends that we as analysts relinquish our theoretical preferences and reliance on particular kinds of illusory analytic constructs. It would be extraordinarily naive to think of our allegiance to a model as so easily prone to persuasion. Our allegiance to a theory is based in deeply personal and bodily attachments and, as well, to what has been therapeutic or growth producing with parents and analysts. To use a developmental analogy, what I am suggesting is that we approach our preferences and the pluralistic realm of theory more like that of a postoedipal child—with healthy doses of both love toward our theoretical predilections (helpful, guiding, and well-intentioned parents) and skepticism.

It is also important to note that the concept of the pluralistic third could be translated crudely to mean that we, the analysts, should always be questioning our decisions and interpretive directions from various perspectives. Nothing could be more inaccurate. A translation of that sort sounds like it might create a highly obsessive and intellectualized analyst, perhaps an analyst with a kind of theoretical obsessive-compulsive disorder (TOCD) who is in effect trying to leave no theoretical "stone unturned." Instead, the concept is offered as a mode of reflective function, carried out by the analyst at particular times when the analyst is thinking about his work or, especially, thinking about moments of impasse or slower growth in the analytic work.

A MELANCHOLIC APPROACH TO PSYCHOANALYTIC THEORY

Briefly, I take a problem in the history of the development of relational theory to demonstrate some of the concepts that I refer to in thinking about the pluralistic third and the melancholia of theory.

There are many ways of thinking about dimensions of self-reflection and accountability in a relational model, and the task is a formidable one. First, the word *accountability* is an evocative one, with all of its evaluative and potentially punitive reverberations. Second, there is no one relational model, so particular ways of working need be defined to be assessed. For example, I know that some theorists who call themselves relational might tend to think of my interest in conflict as always better described by concepts such as self-state shifts.

I don't think of a relational theory as a theory of technique. I think of it as a guiding set of principles that have accompanied an integration of Freudian, interpersonal, self-psychological, and independent tradition schools of psychoanalysis. It includes a set of foundation principles—principles such as the dialogic nature of psychic meaning; the value of countertransference experience in understanding the patient's internalized world; and an ethic of disciplined experimentation.

If I were going to break down the matter of how one holds oneself accountable within a relational model, I would ask questions such as the following: How does the analyst continually look at enactment in the immediate context and over time? How do we decide about the tensions between restraint and expressiveness? In particular, how do we decide to use elements of our disjunctive subjectivity from that of our patient? In abandoning more linear models of development, how do we evaluate the patient's experience and associations as emanating from regressive or progressive vistas?

Many changes in technique and theory have been established as a part of relationally oriented analysis, raising questions about how to evaluate the work and how to hold the analyst accountable. How do we determine which enactments are inevitable and which might be unusual in terms of being deeply embedded in particular aspects of the dynamic makeup of the analyst? What are the guiding principles that dictate various aspects of the analyst's countertransference expressiveness? When is it the case that analyst and patient in a relational model get caught up in dyadic realities without the helpful or requisite presence of the third? Since some of the most interesting and influential articles from the relational tradition address moments of impasse, what are the applications to relational theory to exploring more routine moments of analytic work? For example, what is the place of the analysis of defensive vicissitudes within a relational model, and when does the analyst's attention seem to focus more exclusively on these defensive vicissitudes?

One of the most interesting debates within relational psychoanalysis involves what guides the analyst's decisions to utilize aspects of his subjectivity and when to do so. In an interesting article, Slochower (1996) discusses how she works with some patients for whom the sharing of the analyst's subjectivity in the formation of interpretations creates a toxic reaction to knowing the analyst. Steiner (1993) has written about this dilemma from a contemporary Kleinian perspective as well. In these instances, the patient is said to not yet be able to stand a mutual analytic experience. During what Slochower regards as a kind of analytic "holding," the patient experiences an illusion of analytic attunement, requiring of the analyst a containment of his or her disjunctive subjectivity, not an abandonment of his or her subjectivity. In fact, Steiner refers to patients for whom even an interpretation that takes into account what the patient might be feeling about the analyst is an assault. Slochower argues that for patients for whom externality is equated with either abandonment or rupture, the movement toward mutuality will require that the analyst begin to fail in ways that increasingly expose the patient to his externality and thus his subjectivity to the patient.

Slochower (1996) essentially argues, as a relational analyst, that there are patients for whom knowing the analyst's subjectivity (e.g., interpretations that integrate aspects of the analyst's experience) requires of them to be pseudomature adults. One scenario, among many, is that a false self can develop in which the patient obscures aspects of painful encroachment or the false self falters and the individual becomes more blatantly derailed. For Slochower, holding involves a situation in which the patient cannot challenge or is less likely to challenge the boundaries of the analytic holding experience. Instead, patient and analyst implicitly agree not to question the analyst's largely good intentions, emotional resilience and reliability, or capacity to hold for some periods of time during analysis.

In a critical essay discussing Slochower's (1996) article, Bass (1996) suggests that Slochower might tend to bring to the analytic situation the notion that her subjectivity connotes aspects of unreliability and a lack of safety. Bass proposes that attempting to elude or obscure rather than to explore the ways that the patient may find his safety compromised through the analyst's presence tends to increase rather than resolve whatever difficulties are posed by the analyst's presence and interventions. Bass would suggest that this type of holding involves a degree of sleight of hand in which the analyst's subjective presence is seen as likely to contaminate or interfere with the analytic process in contrast to a relational approach that emphasizes the "inevitable, ubiquitous and potentially constructive presence and impact of the analyst's personal self" (p. 367).

Finally, Slochower (1996) counterargues that there is no one-sided sleight of hand on the part of the analyst within the holding that she describes. Instead, holding describes the coconstruction by analyst and patient of an illusion of analytic attunement in a way that temporarily puts into the background certain disjunctive aspects of the both parties' experience that will later give way to the interpretive work for which she eventually aims.

As you can see, even within the group of analysts who think of themselves as "relational," there are differences in how they define intersubjectivity, mutuality, and holding within the analytic process, and this is but one of the several interesting debates within relational theory. (In general, the treatment of idealizing transferences is a point of fascinating debate among analysts; e.g., Hoffman, 1994; Renik, 1995.)

So, what kinds of conclusions can we draw from these differences? At the least, the criteria for accountability that Slochower (1996) would demand of herself would likely be quite different than those used by Bass (1996).

While the point of the pluralistic third concept is to suggest how we might think about our work using outside models, the differences from within the same orientation seem equally important, as is suggested through the interesting debate between Slochower (1996) and Bass (1996). For example, it seems to me that an analyst who is sensitive to the kinds of issues that Slochower has elaborated so beautifully would do well to consider the warnings by Bass that the determination about a patient's sensitivity can involve assumptions overdetermined by countertransference predilections. Similarly, Bass's ambition regarding taking up the potentially disruptive impact that his subjectivity will have on the patient may be tempered by considering Slochower's emphasis (relationally oriented versions of Kohut's, 1969, and Steiner's, 1993, descriptions of the same phenomena) on some patients' limitations to absorb elements of the analyst's subjectivity. Any analyst of any persuasion is capable of using sleight of hand in his position as analyst.

I do not resolve questions such as these through thinking about theory, and I would not be able to say that I agree with one of these analysts more than the other in terms of how I work without having a particular patient in mind. I have felt the constraints and inhibitions that Slochower (1996) highlighted and the freedom in the face of constraint that Bass (1996) suggested is possible. I have also felt the inability for the interpretive freedom that Bass suggested. At these times, the technical suggestions Slochower made are helpful. What I am suggesting is not a solution to a debate such as this except through the value of having these quite different ways of thinking about patients available to us. Many of these kinds of theoretical debates are resolved in the ethical and clinical imagination of the analyst.

This imaginative capacity of the analyst is what I would suggest is a kind of posttribal approach to psychoanalytic theory. The reason for teaching our students a variety of theoretical traditions and contributions from a diverse group of analysts is so that their clinical imaginations will be as free as possible to work with their patients.

My favorite expression in Freud's (1920) writing, from *The Ego and the Id*, is the description of the ego as a frontier creature existing between the internal and external world. I like the notion of thinking about the analyst as a frontier creature also since he lives in the patient's and the analyst's sense of reality, moving back and forth as the analyst helps the patient to dismantle and reconfigure parts of his psychic world. Each of us relies on our orientation and in doing so partly becomes a tamed creature, tamed by his own need for familiarity in the face of this difficult task. By stepping outside our own way of looking, we can sometimes jolt ourselves for potentially useful moments, claiming a new frontier. In parallel to the patient, we dismantle our own settlements and scaffolding. It is just one of the many forms of what Ghent (1990) referred to as "surrender."

This process helps us to engage in the mandate and sometimes folly of facing the intrinsic limitations, fallout, and collateral damage of whatever approach we most value, a melancholic paradox if ever there was one. It is something we do with those and that which we love. It is a part of what I love about psychoanalysis.

Chapter 2

The grandiosity of self-loathing
Transference-countertransference dimensions*

Everyone is responsible for everybody else, but I am more responsible.

Dostoyevsky
The Brothers Karamazov (1880)

I am born into vileness. I am evil because I am human.

Iago Verdi's
Otello (1887)

Villains are the heroes of their own stories.

Christopher Vogler
The Writer's Journey (1992)

We are all worms though I am a glow-worm among worms.

Winston Churchill

There is a frequently told story that goes like this: During a Sabbath service, a rabbi is seized by a sudden wave of guilt, prostrates himself, and cries out: "God, before you I am nothing." The cantor is so moved by this demonstration of piety that he throws himself to the floor beside the rabbi and cries: "God, before you I am nothing!" Watching this scene unfold from his seat in the first row, the chairman of the synagogue's trustees jumps up, flops down in the aisle, and cries: "God, before you I am nothing!" The rabbi nudges the cantor and, as they both look at the chairman, says: "So look who thinks he's nothing!" The joke plays on the hubris of humility an~ part of the joke that humans play on themselves and others in every and in our unconscious minds.

The particular problem of self-criticism when it is related to · grandiosity interests me partly because it can only be deer' through aspects of transference-countertransference e· problems posed in understanding and working through

* Portions of this chapter will appear in revised form in "Self-Grandiosity: Countertransference Dimensions," an article issue of *International Journal of Psychoanalysis*.

of self-criticism are challenging for both patient and analyst. I explore some ways for analysts to think about and use varieties of countertransference experience in connection with analyzing individuals for whom self-criticism and accompanying unconscious grandiosity are primary and debilitating features of the patient's unconscious inner life and relating to others. The analyst must probe deeply into who he is as an analyst and as a person in elucidating the complexities of self-loathing.

Self-criticism appears often as an enduring part of personality organization and may appear in many psychic contexts. At times, self-criticism is a symptom embedded within a neurosis. For example, within many oedipal contexts a patient may titrate anxiety about success or fear of failure through reflexive, unconscious forms of self-effacement or self-criticism. For a boy, the oedipal context often contains an implied aspiration or wish to usurp the place of the father in relation to the mother. The many neurotic resolutions of the oedipal context that do not involve the child's identification with the father include turning against the self as an unconscious method for mitigating guilt and a fear of retaliation.

In both neurotic and narcissistic contexts, self-criticism may appear as a preemptive strike that the individual issues against the self in the face of anxiety about attack from both representational and actual others. Self-criticism may reflect a self-shaming action as a way to be active rather than passively await an unconsciously shaming experience with an internalized object relation. Self-criticism may involve retroflected rage or anger, an attempt to protect the object who is unconsciously hated or envied.

Despite the enduring nature of this symptom and its general presence within the patient in many interactions, it is still essential for the analyst to try to help the patient understand the particular meaning of this symptom or behavior within the context of the analytic interaction. Since self-criticism is often a part of a continual characterologic pattern and since it involves an attack on the self, it often poses particular problems for the analyst in helping the patient to see the multiple meanings of self-criticism.

A particular type of problem for the analyst in analyzing self-criticism involves the presence of unconscious grandiosity that is at odds with the patient's conscious experience of self-criticism. A part of this problem relates to the degree that the analyst's attempts to analyze unconscious grandiosity related to self-reproach are experienced by the patient's harsh, self-critical attitudes. Interpretation becomes another attack on the self and may serve the patient's defensive needs to avoid his grandiose fantasies and hostile feelings toward others, including the analyst. The patient is victimized rather than hostile or hurtful to himself. The patient is self-critical ther than critical of the other.

Feldman (1997) has noted that the patient requires the analyst's experi- or behavior to correspond in some way to his unconscious fantasy and able to make use of any discrepancy, however reassuring we might assume that to be. An interpretation of unconscious self-criticism becomes threatening by dint of being unmatched to an unconscious fantasy.

Another type of problem is when self-criticism is, along with grandiose trends, unconscious. In such instances, individuals have adapted to unconscious self-criticism through unconsciously grandiose identifications and identities. These identifications serve to keep self-critical feelings and hostile feelings toward others at bay.

For that matter, some self-criticism is neither symptomatic nor problematic. Some degree of self-criticism overlaps with what we refer to as a sense of being discriminating, discerning, appropriately evaluative or realistic. It is quite striking to observe young children begin to develop their own independent criteria for what pleases them about their achievements and the ways that self-criticism figures into this developing ability. We admire as a character trait the capacity to question ourselves before questioning or criticizing others. So, what is the point at which this more or less adaptive self-criticism turns into something that we might agree is a symptom or symptomatic of a problem for the individual or those around the individual?

Let us start by expanding on what might be called "normative" self-criticism or the self-criticism of everyday life that also involves unconscious or embedded grandiosity. Over many years of relatively mediocre athletic ability, particularly in the areas of basketball and tennis, I have noticed an aspect of my own behavior that I found unseemly in others and myself and did not immediately understand. After missing shots in basketball or tennis, I would sometimes direct a kind of self-critical rant toward myself, usually silently but sometimes aloud. It might take the form of, "You idiot, how could you miss that shot?" Or, "What were you thinking?"

Over time, I began to be annoyed by other mediocre athletes engaging in some of the same self-flagellation, wondering at times if it was directed toward the self or intended for others to hear. It is not uncommon in a basketball game of middle-aged men to hear some muttering after missed shots. To be sure, there are more confident or less-grandiose players who take it in stride when they miss a shot, but there is also a kind of acceptable, normative, unconsciously agreed-on level of self-reproach (a compromise or social compact) for many. The compromise is self-criticism, and it rests between the silent acceptance of disappointment or shame on the one hand and on the other a clearly disproportionate level of grandiosity about our ability.

The utterances that the imaginary male player would speak of on the basketball court perpetuate a particular kind of fantasy—for either himself or as he wishes to present himself to others—that he really can make that shot, and that it is more surprising for him to miss rather than to make the shot. Thus, the symptomatic compromise also resides in a self-critical home between the fantasies of being better than he is versus accepting the actual status of his basketball ability. At the heart of this type of self-reproach is an unconsciously grandiose fantasy. I encounter this form of unconscious grandiosity quite frequently in clinical psychoanalysis.

It is easy for a psychoanalyst to feel sympathetic and caring toward patients who present their self-criticism and self-loathing. It is quite common for us to see before us a patient who is bright, attractive, and appealing in any one of a number of ways but unable to experience himself in this way. The symptomatic presence of self-loathing often pulls for a countertransference wish or fantasy in which we seek to convince our patient to give up what can become his or her constant refrain of self-reproach. However, generally speaking the goal of our work lies in finding out why our patient feels this way about himself and perhaps, if we are fortunate, uncovering some of the unconscious determinants and functions that self-loathing might serve.

I find that one of the most conspicuous features of working with self-reproach is how my experience of it changes over time with each patient. It is over time that my experiences of compassion for the patient's conscious experiences of self-reproach are accompanied by other experiences and ways of thinking about the meaning of unconscious fantasy embedded or related to the self-reproach.

For example, it is always interesting to me when a patient's self-loathing becomes so prominent that it begins to sound as though the patient's self-absorption with his badness does not allow for consideration of others' responses as independent of the patient's badness. In these instances, the patient is so solipsistic that a bubble of self-loathing surrounds him or her, preventing the patient from seeing the outside world. At these moments, the analyst's attention moves into a greater awareness of how the patient's self-absorption makes him or her the center of a story that sometimes does not include others. Sometimes, these shifts are also related to ways in which the analyst is rendered secondary to the patient's relationship with his self-loathing and his self-absorption. The patient is in a sense the villain of a personal story that is told and retold. The analyst has become well acquainted with the patient's solipsism and may begin to feel annoyed or excluded. For example, if the analyst yawns and the patient says something like: "You've yawned. It must be because I'm boring," at one point in analytic work, the analyst might hear this self-criticism as an example of the patient's predilection to feel inadequate and boring, essentially part of a powerful sense of unworthiness. Later in the process, the analyst, while aware of all of these processes, might also have accrued enough experience to lead the analyst to consider how the patient cannot allow himself to take in new experiences, particularly an experience that is actually generated by something outside the self-loathing.

It is quite interesting to me when I change in these ways with patients. The first consideration is always that the analyst may be losing his "patience" with the "patient." But, another consideration is that the analyst has been able to get to know the patient better. In a sense, it is the point at which the analyst may be freer to experience the notion of the patient's self-loathing as defensively chosen dominant metaphor for many aspects of self-experience. This is the point at which risk is available, and it can be quite scary in terms of the potential to hurt the patient. However, it can also yield high rewards. I have had patients who burst into laughter when I bring up the possibility that I actually could be yawning for a reason other than their impact on me.

It is also important when a patient's self-criticism creates a feeling in the analyst that there is no way to help. In particular, in these circumstances it seems as though no understanding or formulation about the self-criticism or praise and affirmation can combat the patient's certainty to the contrary. In these instances, the analyst is rendered impotent. Interpretations about the whys and wherefores of self-loathing do not actually provide the patient with what he needs or unconsciously demands—often to be loved or punished. In some circumstances, the patient is unconsciously keeping alive a fantasy that there will be enough affirmation and praise provided in some relationship that would eventually allow him to feel at peace with himself. The analyst is seen as the one who can provide this, and interpretations about these fantasies are woefully inadequate and disappointing. In other instances, the patient's unconscious wish is to be punished for unconscious feelings and fantasies that the analyst cannot yet know about.

From a Kohutian perspective, some of these uses of self-criticism are seen as defensive, utilizing Kohut's (1984) final definition of the term: the attempt through the innate vigor of the self to keep alive a hoped-for empathic object from childhood where there was not one before. Self-loathing communicates, in a sense, the need for this responsiveness. But this is, of course, an experiential/metapsychological perspective. Conceptualized from the point of view of self-loathing as a communication to the self and another, it might also mean, "If only I were this or that, I would be able to receive what I wish." Or, "If only I could be this, I wouldn't ever fail as I do in my performance." A view of the latter as grandiose, then, has nothing to do with an experience of grandiosity. Instead, it is an inferred formulation about an underlying fantasy about the self that, as the analyst comes to know in more intimate terms, creates myriad potential feelings in countertransference experience.

Thus, for some patients, the analyst's interpretive efforts to understand self-criticism may be experienced as a loss of something that the patient needs to feel integrated and whole. In these circumstances, self-criticism is a compromise between unacceptable forms of grandiosity and the release and relinquishing of heroic expectations. The analyst either is seen as a threat to this valued undercover self-representation or composite self-state experience or is seen as a receptacle for the degraded parts of self. The analyst is robbing the patient of valued and compensatory self-states and fantasies. In a sense, the patient wants to hold on to being the hero of his or her story even if vilified by him- or herself.

Often, the analyst is clued in to these unconscious forms of grandiosity through a shift in his or her countertransference reactions to the patient. A feeling of compassion for the patient turns to a sense of futility about being able to help or annoyance with the patient for wanting so much. Sometimes, the analyst may also experience a feeling of being degraded by the mounting awareness of the patient's unconscious superiority. Naturally, in analyzing grandiose parts of patients who vigorously hate themselves, the analyst needs to consider whether his reactions to the patient derive from impatience, envy, or helplessness in the face of the patient's limitations in making use of what the analyst has to offer.

JAMES

When James began analysis, his complaints about being less bright than his law partner often struck me as exaggerated and did not ring entirely true. I had the sense that he was enormously self-critical, and after hearing more about James's history I wondered if some of his self-reproach was overdetermined by his mother's preferences for his older sister when they were growing up. James felt that his mother was likely to see his sister's accomplishments as superior to his, and that she seemed to enjoy spending more time with his sister than with him. He also seemed protective of his parents, particularly his mother.

When James would talk about his lack of ability in comparison to his partners, I did not know how to evaluate this observation. I thought that James was an extremely bright and appealing man—funny, articulate, and physically attractive. He seemed to have a hard time accepting praise from his wife and children. He was quite modest, and it was only over time that I discovered many of his academic and athletic accomplishments. For example, his mountaineering abilities were initially described as "an interest in hiking"; then, a year into his analysis James revealed that he was planning a 2-week expedition involving an extremely challenging peak, Likewise, it was also only after a year of working with James that I learned of the academic awards that he had won both at his extremely competitive high school and at college.

When James and I began working together, I initially viewed his self-criticism partly as protection from his disappointment by his parents, especially his mother's perceived preference for his sister. It seemed like he was prone to beat himself up rather than be critical of others, essentially using self-reproach to defend against his own hostile reaction to his parents' disappointment in him. I saw indications of this in his work and his relationship with his law partner. When his partner made mistakes, James would tend to minimize these errors, but if he failed in similar ways, he was quite harsh with himself. James was prone to blame himself for things that went wrong at home and accepted his wife's criticisms of him without much apparent resentment. I often had the sense that for James, daily life would inevitably reveal his limitations. He seemed to feel bad for those around him who hired and married him.

Over time, I began to be struck by a particular way that James had of putting things in relation to his mother and his partner at work: "They depend on me, and I disappointed them." I was struck by the potential complexity of what this "depending on" might mean. Was he the stronger in his own mind or in theirs, and did they depend on him more than he depended on them?

There were ways in which I felt myself admiring James's modesty and generosity during our first year of analytic work. He was the kind of person who would always be less likely to cast stones, and he had a clear sense of responsibility and commitment to others. As he began opening up in our work, I learned of other sides of James. I began to feel less sympathetic toward James when he would criticize himself. It was not easy for me to understand these feelings. At first, I thought that I might be feeling helpless to aid James with these feelings. His self-reproach had an impersonal quality to it, as though nothing I would be able to say or point out to him would have an impact on him. While this was true to some extent, that did not explain why I was starting to feel something else from James, something that made me feel less sympathetic to him.

What emerged over time was that beneath his more apparent self-critical stance were low expectations for his wife, his law partner, and me. From his point of view, unconsciously, we were less capable than he, so criteria for success were also lowered. He would not accept praise for accomplishments that would have been noteworthy in others because he should be capable of so much more. We began to find out together that, from his point of view, his wife, mother, and partner depended on him a great deal, and that he experienced very few needs in regard to them. I wondered about whether his own needs were scaled off and disavowed.

I began to experience James's self-criticism as a way of rejecting praise and appreciation from those around him because he did not want to stoop so low. His self-criticism began to feel like a kind of active repudiation of our admiration or appreciation of him.

James began letting me know in various ways that his expectations for analysis were very low. We were both somewhat surprised and intrigued to discover that, for James, in many ways his analysis was for my benefit, something that he provided for my enjoyment and livelihood. James seemed to genuinely enjoy discovering these forms of grandiosity in himself, and it was exhilarating for him that I could help him to explore why he would maintain these attitudes. On one occasion following a dream about James doing me a favor, I interpreted something about his unconscious contempt for the analysis and me. The dream was vague, but he had the sense that he had done something for me, a favor, and that I appreciated what he had done. I took up his generosity in affording me this opportunity to analyze him and his gracious pleasure in bestowing this favor on me. He laughed but felt closer to a sense within himself that, in part, this was the way he viewed his analysis and many other parts of his life.

This was an enjoyable phase of work, but it soon passed. James was actually quite angry, especially with his mother, and I had not realized how much my interpretation about his disavowal of need involved an enactment of the very same way that he held himself to be superior. By laughing, he was distancing himself from the parts of himself that needed affirmation from his mother, his wife, his partner, and me—the people he loved and worked with—and he did not want to have to stoop to this level of experience. His laughing enacted a kind of expectation for him to be pseudomature. During his laughter, he had a false sense of superiority and distance from these needs. I was able to talk to James about how it was great to laugh about some of his discoveries, but that I thought that maybe in so doing he was actually laughing *at* parts of him to which we needed to pay attention.

James felt that since his childhood he had maintained quite distinct, separate, and sequestered self-representations and self-states. On the one hand, he thought that he was inferior to his sister by dint of his mother's unequal praise for her. As James became an adolescent, he also had a part of himself that realized that, while it seemed to take very little accomplishment by his sister to receive attention, for James it would take a more significant academic or athletic accomplishment to receive his mother's praise. As it turned out, in most social situations James would slide by with a persona of self-criticism and modesty, presenting himself as a low-level accomplisher. This was the part of James that I had come to know during the early part of his analysis. Another part of James involved having fairly heroic expectations for himself. So, in this light his self-criticism and praise of his partner and wife were unconscious ways of keeping a secret and preserving his elevated expectations of himself.

As our work developed, James began to talk more about what he wanted from his wife, his partner, and me. James felt that he wanted far more than he could get and was uncomfortable without his usual place of equilibrium, which revolved more around his familiar and constant self-criticism. James also began to express feelings toward his mother and his wife that made him quite uncomfortable, including the desire to punish them. He felt that they were perfectly happy to let him go unnoticed, and he hated feeling so angry and resentful about wanting more of their attention. He could allow himself to see how he would try to render these women unimportant by unconsciously patronizing and devaluing them.

I found James more likable when we were able to get his level of contempt for me out on the table. He would laugh awkwardly as I drew his attention to his contempt and helped him to see the ways in which he tried to avoid expressing this contempt. At first, he only reluctantly accepted it. He was giving up his cover story, and he was unfamiliar with this openness. We referred to his self-loathing in part as a Trojan horse that had allowed him to more palatably pass as a mother-lover while disguising the fury inside. I am always struck by the kinds of things that make my sympathies shift toward my patients. Such shifts also occur in my erotic feelings—or lack thereof—or how enlivening or deadening it feels to be with a patient, as well as variations in sadness, fun, and excitement of all kinds.

I was aware that James had limits on how much affection he could experience coming his way from his wife, his partner, or me. At home, when he felt that he and his wife were getting closer after a good weekend, he would often unconsciously end the weekend by doing things that annoyed her. For example, he would forget to mention to her something about an evening meeting for the upcoming week when it would have been just as easy to let her know in advance. Or, sometimes after a good weekend, he would suddenly withdraw, leaving her confused and occasionally angry. I began to think that James might be struggling with the sense that "good enough" experiences of being loved by his wife or appreciated by his partner posed particular kinds of problems. What if that is all that there is? Is good enough good enough?

Similarly, when it seemed that we were making progress or that James was settling into feeling good about his analysis or close to me, he would do something to distance himself. The word *settle* seems apt given that for James it was compromising to accept the limitations of what he might get from me. An example of how James would pull away from me or maintain his heroic expectations occurred in the second year of analysis. James repeatedly started having to miss one of his four appointments a week because of a scheduling conflict with two of the paralegals at work. These two employees of James were quite willing to rearrange their schedules at his convenience, yet he repeatedly sacrificed his analytic appointments to accommodate them. This apparent thoughtfulness toward them made James feel good about his own generosity and willingness to sacrifice his needs for others, and he deflected any questions about these actions making him typically unassailable. In my trying to interpret this "sacrifice" on his part, I was the self-interested one, inferior like his mother and wife for having particular needs and wishes. Far from a simple act of generosity, egalitarianism, and thoughtfulness on his part, James was reacting against the gratitude and dependency that had developed in our work. He unconsciously wanted not to need me too much. At one point as we explored the complexity of his scheduling issues, he said, "Okay, I'm busted."

Arranging for four appointments a week that he would keep, having an analysis, a job, a family, a self were just not enough for James. James and I came to see that the problem with feeling good about him and lovable to those with whom he was closest was that such contentment was all that was available. James did not have to want more when he felt his constant sense of inadequacy and self-recrimination. Self-reproach was a perfect method for titrating this ambition. After this realization, I became much more comfortable addressing James when I felt that he was lapsing into protective positions, states in which he could reflexively put himself in some sort of doghouse at work or home so that he did not have to want more than was available to him. I became more active in terms of pointing out to him when he withdrew from me into a kind of therapeutic nihilism about the analysis, a comfort zone of "perverse hope" (Cooper, 2000b). He could only sustain a sense of hope and enthusiasm for our project if it involved very little actual experience of wish for change.

Interestingly, at the point that James was able to have a clearer sense of what he actually wanted to accomplish in our work and in his career, he had already become a person much less in hiding. His psychic effort was more evident in trying to be a person knowable to others and to him.

THE GRANDIOSITY OF NOT BEING A PERSON

Leonard had grown up believing that the key to his parents' love and admiration was not to act like a little boy. At a young age, he was verbally facile and intellectually precocious, ensuring the likelihood that he would curry favor with each of his parents. He had grown up in a religious community in which community service and liberal values were emphasized, and he became a youth leader and public speaker during his adolescence. He had memories of feeling embarrassed and ashamed when his lack of information about the world became apparent in conversation with others. In a sense, he was trying not to be who he was: a little boy learning about the world. Instead, he felt that he should already know.

Some of these feelings of embarrassment about vulnerability would come up in adult life. He was prone to feel critical of his friends when they would expose any naiveté or lack of knowledge in public. Traveling in a European country with a female friend was torturous because she would sometimes carry around a guidebook. Leonard was very sophisticated about this country and did not need such a guide. He was repulsed by her palpable demonstration of need and dependence even as he chastised himself for his reactions.

Some of these patterns were reinforced by each of his parents in various ways. His mother liked him being "her little man." She was content with her husband, but Leonard felt that she was not deeply emotionally engaged with him. Instead, Leonard felt that she was closer to him than to either his father or his 5-year-younger sister. As an adult woman, Leonard's sister complained that his mother's world "revolved around Leonard," and that no one else seemed to matter. His father never really spoke about himself and seemed only to comment on others. His was a more panoramic view of the world, and while not an angry man, he seemed to view many around him with a mild level of contempt. Leonard feared being regarded by his father as one of these small people with their petty concerns.

Leonard began an analysis with me in his early 40s because he felt a sense of dissatisfaction with his work. He was an academic physician who was in the process of achieving considerable fame for his research, but this attention had led him to feel elements of insatiability. He felt that nothing satisfied him, neither the local praise he received for his work nor the constant flow of invitations to present his work to others. As he became better known, his travels became more frequent, and he had developed two romantic liaisons with women in other cities.

Leonard had married in his late 30s and had divorced after 3 years. He felt that he was never connected to his 10-year-younger wife despite his admiration of her. She wanted to have children, a prospect that terrified him despite his promises during their engagement that he also would want to have a family. Leonard began to feel more and more despondent about a lack of connection to other people. He imagined feeling that his life would consist of a series of different affairs with women. He enjoyed these relationships, but he also felt an increasing sense of sadness and perplexity about his inability to feel close to anyone. He said that sometimes he felt as though he was leading someone else's life.

During one session in the sixth month or so of his analysis, he was relating a story about waiting in line for a ticket of some kind and hearing the clerk call out his name. This horrified and embarrassed him. Something about hearing his name, its specificity in particular, was humiliating for him. In discussing it with him, at one point I recounted the structure of the narrative. I referred to him by his full name. He was struck by a realization that he did not really think of himself as a person, a particular person. He referred to himself as "the man who had the very strange symptom of not being a person."

For years, Leonard and I explored his anxieties about being a particular person. These reasons were quite complex. He had oedipal anxiety about being Leonard ____, a favorite child of his mother and also her man-boy. He wanted to have his father's approval not just as a small, actual, specific person but instead as large with a bird's-eye view of humanity. He did not want to be one man with one job, one relationship with a woman, one actual analysis, or of course, one life. In respect to these oedipal conflicts, Leonard partly ensured his safety by identifying with his father.

The factors that allowed Leonard both to begin to be a person with me and to more fully explore his nonpersonhood are important in understanding transference-countertransference engagement. Something that interests me about my work with Leonard is that the arc of how this work developed was quite different from what I might have expected. I would have guessed based on previous work with other patients that I might have become more aware of and perhaps even frustrated by a growing sense of Leonard not feeling himself to be a person. Instead, I think that what happened in this work was that Leonard brought up his "peculiar symptom" as a result of already feeling himself to be more a person with me. In a sense, he felt more freedom to start being more personal in his analysis. This idea of being more personal in analysis is, of course, the irony of all ironies. I think it likely that he was feeling safer to be specific and to be revealing.

Why I said Leonard's full name in the same session that he revealed his humiliation when a clerk did so is an important question. My guess is that without being fully aware of it I had been hoping to know Leonard more as a person, an individual. I was not aware of feeling hostility or frustration toward Leonard, although I suppose this is possible. Instead, I tend to see my actions as what I have previously referred to as "good enough impingement" (Cooper, 2000a). I was aware that I found it humorous to say his name, and he would laugh with me about it quite often, even inviting me to say his name aloud in a form of play. I think that when Leonard told me the story of the clerk who called his name, without realizing it, I may have felt free also to say his name. It is also fair to speculate that there was a sadomasochistic element to my joking with him. Was I trying to hurt him or inoculating him with the toxic matter of his name? When I have thought about why I might have enjoyed saying Leonard's name, apart from the gratifying part of helping him to be a specific person, I have wondered about whether I had felt implicitly devalued by him because I was a person when, in Leonard's psychology, he had been so much more by not being a person. However, I was never aware of this feeling as I have been with some patients.

This place where I found myself in relation to Leonard I think of as *working backward*. In this mode, I ask myself why I am saying what I am saying in order to better formulate a new understanding of clinical facts that was previously hidden or unknown to me. In this way, I have been reminded of some of Ferro's (2004) similar observation that this can sometimes further the analyst's "contact with the dream-like functioning of the mind..." (p. 9).

The notion of working backward is, even as it is spoken, so flawed with the illusion of linearity and a presumed figure ground relationship to how the analyst "should" work that rarely fits with experience. Loewald (1960) emphasized how interpretations are often expressions of the analyst's anticipation of the patient's psychic future. This view of clinical process was also well captured by Ricoeur's (1970) deliciously subversive and astute statement that psychoanalysis involves the hermeneutics of suspicion. Everything is worth questioning, and what may appear as an unformulated area of discussion between patient and analyst may involve elements of actual interpretation. Similarly, the analyst's interpretations of the past may sometimes involve unconscious anticipation of the patient's new ability to integrate previously unconscious experience (Cooper, 1996).

Over time, as we pursued the difficulty in being a person, we developed a particular form of play. For example, I would try to analyze something about the anxiety or prohibition related to the specificity of being a person, and rather than refer to him with the usual pronoun, "you," I would instead get ready to say his name, Leonard ____. He would smile and reluctantly finish my sentence for me, saying his name. It seemed like he was in a bit of a desensitization paradigm with me. As an enactment seen with a developmental lens, perhaps I may have also unwittingly been playing the part of a father who, unlike Leonard's actual father, was welcoming of his specific personhood.

Over the course of several years, as Leonard delved into these matters he also came to discuss how this specificity was linked to the ways that he reminded himself of his father in both his behavior and his appearance. As he was aging, he would often hear his old friends and his father's friends mention how similar he and his father looked; he could see this similarity as well. As we examined this, we talked about his parents' sexuality as the proof of Leonard's specificity, of his humanness. His discomfort with the idea of his parents creating him went far beyond the familiar discomfort of thinking about one's parents' sex life. Instead, it put Leonard increasingly in touch with his location in his family and the concrete realization that their sexual liaison was instrumental in making someone named Leonard ____.

Leonard's discomfort with self-criticism about being a person was quite unconscious until we were able to forge more links to his feelings of humiliation for others whom he knew who were persons (e.g., his friend with the guidebook). He agreed that humiliation involved projections of some of his own fears about how he might be regarded. Leonard seemed to be practicing doing something (saying his full name) about which he was phobic. I suppose that he was also, in a sense, submitting to me and my interest in him being a person, a specific person. But overall, I felt as though he was trying something on for size, practicing having an identity with an accepting person.

In a sense, from his earliest childhood, Leonard had felt little room to be a child, to be a little person with very little concerns. As he felt welcomed as a person, he was able to revisit his resulting pseudomaturity. Leonard's transference to me was strikingly positive, not idealizing but implicitly appreciative about my welcoming his status as a person. He never felt noticeable or conscious anger toward me around my wishes to know him as a person or to "make" him be the person he was as I might have expected. He did, however, try to engage me in various sadomasochistic ways either to submit to his authority (pseudomaturity) or to punish him in accordance with ways that he feared would result in his more open declaration of being "the guy he was," as he and I used to refer to it.

COUNTERTRANSFERENTIAL EXPERIENCE IN THE CONTEXT OF ANALYZING SELF-REPROACH

It is difficult for any analyst to hear another person's suffering in the form of relentless self-reproach. It is challenging to explore aspects of grandiosity embedded in self-loathing, but it is a part of the analyst's job to consider the multifarious quality of any experience. While many psychoanalytic writers have tried to compassionately address the complexity of grandiosity (e.g., Freud, 1914; Kernberg, 1975; Kohut, 1966; Volkan, 1973) in the narcissistic patient, their accounts have often focused more on patients who are explicitly grandiose. I think that many analysts experience a countertransference wish to protect patients from the potentially hurtful elements of pointing out unconscious grandiosity for fear that the patient will feel criticized or shamed (e.g., Morrison, 1994).

In fact, in some ways I think that one of the major thrusts of self-psychology was to serve as a corrective on some aspects of classical formulations about narcissistic trends, which in Kohut's view had led to iatrogenic aggression. While it was hardly the intention of classical theory to blame the narcissistic patient, special technical dimensions of working with narcissistic patients were not a focus of the first 75 years of psychoanalytic theory or technique. Kohut revolutionized psychoanalytic sensitivity to the adaptive aspects of narcissistic traits, including the various developmental lines of mirroring, idealization, and the multiplicity of function and meaning related to grandiose trends. Even more important, however, was his ability to place the patient's experience at the center of analytic formulation.

Anton Kris (1990), in his seminal paper on analyzing self-criticism, took up the failure of psychoanalysts over many years, roughly between the 1920s and the 1960s, to appreciate sufficiently the significance of unconscious self-criticism. He stated:

> To put the matter most simply, I believe that analysts have regularly, though unintentionally, sided with self-punitive attitudes of the patient. This failure of neutrality on the part of analysts is in large measure the result of a systematic error in psychoanalytic theory, overuse of the concept of unconscious guilt. I prefer to employ a distinction between punitive self-criticism and constructive self-criticism, both having conscious and unconscious components. (p. 605)

Kris elaborated how unconscious self-criticism can be recognized by its consequences: painful affects and states of deprivation. The deprivation may be as small as an interruption of the patient's freedom of associations in the analytic session when they prove too satisfying, or it may be a form of depriving pleasure outside analysis. Often, patients with punitive unconscious self-critical attitudes tend to attribute the analyst with forms of criticism toward the patient.

The analyst's countertransference in analyzing patients with high degrees of self-criticism often features a dichotomy between the fear of hurting the patient and trying to understand the patient in a way that may be helpful. In that frontier, we are always looking for alternatives to dichotomous either/ or (Kris, 1977) or doer/done-to (Benjamin, 2004) paradigms. Fortunately, many of our patients are also looking for a new space outside this dichotomous collapse of experiential possibility.

Probably the most common experience of analyzing self criticism is empathy or sympathy. In most instances, it is not difficult for me to understand why a particular patient has become overridingly self-critical. It is always interesting to look in a more detailed way at the varieties of sympathy or empathy that I experience in these contexts. One particularly difficult and not uncommon experience, especially in the early stages of analytic work, is the sense of my own intellectual flatness in response to the patient's self-loathing. It is as if the self-loathing is so conspicuous and painful that my curiosity is inhibited about its complex nature. It is easy for a patient's self-loathing to become a kind of dominant metaphor that, in turn, dominates our minds and restricts our freedom in thinking (Symington, 1983) about its multiple intrapsychic and interpersonal meanings. The analyst's often-instinctual acclimation and empathy toward the patient's self-reproach, although initially helpful, becomes a force inhibiting the analyst's ability to formulate and think. The reasons for this vary with different patients, but I think that the most usual stumbling block is fear of hurting or blaming the patient through interpretation.

One of the most inhibiting forms of countertransference may appear when the patient's prominent self-loathing involves continual evacuation and projection on to the analyst of the patient's self-criticism. The analyst may feel over time an inhibition in his or her thinking because this thinking is, for the patient, equated with criticism. Bion (1978) described feeling constrained and restricted by the patient's need to know what he was thinking. The patient was only able to imagine that his silence must mean that he was finding her to be defective in a number of ways. At some point, he imagined that he might want to point out to the patient that she was afraid of him having his own private thoughts. The analyst must risk the possibility and sometimes the probability that the patient with a high degree of self-loathing will be likely to experience an interpretation of this sort as one more form of criticism. This point of transference-countertransference entanglement has been described well through Symington's (1983) concept of the "corporate entity" shared by patient and analyst.

There are many forms of countertransference-inhibition and guilt that accompany analytic work related to analyzing self-criticism. Since self-reproach is among the most common clinical phenomena (e.g., Kris, 1991, 1994), it is something that psychoanalysts must get comfortable with analyzing. This is a good thing because most self-criticism burdens the sufferer and can benefit from analysis of its origins and functions. A great deal of self-criticism does, as Freud (1914) and Kris (1990) suggested, protect those we love from negative feelings, criticism, and especially anger. It is often a way to titrate anxiety and sadness intrapsychically and to maintain or restore internal homeostasis. But, not all self-criticism functions in these ways in the context of relationships with others, and it is only in the particular and peculiar crucible of psychoanalysis that countertransference concern and compassion can even be worth examining.

In the same way that tears may communicate to another person that we feel sad, fearful, needy, or regretful and that we need the other person to understand something about that, so also are there interpersonal, communicative aspects of self-criticism. It may be a communication that the individual's pain and self-infliction does not allow him or her to engage with another person or to take on their experience. It can become a way of placing restrictions on the other person in terms of limiting him or her to compassionate or reassuring responses rather than anything more complex or varied. It can involve an apparent act of masochistic submission that in fact unconsciously expresses dominance by dictating the other's response. Self-reproach can invite compliment and support as a corrective, and it can also express the individual's unconscious belief in his or her heroic goals and fantasies of achievement. The phrase "I could have been a contender" can be a realistic assessment of what a person should have been able to achieve in a particular circumstance, or it can be a chronic lament about a larger failure to grieve for the limitations of a real self in a real and limited life—the failure to accept a bad basketball shot from a mediocre player.

When the analyst feels anxious and guilty about trying to help a highly self-hating patient to explore these various meanings, the first line of action is to ask himself particular kinds of questions. A feeling of helplessness in one form or another is never far from the surface. When self-reproach is prominent, it can seem quite refractory to interventions of all sorts, so the impulse to want to do something more active and helpful is quite strong. Interestingly, the analyst's wish to be more active is sometimes implicitly devaluing to the patient if the patient is not feeling better about himself.

Often, the experience of helplessness is related to quite positive countertransference feelings toward the patient, such as the wish to relieve pain induced by constant self-critical refrains. Sometimes, I experience the wish to provide the patient with the satisfaction of feeling adequate, powerful, attractive, or intelligent, in contrast to what I once referred to with a patient as his "poisonous trilogy": "fat, dumb, and ugly." Some patients with enormous degrees of self-hatred that cannot seem to take me in as someone who holds them with high regard have worn me down. Sometimes, the patient cannot use me in the ways that I wish to be used (e.g., Winnicott, 1969). At times it is easy to feel simultaneously sympathetic with the patient's self-reproach and at war with it. The experience of feeling cared for and loved by the analyst, worthy of the analyst's regard, as it were, can become threatening to the patient and prompt the patient to ward it off. The patient's attachment to negative feelings and critical others is often at play (e.g., Fairbairn, 1952; Valenstein, 1972). For some patients, warding off wished-for support can help avoid being flooded by the need for love and approval.

At other times, a shift in more positive feelings can occur when a patient seems more accepting of praise from others with fewer unconscious, implicitly grandiose and disavowed needs for reassurance and admiration. In other words, I will notice that it is easier to like my patient when he or she can allow himself to feel the wish to be liked or loved as opposed to putting himself down and disavowing these needs.

Despite the enormous guilt that may sometimes be engendered, there are instances when a patient's self-criticism begins to feel different in more "negative" ways as analysis proceeds. The concept of the negative countertransference is a simplistic phrasing that fails to capture the layers of "positive" in the negative just as the apparently negative can be filled with warm, loving, or erotic aspects of experience. For example, with one patient, his self-criticism partly became so much more difficult for me the more I cared about him and the more I felt dehumanized by his abstract idealizations of me. But, within this primitive vocabulary of the negative countertransference, questions form, such as the following: Why has my patient's pain become less central in my experience than the sheer insatiability of his or her need for affirmation? Why am I more focused on such different ideas related to the patient's self-criticism than I was at an earlier time? Many important questions also follow related to the analyst's ability to bear affect.

I am not suggesting that changes in the countertransference automatically presage new diagnostic formulations of a patient's psychology. I believe that our consideration of the axis related to the analyst's countertransference and how we formulate self-reproach or any other symptom increases our responsibilities toward how we handle the powers of this countertransference. As Wolff-Bernstein (1999) pointed out, the countertransference is not a royal road toward the unconscious any more than are our other sources of information about our patients.

With these caveats in mind, it is difficult to experience annoyance with the patient's self-reproach as the analyst begins to feel and address some of the increasing demands of unconscious grandiosity. In such instances, the patient may have a feeling that nothing he does is good enough but is often unaware that he or she makes demands on family, friends, and the analyst that the holes in self-regard be filled. This can become draining and in fact may make those around the patient feel degraded, unimportant, or inadequate as well. The delicacy of taking up these matters with someone who desperately feels that he is undeserving of praise, yet constantly requires reassurance, is striking and quite precarious in the context of analytic work. I have previously reported on the case of Susan (Cooper, 2008), in which her demand to be smiled at in particular ways became enormously inhibiting for me and required much hard work between the two of us to understand our particular mode of transference-countertransference engagement.

Naturally, among the first and most important questions for the analyst to ask is whether his shift toward seeing elements of reproach as implicitly grandiose involves the analyst turning against the patient. It is possible that the demands exerted by the patient's self-criticism can exceed the emotional resources to interpret and understand. In turn, this might make the analyst blame the patient for having excessive demands.

It is also important for the analyst not to be crippled by a fear of considering the relevance of underlying grandiosity in relation to self-reproach. Understanding this dimension of self-reproach can help elucidate why it is so durable and refractory to interpretation. The patient has a stake in holding on to this self-punishment because it perpetuates self-regulatory fantasies. These fantasies often have to do with the feeling that "if only" (Akhtar, 1996) this or that, "I will be loved, or I will feel stronger or better about myself." Sometimes, the fantasies are based in competitive or dominant strategies related to wanting to win out over parents or siblings, to retaliate, and the like. I have often felt that it can be incredibly helpful for patients to see this grandiosity as a way to relinquish their self-criticism. It can be one of the most humorous and enjoyable sources of play between analyst and patient as they examine the impossible nature of the patient's expectations.

One patient, Jacob, had huge expectations for athletic performance placed on him, particularly by his peers and coaches in junior high and high school. An extremely talented young man, he was pushed by his basketball coaches to practice hard, which he did. Jacob was a good basketball player but could never achieve his own goals or meet the expectations placed on him by others. He was treated abusively by some of his peers in the high school he attended. Two particularly abusive boys called him "a pathetic waste of height." Jacob's father had been a very good amateur athlete and spent a great deal of time practicing with Jacob in several sports, including basketball. Yet, Jacob never experienced his father as pushy or critical. In his early 20s, when Jacob began working with me, he became overwhelmingly enraged as his intense self-criticism began to be exposed to him as rage toward his peers.

Jacob had grown up feeling inadequate relative to his peers on his high school teams. While he felt intellectually superior to them (Jacob was an outstanding student and quite bright), in relation to these boys he had felt inadequate and self-hating both in athletics and in terms of success with girls. Jacob was shy and felt uncomfortable with his height. As we began to examine more of his own expectations for himself, Jacob began to see that these cruel boys were echoing his own harsh and unrealistic expectations of himself. If he did not make the NBA (National Basketball Association), he was in his mind a waste of height. Jacob kept bumping up against how his enormous expectations for himself both academically and athletically were making him miserable and causing him to feel chronically punished. As he became less focused on those long-ago bullies and more focused on his own reparative, retaliatory, and grandiose fantasies, he began to ease up on himself and again enjoyed sports at the level of his real ability, which was, in fact, quite considerable relative to most athletes.

All psychoanalysts are also vulnerable to grandiose fantasies about what analysis will achieve for their patients. Caper (1992) has written cogently about the analyst's problematic needs to heal that actually interfere with analytic work. For patients with a great deal of self-criticism, the analyst's grandiose healing fantasies will meet a challenge. One outcome is that the analyst may empathize partly as a reaction formation against his frustration or unconscious desire to retaliate against the patient. In these circumstances, it is incumbent on the analyst to become free to interpret the patient's various forms of self-criticism, including the patient's potential to destroy the work of analysis.

Self-criticism—like any conflict, symptom, or self-experience—cannot be fully understood outside the matrices of internal regulatory functions and human interaction. There need not be a fundamental incompatibility between appreciating internal regulation and interpersonal regulation and negotiation. I suspect that the tendency for theoretical dichotomizing between intrapsychic and interpersonal has always been partly related to a form of either/or thinking that Kris (1977) described in terms of understanding some forms of conflict. This narrowness in how we view psychoanalytic theory is likely part of countertransference to the psychoanalytic process itself. Countertransference to the psychoanalytic process (e.g., Freud, 1954; Parsons, 2006) can involve a need to adhere to or to valorize a particular psychoanalytic theory and the rejection of the flexibility to draw on different psychoanalytic theories to understand clinical phenomena and the analytic process.

Symptoms as a distinct subject matter have not been a primary focus of attention of writers within the relational and interpersonal tradition, but many have alluded to symptomatic behaviors and interpersonal patterns that characterize interactions. Bromberg (1998, 2001) wrote about symptoms in various ways, capturing the contextual and constructivist nature of how we conceptualize symptoms while acknowledging the idea that we have enduring solutions to psychic problems. Blechner (2008) also tried to address an interpersonal approach to particular kinds of symptoms, including panic attacks.

I have never understood why there needs to be an antipathy between a constructivist approach to symptoms (e.g., Mitchell, 1991) and an interest in describing symptoms from an intrapsychic perspective. Unless we have in mind a kind of radical social constructivism, the notion of elements of an enduring personality organization is viable. Constructivism emphasizes—and I agree—that the personality organization in question is partly in the eye of the beholder. As Mitchell (1991) clarified, the notion of reified categories of psychic need versus wish are partly related to the analyst's countertransference experience. Thus, an analyst can only make a determination about the patient's need or the urgency of a request in the context of that analyst's empathic capacities and reserves with the particular patient. As I hope I have made clear, the analyst's countertransference experience as it involves understanding the vicissitudes of self-reproach is essential.

Nor do I see any reason to completely dispense with the notion of compromise formation, a concept deeply embedded in conflict theory (e.g., Brenner, 1976) that I find helpful in understanding aspects of intrapsychic conflict and self-regulating. I would, however, extend the notion of compromise formation to include the realm of interpersonal compromise formation, a notion suggested as well by Rothstein (2005). By the latter term, I mean to suggest that all dyads arrive at interpersonal compromises based on the personalities, strengths, and conflicts experienced by each of the participants. All moments in analytic work involve interpersonal compromise formation. Enactment is in fact a kind of interpersonal compromise formation. It might even be speculated that self-criticism is among the most ubiquitous symptoms that human beings experience partly because turning against ourselves rather than our intimates makes us less likely to harm each other.

The vicissitudes of self-criticism, like many debilitating experiences, require us to think about how our patients maintain regulation in the density and "intertwinedness" (Merleau-Ponty, 1964) of analytic interaction. As analysts, we feel the complexity of their experiences of self-criticism. We try, through our own stops and starts, to translate elements of these multiples meanings and the complexity of experience that are embedded in self-criticism in order to open up new avenues of meaning.

Chapter 3

Privacy, reverie, and the analyst's ethical imagination*

There are many registers from which the analyst can illuminate points of transference-countertransference enactment, and our reverie is often quite useful in this process. The modality by which the analyst communicates these formulations of unconsciously held object relations and defenses also varies and includes verbal interpretation through symbolic speech, interpretive action (Ogden, 1994b), and at times, interpretations that involve "analyst disclosure"—a construction of the analyst's subjectivity put forward to enhance the patient's understanding of enactments of the transference-countertransference (Cooper, 1998a, 1998b). In this chapter, I describe varying ways of using and thinking about forms of analytic reverie and the analyst's privacy.

Clinical articles illustrating aspects of expressive use of counter-transference have often addressed points of impasse and stalemate in analytic work. Generally, however, analysts interested in more active use of countertransference have not paid equal attention to "quieter" moments in analytic work. The work of Ogden is a major exception to this observation.

My thinking about the analyst's privacy and reverie in clinical analysis is substantially influenced by Ogden's many contributions (Ogden, 1994a, 1997a, 2004). Ogden has become one of the frontier cartographers of the psychoanalyst's privacy and reverie, particularly the understanding of the "specific unconscious, intersubjective relationship" with each patient (1997b, p. 588). Like Ogden, I formulate reverie as a road to the unconscious, intersubjective objects in the mind of the patient and analyst. However, in my view, the interpersonal is interfused with those of the unconscious, intersubjective internalized object relation described by Ogden. I will try to demonstrate how I expressively make use of reverie, particularly the register from which I sometimes speak to a patient about the bearing of my own experience of intersubjective objects in the mind of the patient.

---

* Portions of this chapter appeared in *Psychoanalytic Quarterly*, 77, 1045–1073, 2008. Reprinted with permission.

THEORETICAL BACKGROUND

Freud's (1912) suggestion that the analyst "should simply listen and not bother about whether he is keeping anything in mind" (p. 112) is a common marker for most analysts who are interested in the reverie process. For Ogden (1996, 1997a), like Freud, the analyst's privacy and reverie afford the analyst a psychic space and actual time to make associational linkages and largely unconscious contextualization for listening to the patient. Ogden's (1996) helpful translation of Freud underscores the importance of the analyst creating conditions in which the analyst can maximize his or her capacity for a receptivity and play of the mind.

It is interesting and a bit paradoxical that in many ways most psychoanalytic models have more procedural transparency regarding maintaining the analyst's privacy than is so for the relational model. For most models, the injunction to be anonymous is quite clear and unambiguous to the patient regardless of how much the patient might protest that anonymity or seek to change, or even destroy, the anonymity of the analyst. For Freud, the analyst's privacy ensures an ideal canvas for the patient's freedom of association and securing the maximal opportunity for the analyst's associational drift. In contrast, in the relational model, there are instances when the analyst might make use of and even reveal aspects his or her experience. Moreover, while many models of analytic work agree with Hoffman's (1983) observation that the patient is often reading us in many ways, the relational model emphasizes the analyst's technical proclivity to follow up on the patient's perceptions as a mode of bringing the transference into more conscious experience (e.g., Aron, 1991; Gill, 1983).

Ogden (1996) draws connections between Bion's (1962) characterization of reverie as the absence of "memory and desire" and Freud's notion of simply listening. In both states, the analyst does not try too hard to remember or even understand too much, instead using personal capacities or states to "catch the drift" of the patient's mostly unconscious experience. In part, Bion's (1962) magnificent poetic of the analytic space—"we're both in this alone"—was his way of describing his own requirements for having access to the patient in ways other than those permitted in conventional forms of interpersonal exchange.

Ogden's efforts place into focus the dialectical interplay of states of reverie of analysand and analyst, resulting in the creation of a third analytic subject. The asymmetrical experiences of the analytic third by patient and analyst promote understanding, verbal expression, and symbolization of the drift of the analysand's unconscious internal object world. Reverie is the state of mind that allows for experiencing and expanding the analytic third.

Like Ogden, I find that many experiences of my reverie are not immediately translatable in a one-to-one fashion about what is going on in the analytic relationship. In my experience, many of the images and associations that come up in response to the patient are just as likely to be defensive as clarifying, and a judicious process of filtering and considering these experiences over time seems well justified. Reverie, like much countertransference data, can be enticing as an invitation to more quickly elaborate confusing and contradictory information or problematic affective states in the analyst and analysand. Ogden was correct to emphasize that these experiences need to accrue to discover whether and how they are meaningful and that we do need to let ourselves be adrift without forcing our forms of reverie into interpretations.

I also like Ogden's commitment to not automatically dismiss our reverie as somehow idiosyncratically personal. While we may have experiences during reverie that suggest a failure to be receptive or understanding of the patient, we usually cannot know that without obtaining more data. At first glance, there are many instances when my thoughts go in directions that seem pressed by my own needs and are not immediately useful to understanding the patient or are active obstructions to understanding the patient (e.g., Schwaber, 1992). Sometimes, however, closer examination might suggest useful connections to points of unconsciously held transference-countertransference phenomena. Thus, I do not subscribe to the notion that countertransference is always best understood as an obstruction to the listening to the patient's experience. Time and repeated experience afforded by the intensity and continuity of analytic work are a great help in the process of deciphering what might be an impediment or an aid in elaborating points of the unconsciously held transference-countertransference experiences.

Obviously, the experiences of privacy afforded to patient and analyst are a part of what allows for the analyst's experience of reverie. Bion (1959) noted that the analyst's abstinence produces what he called "the sense of isolation within an intimate relationship" (p. 73). Reverie within the analyst is intimately, intersubjectively related to the privacy and solitude afforded for the analyst.

It is in order to preserve the place of privacy for both patient and analyst that Ogden (1996) has criticized the fundamental rule of association—that the patient try to say everything that comes to mind. Ogden questioned the rule because it minimizes the dialectical interplay of the capacities of both analyst and patient for reverie. He feared that it can pose the danger of becoming a kind of "frozen injunction" for any analytic dyad. Ogden was concerned that a long-standing appreciation of the place of solitude and privacy, particularly as espoused by the independent tradition of psychoanalysis (e.g., Winnicott, 1958), can be overlooked or even violated in the invitation to say everything that comes to mind. Ogden added to this invitation his statement or reminder to the patient who begins analysis that each of the two participants needs also to have a place for privacy.

I have always had a rather complex reaction to this recommendation to the patient. I have concerns that telling a patient that "we must both have a place for privacy" may run the risk of unnecessarily conveying something about my own wishes for distance or emphasizing my attunement to the patient's needs for distance. In my experience, patients are quite adept at maintaining privacy and editing their thoughts despite the issuing of an invitation to tell me what is on their mind. I can, or at least try to, manage my own needs for privacy. While there may be instances when I tell a patient about my wish to maintain levels of personal privacy, I prefer to talk about that in a particular clinical context with a particular patient rather than as a general statement at the beginning of my work with patients.

Moreover, I am concerned that I might be construed as issuing a kind of nonimpingement promise: that I will try not to invade their privacy. While I think that respect for the patient's privacy is paramount to analytic work, even a precondition for analytic exploration, I cannot promise not to impinge or invade the patient's privacy. I have referred to forms of "good enough impingement" (Cooper, 2000a) as an inevitable part of analytic work involving various forms of misattunement, countertransference enactment, or what Balint (1968) termed "the poverty of interpretation." I have little doubt that, in reminding the patient of his and the patient's need for privacy, Ogden was not promising that he would not impinge. I do wonder, however, whether for some patients this reminder might unconsciously or consciously resonate with either a fear of invading the privacy of the analyst or a fear of the analyst's process of getting to know him or her.

My use of reverie is usually associated with an interspersing of images, fantasies, and recollections, which alternate, with a very conscious form of thought and formulation. My mind is rarely adrift for an extended period of time. Instead, I somewhat reflexively move from types of reverie into much more formulated, private interpretations and often imagined dialogue with a patient about my formulations.

Put another way, it is my sense that in comparison to Ogden's descriptions, my reverie is more fleeting, imperfect, and a more porous vessel. My reverie often leads immediately to private, imagined interpretations of what has been and perhaps is being enacted. These imagined interpretations are, I suppose, a kind of associational linkage, but they are often tried on and often discarded. Sometimes, this "postreverie" thinking leads me quite productively to anticipate how these formulations might also involve particular kinds of enactments, such as truncating various kinds of elaboration of meaning or repeating various patterns of object relating in the patient's life. But often, my reverie and postreverie thinking are what allow me to productively explore how I am enacting patterns of the transference-countertransference as well as the potential meanings and enactment that might accompany an interpretive transition with a patient.

These forms of postreverie thinking all comprise what I call the analyst's ethical imagination. The term *ethical imagination* refers to the analyst's modes of thinking about various forms of enactment of the unconscious transference-countertransference or psychical entanglement between patient and analyst. The analyst's thinking that sometimes follows associational drift is often a precondition for clarifying the unconscious intrapsychic-interpersonal implications of an interpretive shift or transition in our understanding with the patient.

The analyst's ethical imagination covers territory that lies partially outside the kind of maternal reverie described by Bion (1970). However, within this imaginative form of contemplating or formulating reverie, the analyst is adrift in a different kind of way, allowing him- or herself to imagine the usefulness of a form of understanding or the potential impact of such an intervention. The impact might include particular fantasies of helping a patient to understand something new. The impact might also include fantasies of hurting or impinging on a patient — a kind of collateral damage of sorts. Since it is an unconscious aspect of transference-countertransference enactment that I am pondering, it is never entirely possible to know in advance either its usefulness or its accuracy about what we are intending to illuminate. It is because of this uncertainty that I find it useful to think of our imagination, our ability to formulate something as related to an ethic of responsibility or accountability. What characterizes the analyst's ethical imagination is the attempt to think about what we are doing and what we are about to do in our participation with the patient.

Since my imagination is often directed toward the ubiquity of enactment as a feature of analytic process, it is of course a construction of what I imagine I am enacting; it is never entirely possible to know this in advance. This privacy, reverie, and the subsequent formulations I refer to as the analyst's ethical imagination might seem like a kind of injunction that the analyst try to think about what he or she is doing and what he or she is about to do in participation with the patient. I do not view it as a form of technical advice or a conscious attempt to leave no clinical stone unturned, instead believing that to a large extent it is what most analysts do as they utilize forms of reverie and associational linkage, absorption of affect, transference attributions, and the like. We think about the various kinds of impact that have resulted and will result from the choices we make through acts of either extending or constricting interpretive range, through shifts in interpretive focus, or sometimes in holding off an interpretation.

Ogden's (1994a) fascinating discussion of his use of "interpretive action" within the analytic third is an example of moments I refer to as the analyst's ethical imagination. Ogden describes a series of patients with whom he conveys his understanding of the transference-countertransference through what he calls interpretive action. The last might include self-conscious forms of silence at times when he would usually make an interpretation or refusal to engage in invited activities elicited by the patient that he had previously enacted. These are self-conscious efforts to stand outside particular forms of repetitive transference-countertransference enactments and are accompanied by the analyst's silently formulated interpretations. These examples are very close to what I have in mind in describing the analyst's ethical imagination, although I am not referring to "actions" in Ogden's use of the term. Instead, my formulations and interpretations are primarily verbally based understandings about new formulations or interpretations.

One of the most important ways that I differ from Ogden's use of reverie in making interpretation is that I sometimes say something about a construction of my own experience or how I am implicated within points of transference-countertransference enactment. Ogden's use of reverie does not include instances when the analyst uses conscious or deliberate attempts to reveal a construction of the analyst's experience to illuminate the unconscious transference-countertransference.

My intention at these moments of more direct statement of countertransference experience is not to provide gratuitous, exhibitionistic, or diversionary statements of personal feeling. Instead, on those occasions my intention is to express something from the register of my countertransference experience as it relates to particular points of unconscious transference-countertransference. In fact, I do not consider these moments of speaking from this register as best described as "self-disclosure" at all, instead preferring to term them *analyst-disclosure* (Cooper, 1998a, 1998b). This register relates very little to the analyst's person or self and instead, when used judiciously, is the result of highly formulated experience (Stern, 1983). I have suggested the distinctions between analyst and self-disclosure because the subjectivity of the analyst is central to all kinds of interpretive processes in analytic work. I view the register from which the analyst speaks of countertransference experience as embedded within particular aspects of the transference-countertransference and is no more expressive of the analyst's "self" than is any other kind of analytic intervention or interpretation. Like all interpretations, it is partially motivated by unconscious experience. To be sure, there are varieties of countertransference disclosure that emanate more from "unformulated experience" (e.g. Stern, 1983), but these are not the variety of interpretations I am focusing on in this examination of the analyst's use of reverie.

I view analyst disclosure as quite similar to Ogden's formulation of the paradox at the heart of our personal and private reveries in clinical work. Ogden (1997a) highlights that as personal as our reveries feel to us, they are not best understood as personal creations because reverie is at the same time an "aspect of a jointly (but asymmetrically) created unconscious intersubjective construction." Ogden (1994a, 1996) refers to these constructions as the intersubjective third. Similarly, Symington (1983) refers to these phenomena as "corporate entities"—points of shared transference-countertransference that are jointly but asymmetrically held by patient and analyst. These phenomena both illuminate points of unconsciously held transference and can serve as obstructions to better understanding points of transference-countertransference impasse.

Through a series of brief clinical vignettes, I try to focus on the analyst's use of reverie in the area I refer to as his or her ethical imagination. I present vignettes that vary in whether or how the analyst makes use of his or her countertransference and expressive countertransference.

THE ANALYST'S PRIVACY IN THE PATIENT'S MIND

The following vignettes are from the third month of an analysis held four times a week. Sam lies down on the couch and begins the hour: "Your haircut makes you look younger this week. I think it's your haircut. You look younger than your stated age." Sam starts laughing, and behind the couch, I'm smiling, too. He has immediately come to the awareness that I have never stated my age. We start looking into what the notion of "my stated age" means to him.

Sam, a man in his mid-20s often comes into analytic sessions looking at me intently with a probing survey of my mood and dress. He is prone to comment on my appearance, particularly on whether I'm wearing a tie or a suit jacket. Sometimes, I am dressed more formally and sometimes more informally. Sam believes that he is gay although confused about the fact that he is emotionally drawn to women for his closest relationships. He feels that he is not and has never been sexually turned on by women. His best friend is a woman, and they feel that they love each other. She wants to be with him—to live with him and potentially get married and have children despite her knowledge that when they have tried to have sex he found it unstimulating. Sam has been honest with her about his sexual liaisons with men, although he has never had a male boyfriend, instead preferring the companionship of this woman friend and, earlier, other women. When Sam masturbates, he thinks exclusively of men. Sam and his woman friend agree that their seldom lovemaking is not occasioned by his sense of passion and excitement. He has never fallen in love with a man or longed to have a man as a life companion as he has with this woman, despite his lack of sexual excitement.

As we start to look into Sam's beginning statement, "You look younger than your stated age," what emerges in the session is how much he idealizes many around him and me. He says that he always wants to think the best of his friends and professors at graduate school. I am aware of having some new hostile feelings toward Sam as he explores "my stated age." I realize that his attempts to idealize others and me never quite feel positive to me. Instead, they have a competitive and somewhat aggressive feel to them. I realize that, in fact, I sometimes find it patronizing and more hostile than I have previously realized. Then I ask myself, am I registering a competitive feeling from Sam, or is it the way in which he imagines and experiences me (creating a conversation with me as one who reveals something), within a private, autoerotic process that leaves me out?

Sam continues in his associations and says that he is fascinated and humored by his creation of my private self. I privately associate to a business involving a hostile takeover. He keeps laughing and says that in his mind I have stated my age, and it is almost as though he is laughing at someone in his head that is me with whom he is conversing. My thoughts go to how he has privately, psychically, invaded my privacy and taken over a reality that is unpleasant for him—that I have not revealed many things about myself. He has always been angry about my not sharing more about my life. He wants us to be friends and to spend time together socially. He has told me that I am too old for him sexually, but he wants me to be an older friend. He enjoys when we have briefly conversed together more naturally a few times. We have some areas of overlapping intellectual interest, and I imagine that I would enjoy talking to him more about our shared interests than the sense I have of Sam's anger about my not stating things (my stated age) and his attempt to take that matter into his own hands and mind.

As the hour continues, some of my private thoughts seem to become clearer. My private life, my vital statistics, and maybe also my private parts—age, marital status, religion, my private thoughts—all exist in his mind as a "stated something." He speaks more of how much he wants to have access to things he does not have control over. He associates to his tendency to find a way around feeling the lack or deficit and how looking on the bright side makes many of his relationships more superficial. I imagine that he co-opts my privacy into a defense against hostility. He knows that he finds it hard to bear my privacy as something out of his control and that we are bringing it into the open—his privacy is something he is willing to give over to the court of therapeutic exploration and interpretation. Sam associates to his girlfriend's anger at him about not making up his mind about women or men as well as a developing successful professional career, which could lead him in two very different directions in the future. He needs to decide at some point soon about each of these different directions, the choices available to him romantically and professionally.

At some level, the hour is productive and interesting in that we come on this interesting part of Sam's mind or internalized object relation—your stated age. The patient is in conflict about the parts of him that he knows make for superficiality in glossing over what he knows and does not know and that he has to find a way to bring himself more fully to those with whom he is intimate. He has to work with the conflict he feels and anxiety he feels about his anger toward me about not stating my age or not knowing me in the way he wishes to know himself and me. It seems implied that we may eventually be able to explore more about why he may be anxious about asking.

While I am very fond of Sam, I end the session aware that I am no less annoyed now than during the hour. What is it about Sam that caused me to feel annoyed? Over many sessions prior and subsequent to this one with Sam, I visualized Sam at home organizing his surroundings, folding clothes, and cleaning up the house. I fell on these kinds of visual images of Sam despite the fact that they did not come from him. It is not uncommon for me to find that as I listen to patients I locate them in various places, and this reverie can be very useful. Sometimes, the location of a place is related to a point of transference-countertransference that helps me locate a sense of unconscious fantasy or an object relation that I have not previously noticed. At other times, I am aware that I am engaging in a form of defensive distancing, a kind of isolation of affect that allows me to locate the patient outside the consulting room or somewhere other than with me.

Sam's self-sufficiency and organization were adaptations to a family life in which he felt his parents were largely laissez-faire, from his point of view, to a fault. They wanted him to feel that "on his own" he would come to his own sense of values, beliefs, and interests. He was an only child, and while highly valued, he never felt as though he was treated as a child. Conversations with his parents seemed always pitched at an adult level with what he regarded as expectations that he be mature before his time—in fact, pseudomature. He envied his closest friend in grade school and high school, whose parents were directive, opinionated, and sometimes dictatorial. During one session early in his analysis, he associated to his friend's father as dictatorial. In association to "dictatorial," Sam said that he wished his father had had more of a dick. He wanted his father to be stronger with his mother and that he often deferred to her judgment with self-effacing, cheery, cooperation. He recognized some of these character traits in himself, often glossing over differences and sometimes disappointment in others and him.

Over the course of a number of sessions as I began to make use of these images and my continued mild irritation toward Sam's use of the analyst in his mind, my stated age, I became aware of how I felt myself to be continually "folded into," as it were, an internalized scenario that Sam held. When I made interpretations, they often seemed too immediately or easily incorporated by Sam. In turn, his understanding would sometimes seem a bit too superficial. I realized more than I ever had that Sam often seemed quite pleased with whatever I would have to say, and that his affective range was quite focused on being cheery and cooperative. At one point during one of our sessions, my mind turned toward a fantasy of making a mess of Sam's apartment, overturning things that had been neatly stacked and throwing things out of the closet. In association to the "closet" at this point in the analysis, I imagined that Sam's persistent masturbatory fantasies about men and only men might be a clue that he would prefer to be with men, and that his girlfriend might partially protect him from seeking more intimacy with men—thus the fantasy of throwing things out of the closet. This series of thoughts marked a movement away from a particular form of uncertainty I had held in my mind up to this point in the analysis about whether Sam used men as a defense against intimacy with women or vice versa. While I was still quite uncertain about whether Sam would decide ultimately to be with a man or a woman, I began to believe that his confusion served his purposes not to get too close to anyone in an intimate relationship.

These associations began a slight shift in my mode of formulation and interpretation with Sam. I realized that I had been quite content to have Sam work with my stated age in his head, the internalized representation of me, because it would help us elaborate aspects of his unconscious fantasy life. His idealizations of me and senior colleagues seemed too easy to accept, and that I could easily slide into his proscribed roles for others and me. He also seemed so consistently unassailable with his girlfriend. He would say to her that he "just couldn't figure this out yet"—whether he wanted to be with her or with men. He felt guilty that he was making her wait, yet he needed to know what he wanted to do. It was clear to me that he was waiting for her to decide what they would do or perhaps for me to tell him what to do about her, men, or his career choices or even to volunteer my age (although he continued never to ask). He would create a private, "unstated/stated" age or stated position of uncertainty about object choice until pushed to do otherwise. I had been enacting a form of compliance with his unconscious, quiet, but tyrannical hold on my asserting something about my independence from the analyst in his mind. Indeed, in my continued passivity to take this up I was enacting something about being a laissez-faire parent, allowing him to feel, fraudulently, at the helm of his family.

When I arrive at an understanding about something related to what Ogden referred to as the unconscious transference-countertransference or unconscious object relation, interpretations begin to form more clearly in my mind. I also arrive with more clarity at what I may have been enacting with the patient. It is at this point that I am struck with a variety of clinical choices, and this is what I refer to as the analyst's ethical imagination.

The phrase "You look younger than your stated age" now seems more obvious as a complaint cloaked within a compliment—a complaint that he did not know me more intimately and perhaps even that I did not confront him about his wish to know me more intimately. He wanted to avoid expressing his own wishes and needs to know. His language has demonstrated how I had enacted some process of allowing him to be a pseudomature boy, a boy who thinks he knows the facts and who does not know the facts. I began challenging Sam more actively. I told him, "I think that you're waiting for me and others in your life to give you advice and act like parents who are engaged and want to give of themselves to you. Parents should know the facts like what to do with your penis or your career." Sam seemed relieved to be able to speak more freely about these wishes as we began to get more deeply into how insistent he was about wanting this advice. He joked, "That's the idea. So now can we proceed to the advice?"

In essence, I take up what was in some ways obvious all along—Sam's wish to know my stated age without having to ask or to have to show his desire to know. This is what he had been warding off, a warding off of many feelings of sadness and anger camouflaged in some ways by autoerotic and self-sufficient fantasy processes.

My imagination regarding these various kinds of reverie also require me to consider the sobering prospect that as I become more actively confrontational about these processes, I may very well be enacting his wishes for me or someone in his life to be forceful, parental, and guiding and to tell him what to do—a dick as it were. I consider it the work of the analyst to ponder the inevitable continuing aspects of enactment intrinsic to whatever direction our interpretive focus takes us.

This particular set of clinical observations also raises complex aspects of the analyst's ethical imagination. I have to challenge more actively Sam's autistic attempt to experience me as stating my age when I have not while making no promises actually ever to state my age. This is a familiar place for many analysts, who run the risk of needing to make interpretations that may stoke the fire of the patient's curiosity about us as "real" objects while not promising to provide any more information about us as real objects. Naturally, this can become another form of enactment, including the possibility of enacting a retaliatory teasing object as a response to Sam's self-sufficient antidote and private way of not wanting to be in the position of feeling needs or desire to know me more.

Note that in this clinical example I have taken up matters quite similar to Ogden's (1997a) use of reverie as "simultaneously a personal/private event and an intersubjective one" (p. 568). I have not spoken directly with the analysand about my own experiences and instead attempt to speak to the analysand "from" what I am thinking and feeling.

THE CHICKEN AND THE EGG

In this clinical example, I illustrate how my own needs for reverie and privacy help me when I express more direct parts of my experience during the interpretation of points of transference-countertransference entanglement.

Josh was a man in his early 50s who often gets himself into masochistic relationships with others. Josh felt that he could not get his mother's attention as a young boy. From his point of view, she was unavailable largely because of her ambitious career and outside romantic interests. His father was more available to him but not very easy to admire. Josh's father wore his neediness and sexuality on his sleeve. He was damaged in Josh's view, unproductive in a career in which he never lived up to his potential. Josh's father seemed to "hang on" his mother in ways that seemed pathetic to Josh, particularly since she rebuffed his attempts to hold and touch her. She seemed annoyed and turned off by her husband's attempts to be affectionate. Later in his 20s, Josh learned that his mother had been involved in one serious extramarital relationship during his adolescence, and that she had at least a few affairs during his childhood. Josh's parents split up when he went to college, and he now felt as though their marriage was held together quite precariously throughout his childhood.

Josh's transference involved feeling unimportant to me, not wanting to risk whether he mattered. He treated his sessions like they were unimportant to me because they involved him, and I would be more interested in patients who mattered more to themselves and to me. He was often late to sessions, sometimes recounting ways in which he felt unworthy of the attention he wanted from me and others. I regarded our relationship as something akin to what he felt with his mother—that for Josh I was largely unaware of him, finding him unappealing in his view and not really registering any need or desire of my own to get to know him. He would sometimes laugh (with sadness) about this as something that he knew not to be true but that nevertheless he felt "in his bones." From the beginning, I had wondered if Josh's mother was as inattentive as he had experienced or was his identification with his father as someone rejected by his mother quite important either to assuage his guilt or to remain close to his father.

Josh arrives at his session at the beginning of his second year of analysis and starts talking about his law partners, two female and one male, whom he feels devalue his work relative to their own. He feels he sometimes does not exist in the room with them. I hear this as an allusion to a way he feels he does not exist for me. I find myself getting distracted, thinking about what I will be doing that night and later that day, work I have to do, and some creative writing I have been experimenting with lately.

I hear Josh say to me through the distraction of my reverie: "I want to know what you think about this." He is referring to the ways in which he does not exist in the room for his colleagues and how devalued he feels with them. Of course, I am thinking about the ways I just made him not exist by thinking about some of my own ideas separate from Josh. I was struck by his very unusual inquiry about what I was thinking about this frequent complaint of being unimportant to his colleagues. I am thinking to myself that I want to comment on the more proximate inquiry related to how I understand his experience of not existing with his partners. I am aware that by doing so I get myself out of the very uncomfortable position of knowing that I was enacting something in the room with him that he describes feeling all the time with others in his life. I am not sure I want to talk more directly about that yet, if ever.

I say: "I'm struck that you've asked me about the partners ignoring you in a way that is unusual. By asking, you've done something that's hard for you to do—to legitimize your own need to feel that you matter and that you have the authority to ask. In asking me what I think about that, you'd like to feel that I think you matter or that they should pay more attention to you."

His thoughts go in a direction that is somewhat typical for Josh:

JOSH: I'm thinking that a part of me is glad that you'll be away soon [on vacation]. I usually think that at least you need my money even though I don't think you need or want anything else from me. Then when you go away I get sad because I think he doesn't even need my money.

ME: You feel expendable.

JOSH: Yes, you need nothing from me like my mother needed nothing from me.

ME: But you just disappeared again with me. You asked me directly what I thought about your partners ignoring you, and then you went away and said that you're forgettable to me by dint of my willingness to go on vacation.

JOSH: I was forgettable to her, but I can't help but want to be significant to her. I can't stop trying.

ME: And you feel like if you ask to matter to me or her the less likely it is that she will be there for you or that I will be. She doesn't need you, and I don't need you. So then you disappear again.

In the moment of reverie that I have described, the moment in which I am privately disappearing from him, I am likely enacting the role of his mother. Josh is talking about that experience with his colleagues and perhaps symbolically with his mother and me. He may also be attuned to my actual disappearance with him. I believe that I am enacting this not because it has happened for the first time but because it is the first time that I became aware of it when he is alluding to it in displacement. This way of knowing for me is private at this point, but he may feel it. I am not ready to tell him because I fear that by telling him that it is so, I might be enacting something even harder for him to deal with, which is that I am pulling away. I worry that he will conclude that it is because he is not worthy of being memorable or loved. I know that this will have to be discussed, or do I? My thought at this point is that I may very well tell him about this interaction if it is happening repeatedly, but I am not ready to yet. I need my privacy to think about this and see whether it keeps happening. But, I suspect that he and I are in a chicken–egg process, a mode of reciprocal influence in which he may feel me disappearing, so he disappears. But, he may also be reacting to an internalized maternal object he experienced as neglectful. I feel him disappearing, and when he does, sometimes instead of pointing that out to him, at times I go off somewhere else. Where it all begins is, of course, hard to say.

In these moments, I ask, Why do I need some privacy? I am aware that I am afraid of hurting him. By underscoring my moments of distractibility, I might be requiring of him a capacity for reflection that exceeds his ability to regulate his self-esteem. Is the fear of hurting him real or imagined by me? Another side of my ethical imagination is to think about whether I am protecting myself from conveying to him in vivid, more observable terms how I was leaving him and relegating him to the realm of the unimportant. Might it let him see more about the impact of his own self-imposed disappearance on others? Would showing him this allow him to consider more the plausibility reality and substance of his inner life and cognitive process in contrast to how he often reflexively dismisses this level of experience? Will showing him the analyst's correlate experience allow him to feel something about how I am assailable and culpable in this way, or is it a way to unload my own sense of guilt and culpability. He has a right to be angry with his mother and me. More importantly, he has a right to trust himself and his own authority. Like any dilemma involving complexity, I need to be able to sit with the affective implications or fallout, which comes from anything, I decide.

Outside the hours with Josh, my thoughts sometimes go in a more theoretical direction to articles by Steiner (1993) from a Kleinian perspective and Slochower (1996) from a relational perspective; each described patients for whom interpretation that implies aspects of the analyst's subjectivity can be destructive for periods of time during analysis. Steiner described how sometimes "patient-based" interpretations feel too blaming or intrusive to some patients. Similarly, Slochower described patients for whom the act of revealing aspects of the analyst's experience can repeat the patient's earlier experiences with parents who were overinvolved with their own experiences and neglectful of their children. Then, I think of a contrasting view of Bass (1996), who suggested that if we make this assumption about the destructive use of the analyst's subjectivity, we may be more likely to find it. In my view, this to me is not a debate that is possible to be resolved except in the privacy of the analyst's imagination and through discovery with a particular patient. It is a kind of ethical imagination of the analyst in which the analyst's reverie and need for privacy can play and work. This debate does not resolve itself in any way other than that these are matters to consider with each patient–analyst dyad.

I use my privacy and reverie engaged in these clinical imaginings, and I try to think about it also from various theoretical perspectives, which matter to me, what I call the pluralistic third. My use of this privacy and reverie, in contrast to Ogden's wonderful illustrations of the use of reverie, may result in direct statements of affect, ideas, or behavior, which the patient would not have a way of knowing without what I refer to as *analyst disclosure*. I refer to it as analyst disclosure rather than self-disclosure (Cooper, 1998a, 1998b) because it relates to the use of my privacy. I retain a strong sense of a private self when I disclose affects, ideas, and behaviors that are part of the interpretive work. Privacy and reverie are what allow my private self to bring forward parts of me that I try to help the patient to understand about him- or herself in relation to me.

On occasion, the pattern of my own distractability matched Josh's description of important others (e.g., mother, me, and colleagues) who did not seem to register his presence. Eventually, I did in fact talk to Josh about this pattern of my inattention that accompanied his experience of other's inattention during a session when I was *not* distracted. He seemed increasingly present, telling me more directly that he did not feel memorable to me and important. I told him: "I notice myself being most likely to be distracted with you when I experience you as giving up on yourself, particularly when you're withdrawing from alive, sexual, funny and hostile parts of yourself." He said, "Maybe when I need you most." I said, "Yes, I imagine that it is when you need me most to show you what you're doing or encourage you to do otherwise." At the point that I chose to talk to him from this register, I could do so particularly because I was not in the middle of feeling overwhelmed by my own feelings of guilt about my withdrawal from him. Josh was becoming much stronger, trusting himself more, and willing to talk to me more directly about what he wished from me.

I do not want to suggest that this is a necessary technical prescription for anyone else. While it was my guess that Josh would have had a hard time with a more direct disclosure at the moment when I initially became aware of this confluence of intersubjective events that I have described, it is quite difficult for me to know. Instead, I made my clinical decisions based on my own sense of what I was able to convey about how his tendency to feel forgettable might sometimes engender or augment that experience in others. In fact, we discussed how much his growing awareness of feeling unimportant to others and recognizing these feelings in others, while not always correct, were probably part of his own process of growing trust in his own mind and experience. This clinical moment began a process by which Josh became more aware of trusting some of his own experiences of neglect and his own agency in seeing how unconsciously he disappeared from others before they could withdraw from him.

SOME PARADOXICAL ASPECTS OF BEING ONESELF AS PATIENT AND ANALYST

In this brief example, I illustrate a register close to what I have previously referred to as analyst disclosure in the analyst's use of privacy and reverie. While it is a different register from that utilized and elaborated by Ogden (1994a, 1997a), I think it shares his appreciation of the paradoxical interplay of private yet deeply personal reveries and how these reveries help us create unconscious intersubjective constructions, which illuminate points of transference-countertransference engagement.

Susan is a very effective and in many ways satisfied mother and attorney in her early 40s. Her main complaint is an inability to stop feeling a relentless pressure about making everyone in her life happy. She is hypersensitive to disappointing her husband, her two children (an 11-year-old girl and 7-year-old boy), her colleagues, fellow partners at her firm, and now in our analytic work particularly me. During the third year of her analysis, we have come to a point at which she feels, very problematically, that I do not smile at her enough when she is entering and leaving my office.

She has some potent and durable theories about this. In fact, at the time of this vignette she is worried that her concern about whether she pleases me is privately off-putting. In Susan's mind, I am drawn to a very secure and strong woman who is beyond the need for affirmation.

I admire and think of Susan as smart, funny, and physically attractive. In my view and Susan's, she is partly experiencing me as her father, who withdrew from her when she was 14. She felt that he was critical of her as she diverged from him in terms of becoming somewhat iconoclastic in her intellectual and artistic interests. She felt that her mother silently approved of her choices but would never speak on Susan's behalf or her own. Her two older sisters worked in the family business during high school and after college. In particular, her oldest sister was regarded by Susan and her parents as almost being the same person as their father. As Susan's adolescence continued, both sisters became critical of her, and she felt that she lost their interest and pleasure in her as the youngest, cute little sister. They saw her interest as constituting a betrayal of the family's ideals, particularly regarding her growing interest in art and left-wing politics. She married a man who was from a different religious background than hers (Susan is Catholic and her husband Jewish), which seemed to cement her status as an outsider.

During the first year or so into this analysis, I often felt a kind of ease with what I regarded as an "empathic" attunement about her longings to have her father's approval despite her being different than he. She had struggled throughout her life with a conflict about wanting to show and not show herself, often trying to camouflage those interests that diverged from those of her family. She seemed to feel relieved that she could show herself to me in the analysis. I had been taking it up in terms of how this expressed a longing for affirmation and a set of needs from her father that she was feeling and letting me know about in her analysis.

At the time of this vignette, during her third year, Susan became more vigilant to whether I was smiling but not particularly curious about why this was so. I was not aware, initially, that this was the case and instead thought that she was moving into a deeper set of wishes to be able to express how much more she wanted. She disagreed, instead insisting that she had reached some tipping point with me, and that I did not really like who she was. Over many months, I, indeed, began to feel that empathy for Susan's sadness and anxiety was tempered with another feeling more controlled by Susan. In fact, I was aware that, at times, I even felt burdened by her sense that if I did not smile at her warmly when I greeted her or said goodbye (often something of which I was unaware) she felt rejected. I was reminded of the feedback she received at the beginning of our work when she made partner: that the partners wanted her to work more independently and to ask for reassurance less frequently.

At this point in our work, during one session I was thinking about how diminutive Susan was in relation to me. She is very petite, rather small in stature, and has a beautiful but soft voice that I can barely hear behind the couch at times. At this moment, I felt a bit like a bull in a china shop in comparison to her. Sometimes, I visualize this. But in this session, my mind moved to Gulliver with the Lilliputians and then to Dr. Frankenstein's son, Frankenstein, who come to mind from time to time in my work. But, I began to think less of the impact of Frankenstein or Gulliver on those around them and more about them each as misunderstood giants. Frankenstein did not ask to be created. He was the victim of his father's promethean ideas and fantasies. Was I thinking about how Susan was asked to be her father's creation, and how she did not know how to be herself and still loved by him? Then, I went back to my sense of how much power I had over Susan from her point of view and how now I felt controlled by her from mine.

This reverie began a process of thinking more fully about my negative feelings about being this transference object for Susan. I *imagined* something like the following verbose formulation: "I'm feeling controlled by your insistence that my not smiling enough at you means something negative or that I don't like you. Maybe I'm actually not smiling at you in the same way when I greet you. You want me not to have a private life in which I might be thinking and feeling any one of a number of things about you or other matters that you won't know or can't know. I want to have that privacy, just like I think that you wanted to feel like you were loved by your father while having yours, individuality, privacy, and separateness. You're afraid to have your privacy and risk being unloved and letting me have mine. You're trying to make this better by (unconsciously) being like him rather than seeing if you can feel safe being different from him or me and us each having our freedom to feel what we feel." I felicitously call this a variation on reverie, "rougherie."

In my imagination, I am aware that by putting Susan's identification with her father front and center, I am at a great deal of remove from Susan's anxiety about what my not smiling in the way that she wishes might mean.

My mind goes to feeling constrained by this set of feelings and choices or lack thereof. I feel as if I cannot be "myself" as Susan's analyst, an ironically held conflict if ever there was one. I can hear the irony of an analyst who is in some ways never "himself," yet the words seem meaningful. I imagine that this lack of choice, this conflict may also be something like what Susan feels, and I try to talk to her about my dilemma rather than choosing a particular side of this set of experiences and conflicts. The next time that Susan brings up her anxiety about my failure to smile at her in the way she wished as she left the previous session, I say: "It's so tough for you to be yourself at work, with your father and me and still feel our approval, our smile. It's tough for me to find a way to be myself with you as your analyst without making you feel betrayed, hurt, and worried about how I feel about you. It may even be making for less of a smile. You don't like your choices, why should you? And maybe in a way that's similar to the way I don't like mine."

Susan had many reactions to this shift in my interpretive position. She was initially relieved that I could voice this to her, and she recognized the similarity in our positions. She also felt degraded and inadequate that she was not being a good patient because she feared that she had succeeded in creating a form of analytic impasse. We looked at how some of these feelings of inadequacy and badness were a familiar way for her to resolve differences and standstills with her frustrated love in relation to her father. I suggested that by blaming herself she was able to preserve her relationship with her father and me. The complexity and layering of even this brief part of the analytic process is far beyond the scope of this chapter, but it is important to say that the density of these points of transference-countertransference experience and enactment were the stuff of our work together and allowed her to get much more into some of the erotic and aggressive aspects of the wanted smile. Much later, in a moving moment of parapraxis, Susan was speaking of why it was difficult to get started in her sessions. She wished to say, "I wonder why I can't get started." Instead she said: "I wonderful." She burst into tears as she knew quite well what this was all about.

CONCLUSION

There is some overlap with what I call the analyst's ethical imagination and what Benjamin (2004) referred to as "the moral third." Benjamin included that part of the analyst's mind and experience that considers how to reach a patient and aspects of moral responsibility in doing so. It also overlaps with the notion of the "future of interpretation" (Cooper, 1997), and it borrows from Loewald's (1960) model of how interpretation takes a patient simultaneously one step into regression and one step into an unknown and new psychic future. Sometimes, the analyst's anticipation of this psychic future is helpful in challenging a patient to examine new dimensions of conflict or self-state experiences, while at other times it may enact too far a psychic reach, unanticipated or underappreciated by the analyst.

These moments of repetitive transference-countertransference enactment sometimes also invite the opportunity to think outside the boundaries of our own theoretical preferences. When I have this kind of privilege in my analytic work, I also use what I have called the pluralistic third (Cooper, 2007b), which includes the opportunity to think about these choices from several differing perspectives, including theoretical choices that are different from the one that I believe I have used. This pluralistic third includes the analyst's attempt to think about the transference-countertransference especially by trying to step outside what might be my "overvalued ideas" and "selected facts" (Bion, 1963; Britton & Steiner, 1994) to build on my understandings. In other words, the analyst's dyadic relation to his or her own theory creates its own blind spots in integrating forms of reverie or any other form of clinical data. The pluralistic third, like the analyst's ethical imagination, are ways of thinking about spontaneously occurring events within the analyst's mind. It is a way that we sometimes reach outside our usual modes of thinking to draw on our body of ideas and cumulative knowledge in clinical psychoanalysis (e.g., Pine, 2006). It helps develop what Britton (1998) termed "vulnerable knowledge" of our patient rather than fixed belief.

I have illustrated some examples of varying ways in which I try to make use of forms of analytic reverie and my privacy. I have also illustrated a few different registers from which the analyst can illuminate these points of unconscious transference-countertransference enactment. The goal of using such reverie in the course of analytic work is to help show the patient specific and hopefully rather immediate dimensions of the analyst's understanding of the transference-countertransference enactments that have and continue to exert influence within the work. It is likely that the analyst's use of reverie is vitally related to therapeutic action in ways that relate not only to the analyst's "uncovering" of unconscious phenomena but also to the analyst's curiosity about his or her own mind. The patient has an opportunity to see the analyst's mind at work, using his or her experience and the imagery that emerges to know the analyst's own mind in order to know better his or her patient.

Chapter 4

The analyst's experience of being a transference object

An elusive form of countertransference to the psychoanalytic method?*

> The first lesson that innocent Childhood affords me is—that it is an instinct of my Nature to pass out of myself, and to exist in the form of others. The second is—not to suffer any one form to pass into ME and become a usurping Self in the disguise of what the German Pathologists call a FIXED IDEA.
>
> Samuel Taylor Coleridge

Psychoanalysts are always in a relationship not only with their patients but also with the particular way or method that we engage in a relationship as a psychoanalyst. While there are many elements of the analyst's object relationship to method, I will focus on one that is at the heart of method—the analyst's reactions not only to being a particular kind of transference object but also to the fact of being a transference object. I chose this topic since its centrality to method makes it difficult to think about it.

Psychoanalysts almost reflexively or axiomatically think about this kind of transference or countertransference to method as overdetermined by work with a particular patient. Yet, there is reason to believe that as individuals we differ in our relationship to receiving and participating in the analysis of transference—that is, in how enthusiastically we embrace, feel gratified by, idealize, devalue, or in sum have conflicts about the psychoanalytic process that features the analysis of transference. We are all different in the degree to which we are likely to feel ourselves at home with being an object of transference or are alienated by the notion of transference, and the like. Of course, there is also the general matter of whether a particular analyst is most at home in working with transference through displacement or taking it up more directly.

Parsons (2006) suggested that all analysts have various versions of countertransference to the psychoanalytic method, and my discussion focuses on only one dimension of that method. Perhaps one reason that we have not vigorously explored the analyst's experience of being a transference

---

* An earlier version of this chapter appeared in *Psychoanalytic Quarterly*, 74(2), 2010, pp. 349–382. Reprinted with permission.

object is our fear that, in doing so, we might undermine the method itself. If analyzing transference is our job, our medium as well as understanding the countertransference, why would we legitimize thinking about how it feels to be a particular kind of transference object? It is not unlike the joke about two young fish swimming when another fish swims by and asks, "How's the water?" One of the fish looks to the other and asks, "What's water?"

We encourage patients to give themselves over to experiencing transference. As analysts, we learn about the value of surrendering to being transference objects. When we work with our reactions and experiences about being transference objects within the particularities of any analytic dyad, we always run the risk of collapsing the patient's analytic space, taking away this precious opportunity to understand our old objects, the ghosts that haunt us and accompany us in the present. Unconscious enactments related to our feelings about being objects of transference, since this is the very stuff of analytic therapy, a lynchpin of technique, may sometimes be quite difficult to see. The act of giving ourselves over to receiving the patient's transference partly defines us as analysts and shapes what we are trying to accomplish.

Psychoanalysts have been more inclined to focus on the patient's resistance to the transference (e.g., Sandler & Sandler, 1994) than on the analyst's resistance to observing the transference. Bird's (1972) description of these forms of resistance in the analyst is an exception to this generalization, as are the important contributions of Joseph (1989), Feldman (1997), and Smith (1990, 2000). The notion of the analyst's "being" a transference object does not imply that the analyst occupies a static, unidimensional form of object relating or a single affective experience for the patient as the patient expresses unconscious feelings for the analyst in the form of transference. In speaking of the analyst as "being a transference object," I am simply referring to the patient's conscious and unconscious experience and participation in that affective realm that patient and analyst recognize as a part of transference. Patient and analyst are mutually influencing each other in the formation and development of the transference and countertransference.

To be sure, our more general reactions to being a transference object often help inform us about the nature of specific transference and countertransference reactions with particular patients, just as these reactions are affected by the content of particular transferences. For example, the analyst may feel that he has only a distant relationship to the patient's attributions to him or he may have an intimate experience of these attributions. This may be related to defensive aspects of how the patient is relating to the analyst or may relate to the analyst's particular kinds of experience in response to the patient. The analyst's wish for recognition may become prominent at various stages of analytic work (Steiner, 2008), just as there are parts of the analyst that the analyst may wish will not be recognized by the patient. It is easy for the analyst to attribute or consign disavowed parts of himself to the patient's "transference" or to be overly literal in failing to see as transference certain elements of the patient's perceptions of him that resonate with the analyst's perceptions of him- or herself (Feldman, 1997). Experienced analysts have the opportunity over time to determine whether they tend to be more comfortable with elements of erotic transference or hostile ones and of course to observe whether they tend to experience one form of transference more frequently than another.

I view it as axiomatic that the analyst is always in various degrees of conflict with the idea and experience of being a transference object just as he is in a state of conflict toward everything else in psychic life (Brenner, 1982; Smith, 2000). As Smith (2000) put it:

> The analyst at his or her best is not simply responding affectively and cognitively to the patient's material, but enters into a complex conflictual engagement with the patient that includes all the components of conflict, including anxiety or depressive affect; defense; fear of punishment; and erotic and aggressive wishes. It is these components, which define the analyst's ongoing object relationship with the patient, that have largely been overlooked in the literature, except as pathological interferences. (p. 125)

One part of the various sources of conflict and ways that conflict is expressed is the analyst's relationship to the method of working with and experiencing in the transference, notwithstanding our conscious dependence on and valuation of the transference in our work.

It could be said that we construct particular forms of compromise related to being transference objects that involve occupying a position between a methodological ideal (i.e., what the analyst aims to receive and interpret) and a clinical reality (the analyst's constraint in interpreting particular clinical phenomena). When the analyst notices that he or she is in a kind of postured position with a patient related to this type of compromise, it is often a sign that he might benefit from trying to understand the relevance of this countertransference situation to the notion of transference in the "total situation" of psychoanalysis (Joseph, 1989). In other words, the analyst might question what these compromises repeat or how they might be seen as a form of enactment of previous or new forms of object relating.

This view is consistent with Feldman's (1997) description of the analytic situation as one in which the patient projects both a fantasy of an object relationship and a propensity toward action. Within this view, the patient is trying to reduce the discrepancy between an internalized object relationship and experiences in the analytic situation. If the analyst receives these attributions with too much of a sense of congruence between the patient's internalized object relation or fantasy and the experience of the analytic situation, the analyst is often unable to observe various modes of conflict and defense related to the meaning of these unconscious object relations.

A blatant and crass example of my own experience of being a transference object occurred a number of years ago when I was consulting with a close colleague about a patient who was feeling particularly envious of me and angry in the transference. I was seen as a father who had much to give but who selfishly refused to do so, and instead decided to withhold love from him. My colleague also talked to me about some of his most challenging patients. At some point in our conversations, we humorously imagined a *New Yorker* cartoon depicting an analyst's office with a sign on the wall that read: "Transference Costs Extra." When this joke about our method developed, I found it immediately helpful with regard to this particular patient as it seemed a rather obvious signal that I felt something was being extracted and stolen from me, something I was afraid of losing or I wanted to get back. My vengeful thoughts about charging extra for transference seemed to relate to a fantasy in which the institutionalized methodology of psychoanalysis would change and conform to elements of my frustration with my patient, given that I had felt that I was giving my all, and it was not enough. At bottom, my patient wanted me to change the inherent and institutionalized restraints of being an analyst so that I might spend more time with him. Interestingly, my vengeful fantasy reflected my actual inhibition about more actively interpreting his feeling that not only was I not giving enough, but also that I could not give enough.

This example is not unlike one summarized by Joseph (1989) in which a case seminar discussion resulted in the participants feeling uneasy about the nature of what was going on between analyst and patient. The seminar concluded that their countertransference of needing to guess about the inner life of the patient, feeling pressure to understand at all costs but never quite feeling that they could get it "right," enabled them to be in touch with projected parts of the patient that never felt understood by important objects in the patient's life. Ferro (1997) has highlighted how he learns about his patient at times through what he himself has but not yet fully understood until he speaks. I have referred to this as a form of the analyst "working backward"—discovering and hearing a new formulation that is implicit or embedded in a comment that we have just made (Cooper, 2010).

CONFLICT AND ENACTMENT EMBEDDED IN THE ANALYST'S ATTITUDE TOWARD TRANSFERENCE

I suggest that there are at least two dimensions of countertransference that specifically relate to being the object of the patient's transference. While they are not entirely separate from one another it may be useful to tease them apart. In so doing, I hope to illustrate how these dimensions illuminate conflicts for the analyst in understanding enactments in relation to experiencing and interpreting the transference. In particular, these dimensions of the countertransference exist in dynamic relationship to one another and are often embedded in enactments between patient and analyst.

The first is a level of more immediate experience, something that the analyst senses about the patient's way of seeing the analyst that includes perception and attribution. The other level is a technical ideal that we hold about how to use countertransference which demands that we not consciously attribute negative or positive feelings too quickly or concretely, too categorically, or too simplistically to any particular meaning. Above all, this technical ideal emanates from a belief that the patient's transference helps the analyst understand elements of the patient's inner life and the inner life of the analyst as they are intertwined in various forms of enactment. Our technical ideal also holds that patients are always trying both to change and to hold on to their current self-organization in a way that creates conflict within the self and within the analyst.

Countertransference includes all feelings that the analyst holds toward the patient including those stemming from his experience of being a transference object, his feelings about being a person in relation to the patient, and his responsibilities and technical ideals as an analyst. Yet the experiential level of countertransference to the patient's transference does not entirely overlap with a theoretical commitment to the proposition that all countertransference experience (like all transference) is complex and serves to both advance and limit analytic progress. In other words, we feel what we feel in the moment to moment experience of being an analyst. We use this level of feeling by incorporating it into our commitment to a kind of analytic ideal about understanding how our experiences help us understand the patient.

Within this experiential level, the analyst is to some extent at any given moment operating with a sense of what is an "objectionable" and "unobjectionable" set of feelings in relation to the patient's transference regardless of his technical ideal not to think of any countertransference experience as technically "objectionable". The analyst may begin to experience something about the nature of transference as a binary (e.g. erotic or hostile, good or bad) as he begins to formulate the meaning of transference in language that gets at the "thickness" (Tronick, 2003) of meaning. For example, a patient's lack of apparent progress is likely to feel more frustrating or problematic at one point than at another. With another patient, the analyst may gradually notice himself shifting in his experience of the patient's idealizing transference; he may note that in some respects he finds this idealization impersonal and reflexive or even hostile and patronizing. Like any other form of countertransference this is partly unconsciously motivated and might very well be more or less noticeable or unobjectionable or objectionable to another analyst.

But these experiences of what at any moment feels "different" or more noticeable in the analyst's reactions to the patient's transference are not objectionable at the level of being technically or analytically problematic. On the contrary, these shifts in the analyst's experience of the patient's transference are nearly always a sign of movement, a kind of tipping point, in trying to understand levels of enactment or mutually held forms of resistance within the analytic dyad. These are "cues" (Smith, 1990) about a level of experience related to resistance or enactment that is becoming more conscious. Smith's (2000) explication of the "benign negative transference" demonstrates how many subtle experiences of the analyst may be more broadly applied in understanding levels of enactment and resistance in the analytic dyad.

It is important to emphasize that some analyses are compromised by the ways in which our technical ideals about welcoming and containing the patient's transference sometimes make us less attuned to the useful signals provided by our more immediate experience of being objects of transference. Other analyses may suffer from the opposite problem, one in which the analyst's affective experience about being the object of transference is valorized in ways that compromise his ability to contain and make use of countertransference.

An area that is particularly complex and important to explore is that we are also probably quite different from one another in terms of how we both metabolize and express affect. For some analysts a change in countertransference may feel as though a switch has been turned on while others are far more able to have a more continuous awareness of affects about the patient's transference. That is, some analysts become more aware and conscious of what they are feeling about the transference in a sudden way that may be more similar to the ways that dichotomies such as objectionable and unobjectionable describe experience. There are also differences in the promptness with which analysts initiate interpretations about enactment, experience, or conflict, with some taking up these matters gradually and others more abruptly. Some debates between various schools of thought about the use of countertransference are, at root, debates about to what degree the analyst speaks from "unformulated experience" (Stern, 1983) or a personal register (Bromberg, 1998; Cooper, 1998; 2008) more than they are debates about how these experiences are ultimately conceptualized in clinical work.

My view of these levels of countertransference overlaps a great deal with Smith's (2000) view of the "benign negative countertransference". Smith describes the analyst's awareness of subtle shifts in repetitive but not always fully seen and enacted elements of the transference. He would encourage analysts to more closely attune themselves to these kinds of experience in working with formulations about transference and enactment. In my attempt to tease apart the analyst's initial, affective reactions as distinct from our technical dedication to working with these reactions, I am trying to highlight something that Smith called, "a personal response from the countertransference" (1990, p. 223) that triggered his thinking about the complexity of enactment with any particular patient. Greenberg's (1995) notion of the interactive matrix is also relevant here since he suggests that the analyst's focus on interpretation will depend on what is seeable to him at any particular time—essentially, what is syntonic or dystonic.

While on one level it seems obvious to apply these notions of counter-transference to the patient's transference, in fact I believe that this is not so clear-cut. If we believe as I do that the patient's transference is to the "total situation" (Joseph, 1989) then the patient will be reacting to every-thing that the analyst does from a total psychic organization. He will be responding to various elements of how the analyst responds to analyzing and expressing his reactions to the patient's transference, including changes in how the analyst responds to elements of the transference. The patient will also notice, sometimes without being conscious of it, that there is a dif-ference between the analyst's affects about receiving the transference and his capacity to dedicate himself to working with it.

Also relevant to this discussion is Feldman's (1997) comment that, if the analyst feels his role is too congruent with the patient's internalized fantasy of an object relation, the analyst's ability to recognize the patient's unconscious fantasy is compromised. In light of the two levels of theoreti-cal discourse about our use of countertransference that I am highlighting here, Feldman is suggesting that when the analyst feels the transference is concordant, he may sometimes fail to engage in the second level of work with the countertransference—in his terms, to explore an internalized fan-tasy or, in my terms, to more fully investigate levels of enactment between patient and analyst that we may be alerted to through these experiences.

Put another way, the more immediate form of experience that Feldman is speaking of, and that I am describing as well, is another "cue" as to the nature of forms of resistance on the part of the analyst (Smith, 1990). Similarly, Mitchell (1991) proposed that the analyst changes in his experi-ence of the arrangements of analytic work in ways that make him more or less likely to see and interpret particular types of clinical phenomena at various points in the work. These analysts suggest that whatever the ana-lyst interprets is related to how psychic phenomena are juxtaposed in the context of the analyst's changing psychic reality.

It is likely that many analysts struggle with feelings about the transference being noxious, annoying, or unwelcome, given that we invite the transfer-ence, indeed rely on it, for our work. Smith (2000) prefaced his discussion of the "benign negative transference" by saying that it may be "impolitic" to try to discuss this matter while, earlier in this paper, I referred to my imagined *New Yorker* cartoon as potentially "crass." Yet I think that our patients sometimes have a realistic sense of our range of feelings about being transference objects despite their awareness that we aim to work with and understand the complexity of these feelings.

Sometimes this becomes a kind of "before and after" situation for the patient—"How come you seemed to welcome my anger before and now you see it as my blaming and avoiding taking responsibility?" Thus many of our patients, fundamentally not interested in our technical notion of finding all levels of our own feelings workable, would describe our reactions to their transference in the binary of "objectionable or unobjectionable". For example, the patient might notice an instance when the analyst shifts his interpretive position in relation to the transference, perhaps partly because it has become painful or challenging for him to work with. In this sense, laments of "you used to love me," "you used to see my side more" (even when the patient consciously agrees with the analyst's interpretations) become defensive positions that are more comfortable to hold on to, than it would be to entertain the complexity of new shadings and perspectives on the patient's conflicts.

A more accurate way of describing these various levels of countertransference experience is to say that we are always in a state of conflict with our patient that both advances and impedes progress in getting to know him. We are also in a constant process of change in our relationship to our patient's experience and our arrangements in working with him as described by Greenberg (1995) and Mitchell (2001). For example, a patient's version of psychic reality in which he feels victimized by his parents in some way may be largely resonant with the analyst for a period of time until at some later point when the analyst becomes more aware of the patient's identification with these hurtful others or even of the patient's unconscious efforts to arrange for a repetition of these kinds of interactions or experiences with the analyst. In a sense as the analyst gets to know his patient more and more, he changes in terms of how much and how deeply he feels different parts of the patient and consequently his interactions with the patient may also change.

As analysis progresses, the analyst also (hopefully) feels a greater degree of freedom to think and to express his thoughts and perspectives to the patient (Bion, 1956; Symington, 1983)—what Caper (1997) referred to as the analyst "having a mind of his own." Some of the time I suspect that our feelings about not wanting to accept particular forms of transference are important because they lead us to a further exploration and awareness of more comprehensive versions of the transference. At best, dichotomies such as unobjectionable and objectionable or negative and positive help the analyst locate his experience in order to understand new elements of transference–countertransference engagement.

For example, some analyses that tend to provide destructively false "alternative realities" do so by ignoring some of the analyst's realistic feelings about being a particular kind of transference object. Blatant examples involve the analyst's reluctance to interpret hostile elements of erotic transference not only for fear of hurting a patient but also because the patient's longings and attributions are congruent with how the analyst feels toward the patient or wants to feel toward the patient. This is a point at which rationalizations related to "needs" that the patient has to experience love, while partly true, may be valorized to the exclusion of more complicated, multifarious elements of transference (the mixture of loving and hostile feelings) that the analyst avoids taking up with the patient.

I have worked with patients who had previously seen analysts for protracted periods of time in which the patient was feeling lost in an erotically masochistic relationship to the analyst. Sometimes, the analyst in these circumstances is afraid of hurting the patient by more actively analyzing the meaning and origins of some of these fantasies. Sometimes, the analyst is gratified by these fantasies and unwittingly blocked in making sense of them to this patient. The fear of hurting the patient through interpretation of these desires may lead to the analyst's concretization of these fantasies as "real" in the patient's mind, as a kind of object relation, instead of the analyst's working with the fantasies as complex expressions of affect and desire that can be investigated. Feldman (1997) made the cogent observation that the patient's transferences include particular proscribed ways of behaving in response to the patient's unconscious inner life. The analyst may be blocked in his ability to think about this patient "falling in love" because he wants to welcome the patient's capacity to resume experiencing longed-for empathic objects.

On the other side, however, the analyst's constraint in interpreting some of these fantasies can engender and catalyze the patient's fantasies or wishes about the analyst being in love with the patient. In this sense, interpretation nearly always contains a component of rejection and repudiation of a patient's transference fantasies. It is an act of separating the patient's mind and the analyst's mind for a moment in time. Sometimes, these moments occur very early in a treatment.

Consider the following clinical example as an illustration of how differently two analysts hear and understand elements of transference. I aim to illustrate a number of issues related to our varying feelings about being transference objects and what these feelings may tell us about our patient. I suggest that this dimension of analytic work may inform us about implicit and explicit attitudes embedded in our theory about how the analyst uses his experience of being a transference object and about various forms of analytic posturing.

EDWARD

I saw Edward, a man in his mid-fifties, as part of a consultation process 3 months after he had begun an analysis with Dr. G, a female analyst. Edward had been in a previous analysis for 2 years with a different female analyst, Dr. H, until his move to a new city. My initial impression was that Edward had developed what appeared to be a highly eroticized form of transference with Dr. H, his former analyst. He had enjoyed seeing her despite feeling that he had not really changed as a result of their 2 years of work together. I was struck by his lack of frustration about his lack of progress. According to the patient, Dr. H had not really offered any formulations of what these erotic feelings were about in dynamic or developmental terms, leaving him feeling that his erotic sentiments were "really just about being attracted to her and I think her being attracted to me."

I found this puzzling and of course I considered whether Edward simply did not want to hear or remember what Dr. H had said about his feelings. Yet, I found his version of things plausible, particularly after a discussion with Dr. H.

Edward had grown up feeling that although his mother showered him with praise, her observations and engagement with him were superficial. While his 3-year-older brother felt envious of the flattery that Edward received from their mother, Edward envied his brother because "she was honest and direct with him like she was with my father, opinionated but engaged." He felt that his mother actually attended to his brother's schoolwork, critically evaluating both his athletic and academic performance. In contrast, Edward's mother reflexively praised his activities, he felt, in ways that began to enrage him during adolescence, making him feel unimportant to her and weak. In contrast, Edward trusted his father's evaluation of both his own and his brother's performance. He felt that while his father was supportive, "he could be honest, too."

Edward told me that he had ostensibly been seeing his former analyst, Dr. H, to improve his relationship with his wife. Yet, it occurred to me in our several meetings that unconsciously he was seeing her, at least partly, to gratify some of his erotic needs and fantasies that he was unable to bring to his marriage. He found Dr. H very attractive and thoughtful, and the two of them lived together in his mind in an idealized marriage. Unlike his wife, Dr. H had been interested in him and had laughed at his jokes. In contrast, Edward said his wife found his sense of humor "stupid" and childish.

Edward said that his analysis had helped him stay in his marriage, but it was not clear whether this was because of what he had learned about himself or because the analysis functioned as a kind of adjunctive relationship that titrated his disappointment and anger with his wife. It also occurred to me that his analysis had functioned as a kind of compromise between staying with his wife in their relatively disconnected state and having an actual, secretive affair that would cause him more guilt than he was already experiencing. I had some sense that perhaps he had found another way not to need anything of an emotional or sexual nature from his wife.

Edward consulted with me almost immediately because he had concerns about Dr. G whom he had been seeing for 3 months. During our consultation, I spoke to each of them separately for a few sessions and with Edward's previous analyst. In my discussion with Dr. H, it appeared that the analyst felt that Edward's experience of her related to a longed-for maternal object—a sense of loving and being loved that he could trust. I found Dr. H to be thoughtful but quite general in her descriptions of the analysis. She had found Edward appealing in his intelligence and experienced him as quite lonely and unhappy in his marriage. She had been encouraged by his ability to give up a series of affairs when he began analytic work with her.

When I told Dr. H about Edward's statement that she "hadn't made interpretations about his affectionate and loving feelings for her," she was surprised since she thought she had linked these feelings to the patient's wishes for a mother who would love him and engage with him. Yet, she did say that she had been considerably less active with Edward than was her custom with most patients, and that his transference had been striking in how quickly it materialized and how homogeneously it was expressed.

My overall impression of this work was that Dr. H had been recruited through Edward's projections in ways that were relatively comfortable for her but that she may not have been aware of how he may have also been shaping and delimiting the analytic situation in important ways. I wondered more specifically about how the homogeneity of this "transference," rather than involving primarily "loving" feelings, may have also expressed repetitive elements of generalized, generic loving, not specific ways of knowing and being known that he had longed for with his mother. That is, it occurred to me that Edward had partly re-created an old situation of feeling "loved" while not feeling very well seen or understood.

Within the first few months of his new analysis with Dr. G, Edward had developed very strong erotic feelings and fantasies toward this new analyst, not unlike what he had experienced toward his first analyst, Dr. H. The new analyst, however, had begun to take a very different interpretive direction. Early on, Edward asked Dr. G how she felt about his having such strong and intense desires for her. Dr. G surprised Edward by telling him that she was puzzled by his feelings and intrigued by his question. She told him that she did not yet know what his desire might mean, and that she wanted to understand these feelings with him.

Dr. H had told Dr. G how she had viewed Edward's erotic feelings as related to longings for his mother to let him love her, be excited by her, and be loved by her although she had actually not made this interpretation very well known to Edward. Dr. G thought that this formulation was partly correct. She also had the sense that Edward was trying to revisit the question of whether he could love and be loved in a way that would allow him to feel that his mother was sincere and engaged and that he could trust her in ways that he had never been able to feel.

Dr. G partly came to this conclusion based on her experience of Edward's affect when he probed her about how she felt about his desire. His question seemed riddled with anxiety and had a demanding quality, as if to want to lock in her affection and attachment to him. Because he was a man of some subtlety and nuance, the question also struck her as incongruent with his other ways of relating.

After several months of analytic work, Edward continued to ask Dr. G how she felt about his desire for her. At this point, she wondered with Edward about whether he was unconsciously avoiding or minimizing anxiety about his attachment to her and, in fact, working hard to replace anxious feelings with feelings of desire. She told Edward that he might be seeking for her to act and feel in ways that were not unlike what he himself described feeling in relation to what his mother had done to him—that is, his mother would often tell him how much she loved him, but he felt it was disingenuous and insincere. During his adolescence, Edward had felt guilty about not believing his mother and would sometimes criticize and attack her. Furthermore, he would at times feel "dropped" by his mother when she would seem to be close and then all of a sudden prefer his father or older brother to him.

Dr. G suggested that Edward's tendency to "fall hard" for Dr. H and Dr. G herself made her think that his desire was at least as much a request or demand for both analysts to be more trustworthy than his mother. In a sense, he was providing an apparent opportunity for a disingenuous form of engagement, probing Dr. G to determine whether she, like his mother, would offer meaningless expressions of love that he would then question (yet desperately continue to seek).

The patient came to me to talk about whether he should continue to see Dr. G and asked what I thought of her work so far. He was confused. He was puzzled and intrigued by Dr. G answering a question (even though the answer was more an interpretation about what Edward was seeking through asking the question). Dr. H never answered the question about how she felt about Edward's desire, instead conveying to Edward a silent acceptance of his desires. I developed the sense that, at least for Edward, they seemed to live in a world outside of interpretation, and the analysis partly seemed to fuel Edward's fantasies about him and Dr. H as objects of desire for one another. He also thought that Dr. G might be right, but he felt threatened. He was concerned that she was "tough and rejecting." In our three sessions together, I became convinced that Edward was beginning to experience Dr. G as rejecting in ways that he experienced with his mother, and that, while painful, this might be quite productive for him.

I think it was a useful consultation. Edward and I talked for a few sessions about his experience of Dr. G's interpretation. He spoke to me about how he had sought intimacy with women through a series of affairs, and said that he felt hopeless about finding closeness and sexual gratification in his marriage. During his earlier analysis, Edward had stopped his extramarital affairs. Edward agreed that his earlier analysis had to some extent enacted a compromise in which he found intimacy with a woman without having a real affair. Analysis had provided him with not only an opportunity to feel understood but also a way to reject his wife and mother. It had partly been a safe place to hide. He decided to take this on with Dr. G, agreeing that something in his question to his new analyst about her experience of his desire was a test. Of course, this was an adventurous interpretation and hunch by Dr. G, but it was offered with a considerable degree of modesty, warmth, and speculation, inviting the patient to discover his reactions.

What I want to explore for a moment is how Edward asked a probing question of Dr. G about how she felt about his feelings toward her. Dr. G's response to him utilized her countertransference experience with considerable freedom. By her own admission, in this situation she did not actually like being the recipient of these feelings so suddenly and without a sense of the source of these feelings. She wondered whether her sensation of mild irritability reflected an inability to contain Edward's wishes and longings.

For good reasons, we are trained to be suspicious of our wishes *not* to receive or contain our patient's feelings and attributions before making use of them; it usually takes a while to get a sense of what these feelings are about. Dr. G told me that she was usually quite open to patients who express such feelings, and that she often found these feelings quite gratifying. But, in this case she felt suspicious because she felt quite unknown by Edward; it was as if this "transference" had a life of its own. She also felt controlled by Edward, and this feeling of control led her to consider whether the patient was beginning to elaborate an internalized sadomasochistic object relationship; this relationship involved erotic feelings organized around submission to what he construed as a maternal lie.

The issues confronting Edward's new analyst were quite complex, and by no means can any aspects of technique be generalized from this consultation, particularly with reference either to the complexity of erotic and hostile transference or the virtues or problems with early interpretations of transference. For Dr. G, the early, nearly automatic appearance of strong erotic feelings became an occasion for her to think more quickly and perhaps more daringly about some of the underlying transference phenomena than she would have done had Edward's feelings developed over time. She probably also benefited from knowledge about his previous analysis, its strengths and limitations.

What is most important to my discussion of the analyst's experience of being a transference object is the notion that Dr. G made more liberal use of her trust of what was "normative" in her experience of doing analysis. This resulted in her sense of questioning something about the complexity of Edward's experience, an objectionable sort of negative countertransference and something that was at odds with the patient's psychic reality. This reliance on a kind of external reality (her perceptions of the patient's "desire") provided her with a pivot point from which to understand his unconscious expressions of desire, enactment, submission, and the attempt to secure an attachment.

It is important to pay attention to both our more normative and subtle reactions to being a particular transference object. By attending to this set of reactions, we may become more attuned to Edward's actual interest in his new analyst as an object external to the internalized fantasy with which he held his previous analyst (e.g., Bromberg, 1995; Feldman, 1997; Winnicott, 1969). After all, he is engaging in elements of curiosity toward an object external to the internalized maternal object by asking her how she feels in response to him. In fact, Dr. G and I considered whether there were ways in which Edward might even be permitting himself a form of useful therapeutic regression by asking this question—a revisiting of the experience of betrayal with a difficult-to-read, often disingenuous mother. I also think it possible that Edward may have been responding to elements of Dr. G's attitudes, feelings, and reactions to him that were quite different from what he might have prescribed for her (Feldman, 1997; Hoffman, 1983).

Analytic work and a commitment to the analysis of transference need not involve a suspension of the obvious reactions that our patients feel and that we feel in the countertransference (i.e., a kind of reality testing). When someone immediately feels "in love" with his analyst and the analyst in turn acts as though this is immediately understandable in ways that it actually is not (once we integrate her various countertransference reactions), a particular kind of disconnected posturing on the part of the analyst may be involved. On the other hand, to contain affects and attributions that we do not yet understand is not necessarily posturing but involves an active process of trying to make sense of transference.

Dr. G, at least with Edward, was not prone to that kind of counterphobic or disconnected receptivity. I believe that this analyst, in a highly thoughtful, careful, though daring way, was trying hard not to push Edward away from his feelings of love and attachment. Instead, I think that she wished to show him how he might truck with erotic feelings that were far more complicated than he had let himself investigate in his previous analysis.

I find it interesting that Dr. G's initial thoughts began with a particular kind of questioning of the patient's transferential attributions to her or perhaps even showed a resistance to being the transference object Edward wished her to be. She felt unknown by him, made into a creation of an internal object in his mind. This is what she was beginning to try to analyze—that Edward subverted the reality and externality of the object to enact internalized scenarios in his mind. Dr. G decided early to try to begin an analytic process by making it their project, in a sense, to look into and investigate that.

Dr. G made use of her countertransference to being a particular kind of object for Edward, as sort of a signal of something problematic—a disturbance in the field. She experienced a kind of countertransference to being a prescribed object involving Edward's unconscious transference of wanting her to submit to his demands to love him by "believing him." She learned that Edward had felt seduced and abandoned by his mother. Interestingly, it is a method through which Dr. G was able to make different transference interpretations to Edward. She could try to help him see why he needed to feel things from his analyst that might not be very related to what she really felt.

Edward's new analyst was much more focused on Edward's unconsciously embedded transference and less focused on his accessible awareness of his experience of the relationship. In this instance, I very much agreed with Dr. G that she, in this way, was helping Edward make contact with parts of himself that he was continually enacting through his adaptations, including in his enacted version of repetitive scenarios with his former analyst. This technique of using a variety of levels or types of transference is to me a living example of the way in which Freudian, Kleinian, and relational versions of transference can find a home together.

If we frequently dismiss or override our reactions to being an object of transference in clinical work, then we are throwing out huge amounts of clinical data and opportunity. Another way to say this is to note that the interpretation of transference as a form of enactment has been a relatively neglected area of focus in analytic work, due to the fact that the interpretation of transference is our most revered form of technical activity. But, it is no less likely to involve compromise formation, repetition, and enactment than other types of interpretive activity.

Often, a patient such as Edward thinks he is expressing feelings about the "transference" and concretizes these feelings, unable to experience a disavowed or dissociated opposition to another set of feelings. His modality of "have erotic transference, will travel" constituted a way to repeat an ambivalent attachment to his mother and his accompanying servitude to her. It was also a way to *not* feel the desperate aloneness he felt in relation to his wife and not to feel what he needed from her or anyone else. Dr. G's attunement to her relatively routine negative countertransference was a clue to this defense, but in order to be most effective with Edward, she had to avoid an instinct to accept transference attributions instead of paying attention to this reaction of a benign negative countertransference (Smith, 2000). In the end, I imagine that this put her in closer contact with parts of the transference that were less apparent: the patient's feeling that if he did not manipulate and seduce his analyst with his submissive love, she would abandon him.

DISCUSSION

Feldman (1997) described that what is projected into the analyst by the patient is a fantasy of an object relationship that "evokes not only thoughts and feelings but also propensities toward action" (p. 238).

Thus, a fantasy of an object relationship essentially impinges on the analyst in one manner or another. Feldman stated that the analyst may feel "more or less comfortable with this projection or he may be prone to enact" (p. 233). In Feldman's terms, the enactment may represent the analyst's attempt at restoring a less-disturbing fantasy to the forefront of the interaction. Feldman seemed to be implying that there is an optimal level of receptivity to these projections in which the analyst will not be prone to restoring or revising the patient's attributions.

While I agree with the notion that there is an optimal level of receptivity to the patient's projections, I also believe that the analytic pair is always in some or other form of enactment. I would tend to think that whether the analyst is comfortable or not with these projections, the analyst is positioned in a particular place vis-à-vis unconscious process that may reveal itself at one point or other as a form of enactment. But, I find quite useful Feldman's notion of thinking about projection in terms of the projection of a particular kind of object relationship that evokes or recruits (Sandler, 1976) particular kinds of actions. This points the analyst to consider more specifically how he or she feels about being pointed in particular directions by the patient and how it differs from the patient's earlier propensities for action.

Somewhat similarly to Feldman, Caper (1997) described the need for the analyst to discover his or her relationship to both receptivity to the patient's transference ascriptions and the analyst's need to stand outside these ascriptions with "a mind of his own." When the analyst identifies too much with the patient's projections, what Strachey (1934) called "external phantasy objects," the analyst is unable to survive these projections and cuts off his or her access to internalized objects that allow some interpretive purchase. The analyst may maintain a useful depressive position through differentiating personal identificatory needs with the patient's inner world from the analyst's own inner object world. Caper offered a view of his attempts to position himself in relation to his analytic attitude by emphasizing the importance of the analyst establishing "a mind of his own."

My own orientation as an analyst is overlapping but also distinct from Caper's (1997) in this regard. I appreciate Caper's focus on the need not to be too subsumed by the patient's unconscious wishes to create in the analyst too much receptivity to the patient's projected internal world. Caper's concern about the analyst's susceptibility to be "too receptive" might prevent his or her achievement of the position from which interpretations about the patient's inner life may grow. Caper may have been implying that the analyst's "comfort" with transference attributions is likely to be somewhat telling in terms of the analyst being recruited into particular forms of roles and attributions that compromise his or her ability to observe the transference. Yet, I also try to be attuned to the ways in which the analyst's inner object world is experienced by the patient, and that we cannot always determine that the analyst's "receptivity" to the patient is simply "the analyst's identification with the patient's projections as a form of pathology of his receptivity to the patient" (p. 273). In my view, there are elements of reciprocal exchange between the inner object world and ascriptions of external phantasy objects from each participant.

I think it fair to say that since the method of psychoanalysis is so centrally defined by the analysis of transference we have been prone to emphasize the analyst's attempts and wishes to bring the transference into focus. For example, Steiner (2008) provided a thoughtful examination of the analyst's experience of being an excluded observer in the transference. Sandler and Sandler's (1994) classic article on the antiregressive tendency also spoke to the patient's anxiety and inhibition that prevents the patient from therapeutic regression and the capacity to work in the transference.

Analysts have written less about the sense of alienation that can accompany listening to the myriad ways in which patients experience us in the transference. Sometimes, I think of being a transference object as a kind of uprooting, of being an alien in a strange land; inhabiting a self as experienced by another who is sometimes unfamiliar and at other times uncomfortably familiar in that the patient recognizes parts of us that we might wish were less recognizable. In our acceptance of this role as analyst, indeed our invitation to work with transference without really knowing what we are getting into or how it will go, psychoanalytic treatment begins with an act of uncertainty and risk for the analyst even if the risks are not as great as for those of the patient.

To some extent, the analyst pushes aside personal concerns about this risk in favor of his or her method that he or she believes will be helpful to the patient. I want to investigate this business of pushing aside and want to refer to it as a mix of investment in the patient and the analytic process as well as having elements of potentially useful information that are available to the analyst. An obvious caveat is the need for the analyst to first consider that his or her "objections" to being seen in the transference may involve any of a number of problematic features—a rejection of the patient's unconscious fantasy life; the analyst's need to be seen "as he is" rather than as an object in the patient's mind; the analyst's wish on the part of the analyst to dictate psychic reality rather than explore the patient's psychic reality.

At the beginning of analytic work, there is a kind of analytic compact involving the analyst's invitation for the patient to say what comes to mind. Inviting patients to say what comes to mind, as we know, is a limited invitation since we really do not want our patients to necessarily say "everything" that comes to mind. For example, Greenson (1974) and Hoffman (2006) pointed to the ways in which patients can reduce the analytic situation to an absurd exercise by saying things coming to mind without filter. The invitation is to try to tell the analyst what comes to mind that already, in the idea of "telling," involves elements of secondary process. There are some rules of engagement, however uniquely defined, in sex, visual art, literature, and athletic activity as well. While different from the faith of the patient, the analyst's invitation may involve a potentially counterphobic defense insomuch as the analyst does not yet know whether he or she really wants the patient to say what comes to mind. How can the analyst know that he or she wants this before the analyst knows what the patient will say? Ogden (1996) seems to implicitly address this complexity in outlining his wishes to let his patients know that they, like he, may also want their privacy. With this statement, Ogden may have been, in effect, making an interpretation about the analyst's countertransference to his method; he seems to be noting that there may be a particular kind of enactment in our usual invitation in that it does not pay enough attention to our lack of certainty about what we want or to the need for privacy as well as expressiveness. He is implying the presence of a kind of posturing, as it were, on the part of the analyst's invitation. This partial posturing may be seen as even a kind of institutionalized enactment of our countertransference to the method of psychoanalysis.

I would suggest that the analyst's stance in inviting the patient to say what comes to mind is always an adapted one that the analyst has not come to experience fully as his own position. He consciously wishes to extend the invitation because of belief in the method, but he does not yet know whether he or she really wants to hear what the patient has to say. At the very least, the analyst knows that the notion that a new patient—a stranger as it were—will be telling the most intimate details of his life. What has prepared the two of them for this? The postured part of the analyst's stance relates to the fact that the analyst commits to this method because he or she believes in it. But, he is often filled with complex feelings that are sometimes not attended to and may be important.

Thus, at the beginning of an analysis, our surrender to being transference objects and translators of the language of transference has elements of posture because we do not yet know the patient well or how the patient experiences us. The complexity of this existential position we find ourselves in as transference objects was well summarized by Ghent's (1990) discussion of the role of masochism and surrender in being a member of our profession.

We do not necessarily understand the origins of the ways that the patient sees us—whether it is based in early history or currently unfolding aspects of the interaction with the analyst. We do not yet understand how we have become implicated in the patient's inner object world or how we will contain, enact, and analyze this inner world with its attendant feelings. This lack of personal and emotional experience and knowledge with and about the patient often makes it difficult to understand our participation as analysis begins except to say that it is somehow "unobjectionable." At the outset, the analyst's receptivity to the patient's transferential experience is established more by fiat, the analyst's good intentions, and grows out of our dedication to helping our patients. It is partly a postured stance that is part of our clinical, human, and technical responsibility but probably different than it will be over the course of analysis.

This invitation by the analyst is far more than simply postured. The analyst's genuine concern for the patient is quite important in his understanding of his countertransference to method. I imagine that for most analysts there is a period of time, a transitional time, during which there is a need to translate the method of listening that we use outside analysis to the ways in which we analysts listen in order to understand transference. For example, I notice various forms of constriction in listening when I begin working with a new patient in analysis. I often have an initial intensity of focus that unwittingly limits my experience of my own reactions and person. I would say that I am less "adrift" in my own associations and reverie as I try to simply learn about the patient and get the "facts" surrounding his actual life, not only his psychic one. For example, I and others I have supervised have described ways in which our minds are not as active in the beginning of analytic work particularly with regard to formulations that are at odds with the patient's view of him- or herself. I have had experiences as I begin analysis in which it is common for me to see things very close to the way that my patient is seeing and describing things; I do not have my usual accompanying ability to step back and consider a variety of ways of thinking about what the patient is saying. It is as if I am psychologically devoted to seeing things as the patient does, colonized in an easy and seamless way by the patient's sensibility and concerns, and some other part of my mind is either constricted or on hold. While this empathic capacity is always a valuable, necessary analytic function, during all phases of work, I usually find that it is not sufficient in and of itself.

Over time, my mind becomes freer to work and function as a separate entity. I have, in Caper's (1997) words, more a mind of my own as things develop. I can observe how I view the patient more distinctly from how I believe that the patient sees things. My dedication to the analytic task becomes less postured, more genuine, to the extent that I feel a more distinct sensibility within myself that can move back and forth between immersion in the patient's psychic reality and our overlapping and distinct psychic realities. In a sense, during this early process I have shut down a part of my mind that would think more about the transference and in a more complex and supple way because at some unconscious level I do not feel comfortable thinking in that way with someone I do not know very well. We are taught to not talk to strangers, particularly about something as private as the ways in which one of us has managed conflict, in effect, the patient's self-cure (Khan, 1973). Of course, these are generalizations, and one of the features that makes analytic work so interesting is the analyst's wide variations in listening and participation.

One might usefully ask questions about why I would emphasize, in the act of beginning an analysis, elements of the analyst's posture rather than simply refer to it as a kind of unobjectionable participation or dedication to the work task. I want to emphasize that psychoanalysts do well to stay close to the nature of their personal participation and, if you will, impersonal participation. For example, I think that there are ways to be authentically and inauthentically "anonymous" and authentically and inauthentically "revealing." The relatively anonymous analyst who is devoted in his or her mode of formulating to keeping him- or herself out of the mix as much as possible because the analyst genuinely believes that this is the best way to analyze a patient is probably more likely to be experienced as genuine. I suspect that the patient can feel this dedication, what Glover (1937b) referred to as the analyst's "inner attitude." There are probably analysts who do not use anonymity as a way to know their patients but instead to avoid knowing and being "known" in the way that all analysts, regardless of their stripes, are known. Conversely, there are analysts who may be revealing in particular ways in which they are not actually connected to in their participation with the patient. Making ourselves more explicitly known may be used constructively or defensively. Allowing ourselves to investigate how we are known by the patient is an essential part of how genuinely we can expressively participate. This is related to a joking question that I have posed to students over the years: What is the difference between a schizoid relationalist and an expressive, open classicist? The answer is "a theory."

Sometimes, the line between posturing and our actual view of therapeutic action is a blurry one. For example, Hoffman (1996) elucidated the ways our patients often idealize us that can never be fully analyzed even if it is our ideal to try. His explication of the analyst's "intimate and ironic" authority presupposes that we can never fully analyze these predilections by the patient to view us as authority figures. But, Hoffman suggested that these idealizations are part of what fuels the process of analysis and our own power to influence. I disagree with Hoffman in his deemphasis of the attempt to analyze the patient's experience of idealizing his analyst as much as possible. In fact, I would say that, if anything, idealization is usually as destructive as it is constructive in growth and development during analysis. However, I appreciate that Hoffman was essentially exposing his awareness of a kind of posturing intrinsic to his notion of the method of the analytic process.

I have heard some patients complain that the analyst loves his or her technique more than he loves the patient. To some extent, of course, this is an epic battle for each patient as the patient tries to get the analyst to love him or her while the analyst's job is to understand the patient and show the patient how to understand himself. Partly, the analyst's love of his method allows the analyst to work with and know a patient in a way that is unique and distinguishable from other forms of intimate contact. However, there is some validity in the idea that if the analyst is too absorbed in his expectations of how the transference will be expressed, it can become an obstacle to analytic work. If the analyst is absorbed by his or her method and theory, too much in love with those objects, as it were, then the analyst will not have enough left to engage with a patient. There is a difference between the use of theory as usurping versus facilitating our formulations, interpretations, and participation in the analytic process.

Being too in love with method is a kind of degradation of the psychoanalytic process that, after all, is a method that allows for us to intimately and uniquely understand each of our patients. Just as the analyst helps the patient to examine his or her method of self-cure (Khan, 1973) that interferes with the patient giving up old, ineffective solutions to problems and conflict resolution, the analyst must also examine his or her relationship to self-cure since these inevitably go to the core of the analyst's blind spots in understanding a patient. In this way, the analyst must surrender to his patient. The analyst must move beyond his or her fixed ideas and selected facts (e.g., Britton & Steiner, 1994). This includes examining the degree to which his relationship to a personal method may serve as a resistance to analyzing the patient. In a sense, the notion of the analyst as a new object in the therapeutic action of analysis is not only related to the patient's increased freedom for new affective pathways associated with object ties (e.g., Loewald, 1960), but also the notion of the analyst as a new object for the patient includes the fact that the analyst has to become a new object to him- or herself (e.g., Cooper, 2000b, 2004b; Slavin & Kriegman, 1998; Symington, 1983).

If the analyst is too attached to being seen as a transference object closely tied to the patient's conscious perceptions and fantasies, this can also be problematic. Feldman (1997) put this well when he commented on a "comfortable, collusive arrangement, in which the analyst feels his role is congruent with some internal phantasy" (p. 238). This "comfort" may also become an idealization of being a particular kind of transference object that can, in turn, involve a degradation of the analytic method since it may involve the analyst's compromised ability to reflect on transference in terms of the patient's unconscious participation or the total situation of transference. I do not mean to minimize Gill's (1982) expansion of transference to include the patient's experience of the analyst, but I do not see it as a complete view of transference since a more complete view is often defined by what the patient does not consciously experience or express. Any patient who is able to engage in the process is going to try to find the analyst, some combination of the analyst in his mind and the analyst who is working with him. If the analyst is focused too exclusively on the patient's allusions to his experience of the analyst, then it may well obscure the patient's unconscious experience of the analyst.

The patient is always partly trying to stay the same, and if the analyst too readily or unquestionably accepts the patient's attributions, it may be easy to miss some of the patient's complex feelings hidden and obscured by the "transference." In other words, the analyst will miss out on the communications of defense that are delivered often through conscious associations that resemble transference attributions. The analyst's ability to interpret the patient's unconscious feelings, fantasies, and quests (what the patient is looking for) is what I mean by the notion of an analyst who can be found (e.g., Bird, 1972).

Sometimes, the analyst is too attached to or falls back on encrusted ways of being observed and experienced by the patient that, in turn, become sources of resistance to analytic work. The "method" is memorialized through previously offered interpretations of transference rather than given life in the form of curiosity and exploration. It can be tiring to be stuck in places of transference-countertransference entanglement that are difficult to change. Often, as the patient and analyst get engaged with the patient's most refractory conflicts, they get into habits, if you will, related to this transference-countertransference engagement. As one of Samuel Beckett's characters said: "Habit is a great deadener." I think that every dyad, including in analyses that are productive, going concerns, gets habituated to transference and stuck in particular places that involve acclimating to each other for better and sometimes for worse. For the analyst to get habituated to the patient's perceptions and experience seems as potentially problematic as the patient getting habituated to the analyst's limitations. Didion (2006) wrote of the dissociation related to the stasis of everyday life as a kind of disconnection that can go almost without notice. Sometimes, it is important for the analyst to check in with him- or herself about whether forms of distancing and disconnection are a part of ongoing engagement or disengagement with the patient of the kind referred to by Didion. Method in these instances is associated with deadness.

Thus, the bread and butter of psychoanalytic work, the analysis of transference and countertransference, can sometimes be the stuff of dissociation; the stasis of everyday life; a kind of force of habit for both the patient and analyst. In this context, so-called interpretations of transference provide more distant and static observations rather than new information about the patient's unconscious experience. Yet, the analyst should be prepared for the emergence of aspects of habit. At first, transference is new and in some sense unfamiliar, *unheimlich*. Over time, the very nature of transference as unfamiliar may change and become part of our habitual modes of relating to each other.

Put another way, the interpretation of transference as an action or a form of enactment has been a much ignored and neglected area of focus in analytic work because the interpretation of transference is our most revered form of technical activity. But, transference is no less likely to involve compromise formation, repetition, and enactment than other forms of activity. Smith's (2000) dedication to this observation is helpful in demanding the analyst's continuous scrutiny of this fact of psychoanalytic life.

Thus, there are various types of collapse occasioned by the analyst's dissociated states, from being a transference object or the patient's dissociation within an embedded and repetitive transference experience. It is particularly in the areas of strong affective expressions of affection, desire, hostility, and attachment directed toward the analyst that the patient might become dissociated. Sometimes, the analyst's distancing from these affects involves a kind of compromise between saying more of his or her thoughts about the patient versus not doing so for fear of hurting the patient. Analyst and patient alike can retreat from the daunting uncertainty of new and spontaneous interpersonal relatedness by viewing each other, over extended periods of time, in the familiar safety of mutually agreed transference-countertransference understandings. This retreat is well described as a kind of interpersonal compromise formation and often takes one form or another of analytic posturing.

COUNTERTRANSFERENCE TO METHOD AND THE WISDOM OF THE NEW ANALYST

Highly experienced analysts who are immersed in psychoanalysis day after day may have become so acculturated to the method that they can lose touch, at least partially, with just how subversive the analytic situation really is. Students of psychoanalysis are sometimes closer than more experienced analysts to the radically different nature of what we do in treatment relative to what we learn culturally as citizens. The novice often keenly appreciates the leaps we ask our patients and ourselves to make. Students are generally far less familiar than is the experienced analyst with the powerful and extraordinary ways that analytic regression can allow people to get in touch with affects and fantasies that had heretofore been less available. Yet, in a sense, students are quite conscious of the radical shifts accomplished by the analytic method in relation to the conventions of other types of discourse and treatment. Nowhere is this more apparent than in our experience of working in the transference.

In teaching psychoanalytic candidates over the years, I have often heard them say something like: "Sometimes it seems so narcissistic to make transference interpretations. I think that the patient might be alluding to the transference, but it's such a leap to say something to them about it." The beginning analyst indeed has much to learn about analyzing specific elements of transference and regression, and particularly about bearing and being curious about levels of transference intensity. Nevertheless, I conjecture that the relatively less-experienced analyst may sometimes be less dissociated from his or her experience about being an object of transference in contrast to those of us who have worked for many years with patients and the nature of their transference to us. To be sure, I believe that there are relatively normative levels of dissociation and disconnection from our feelings about being transference objects that if attended to can be of interest.

I bring these matters up because in some ways I think it helps to make explicit the larger context in which analytic work is embedded. Analysis involves a particular set of highly unconventional, subversive, ritualized conventions. Both patient and analyst surrender themselves by agreeing to behave in ways that break rules. Some of the rules are the following: "Don't talk to strangers." "If you start talking about sex to someone, it's usually going to mean that you're going to have sex with them." "Don't discuss digestive and intestinal matters unless you have to." "Never say what comes to mind, always wait a bit." "If you can't say something nice about someone, don't say it at all." "Don't talk about yourself too much." "Always ask someone else how they're doing, get to know them, ask them about their family, their children, where they come from, where do they live now."

In days when psychoanalytically oriented treatment was extremely popular in psychiatry departments and graduate schools, students may have been uwittingly taught to disavow elements of their feelings and thoughts about being seen in one way or other as "transference objects." They may have been encouraged to have a kind of false ease in feeling that they had to actively ignore these questions and immediately assume the mantle of responsibility in making transference interpretations. In general, attention to countertransference reactions in the United States has been increasing since 1985 (e.g., Kernberg, 1993). Contemporary analysts have more opportunity to utilize their varied and more subtle feelings about being incorporated into the transference.

Perhaps we should consider whether we have experienced an institutionalized distancing from our very particular reactions to this aspect of process, leading us to espouse to our students a kind of automatic and potentially superficial receptivity to the patient's transference. In this sense, we might ask ourselves whether we sometimes unwittingly advance an attitude of dissociation toward the transference in our necessary commitment to teaching students to be its recipients. By keying into the complexity, subtlety, and diversity of our reactions to being transference objects, we may facilitate a greater understanding of the patient's complex unconscious conflicts and their enactment. These experiences may be profitably worked with and explored over the course of a psychoanalytic career.

Chapter 5

The analyst's anticipatory fantasies

Aid and obstacle to the patient's self-integration

We are often feeling parts of our patients that they cannot feel themselves. Sometimes, this information is helpful when conveyed to a patient; sometimes, it is even welcome news from an outsider who is able to feel and see things that the patient cannot see alone. Patients are also sometimes predisposed to experience our externality (e.g., Balint, 1968; Benjamin, 2004; Bromberg, 1998; Winnicott, 1969) as a form of control and forced accommodation to our language and way of seeing.

Along these lines, Bion (1959) stated that ultimately what the analysand hopes for is for the analysis to offer them "the exercise of a mechanism of which [they] had been cheated" (p. 310). Bion was describing externality that the patient may welcome based on realistic hopes about analysis as well as at the level of fantasy about magical provision or correction for what is wrong or what is missing.

Bion (1959) went on to say that what seems to be lived in the counter-transference is "a catastrophe that remains at one and the same moment actively vital and yet incapable of resolution into quiescence" (p. 311). Part of the analyst's experience of imagined or experienced catastrophe is that, at particular moments, the analyst's version of what the patient's catastrophe is and will be is not always the same or aligned with the patient's version of what the catastrophe is like or even about. The patient may sometimes be attuned to the analyst's anticipation of the catastrophe, such as a patient who can sense that an analyst is treading too lightly, worried about hurting the patient or afraid of the patient's anger. But often, these kinds of interpersonal events are inchoate, shimmering in and out of awareness on the part of the patient's and analyst's awareness. Here, the metaphors of containment and the interactive matrix are both relevant. The analyst tries to contain elements of the patient's internal objects. The patient also experiences the analyst's stops and starts in this process of containment just as the patient must, at times, contain parts of the analyst in this process (Cooper, 2000a). As Russell (1985) suggested so poignantly, treatment experiences force us "to recognize that there are parts of ourselves, even more than our patients, that we do not yet understand" (p. 15).

In this chapter, I explore instances of routine enactment related to the analyst's feelings and fantasies about how analysis will proceed. I present a patient who was developing a new capacity to experience conflict. I also explore how the analyst's fantasies about the impact of his interpretations may be utilized in helping the analyst to elaborate the patient's anxiety and reluctance to understand and be curious about himself. These fantasies inform the analyst about personal obstacles in helping a patient to understand unconscious fantasies and identifications and unintegrated feeling states. In so doing, we sometimes discover how we are attempting to forcefully influence based on our own version of the patient's catastrophe. Rather than develop language when there was previously no integrative language for the patient's internalized and interactive version of catastrophe, we project particular kinds of expectations into the therapeutic situation.

THE PSYCHIC PRESENT MEETS THE PSYCHIC FUTURE: THE PROBLEM

There is a very particular kind of feeling that looms in the air when an analyst is able to feel affects or parts of a patient that are not yet consciously experienced by that person and decidedly not welcome. The analyst knows that sadness is on the horizon or shame, anger, or a sense of feeling deeply hurt. It is almost like knowing that we will step on someone's toes. The only way not to step on them is to step away, and our patient does not really want that. Besides, stepping away is another kind of stepping on.

This problem is always difficult but less so when the person with whom we are working is relatively more cohesive. Each of us has a set of overlapping schemata of various self-representations and identifications accompanied by affective experiences in relation to others. But, when these various self-narratives are quite discrete, their presence inaccessible to one another, it makes interpretation and negotiation of these narratives challenging because coherence itself may be undermined rather than promoted through language and interpretation.

Feldman (1997) points us to an important obstacle in facilitating integration. In Feldman's terms, the patient is always trying to recruit the analyst as an object who is similar to the internalized object/fantasized object. Interpretations that demonstrate the analyst's difference from the internalized object may make the patient more, rather than less, anxious.

Davies (2004) addressed this feeling of trepidation in poignant terms in an article that examined the complexity of determining whose bad objects are in play at any given point. Davies specifically addressed the complexity of instances when the analyst experiences dissociated and split off parts of his or her patient that the patient is hesitant and terrified to experience. She also addressed how often the analyst is likely to experience parts of himself that are unwelcome as well in this process.

The analyst must reach these parts of the patient not only in an empathic way but also in a way that preserves an interpretive pivot point from which the analyst may find a "mind of one's own" (Caper, 1997). I agree with Caper that the analyst's ability to distance himself from the patient's projections and therefore to interpret them depends on the analyst having links to his or her internal objects that survive the patient's projections and proscriptions toward the analyst for particular kinds of object relationships (e.g., Feldman, 1997; Ferenczi, 1909). Interpretations make the patient aware simultaneously that the patient and the analyst are separate, and that the analyst has a link to internal objects that are not under the patient's control. At the same time, however, what Caper did not take into account is how parts of the analyst are being experienced by the patient and, indeed, are contained by the patient as well through elements of mutual containment. The analyst needs to have a mind of his or her own about the patient, but this mind is always infused with the analyst's experience of the patient's experience of the analyst's mind.

I agree with Benjamin (2004) that the analyst needs to maintain independent thinking—"the third in the one"—but only through his capacity to discover shared reality to accommodate without coercion (p.23). Caper's view of interpretation is embedded more strictly in a notion of interpretation as external to the patient's subjectivity and the shared intersubjective field between the patient and analyst. The patient needs to access the analyst's mind, and Benjamin (2004) has tried to chart the process by which a shared third, a dialogic structure can sometimes facilitate usable access to the analyst's mind. This is also a part of D. Stern's (2009) notion of partnership in the analytic process.

Psychoanalysts require a language that includes both the language of shifting states of patient and analyst and the language of unconscious fantasy and conflict in understanding our patients. I am always trying to find a new integration or frame that might embrace the internalized object world and the interpersonal communication of these internalized worlds between patient and analyst. In my mind, this search renders as problematic the question of "deciding between" elements of contemporary Kleinian theories that focus on the analyst's containment of unmetabolized parts of the patient and relational theories that elaborate an interactive matrix in which analyst and patient communicate to each other varieties of affect and internalized object relations.

A part of why I find a home between focus or unconscious fantasy and various levels of interpersonal engagement is that I believe that these two domains are always in dialogue. In Chapter 3, I tried to integrate how the analyst's reverie relates to elements of the interpersonal relationship between patient and analysts just as they relate to the patient's unconscious conflicts and fantasy. I agree with Bonovitz (2004) that both our perceptions of reality are infused with fantasy and fantasies contain elements of reality. In this chapter, I examine how that analyst's anticipatory fantasies about how things might go are at play in clinical practice.

As Tronick (2003) has suggested, meanings and meaning making are biopsychologically polymorphic. Meanings include not only the linguistic and abstract forms of meaning but also the meanings that we find more difficult to conceptualize, such as bodily, physiologic, behavioral, and emotional processes. It is often at a level of unarticulated feeling or anticipated feeling that a disturbance in the field marks the beginning of a change in what or how new parts of the patient will be recognized or voiced by the analyst. As Ogden (1999) put it: "The art of analysis is an art form that requires not only that we struggle with the problem of creating a place where analyst and analysand might live, but also requires that we develop a use of language adequate to giving voice to our experience of what life feels like in that ever shifting place" (p. 981).

One of the most difficult problems in finding this language is that we are often in the position of anticipating what it will be like for the patient to experience the parts of himself that he or she is working hard not to experience. Part of this anticipation involves an empathic resonance with the ways that the patient is unable to integrate elements of his experience. In addition, however, the analyst may be experiencing trepidation and anticipatory dread related to particular personal fantasies about the outcome of these interpretive efforts. These fantasies may or may not overlap with what the patient has struggled to integrate. It is likely that patients may also have reason to gain a sense of these experiences of the analyst.

One of Loewald's (1960) great contributions to psychoanalysis was his elaboration of how all interpretations communicate a kind of psychic future for the patient that is imagined by the analyst (Cooper, 1996). The analyst in Loewald's terms is able to take the patient into a workable regressive experience in order to grow and experience new parts of the self and new levels of integration. Benjamin (2004) correctly likens elements of this function to what she terms "the third is the one," as takes place when the mother can anticipate her child's movement from distress to soothing. The space of the thirdness must in some way be genuine and palpable to the child (p. 14).

The analyst may also offer interpretations that implicitly imagine a psychic future, not about what the patient will integrate but what the patient cannot integrate interfere with greater understanding, unwittingly minimizing aspects of the patient's experience. Interpretations may hold the analyst's needs for a magical cure or healing that goes beyond what analysis provides; they may unwittingly express the wish to circumvent thorny aspects of conflict; they may ask the patient to change or accommodate in ways that repeat elements of parental wishes. Unconscious wishes accompanying interpretation may reflect heroic fantasies of the analyst or nihilistic trends that reflect the analyst's frustration or despair about the possibility for change in the patient. In other words, the analyst's interpretations express many parts of the analyst that have little to do with what the interpretation is consciously about or means to be saying.

Often, the analyst learns about what he thinks when speaking. The analyst may feel moved to speak at times before even fully conscious of how what he or she offers will be developed. Among the things that the analyst learns about through his words I would include the analyst's view of his anticipatory fantasies, those that resonate with the patient's communication of conscious and unconscious experience and those that don't.

In addition to the psychic future that is consciously or unconsciously imagined by the analyst are the analyst's sometimes unformulated fantasies that belie wishes to, not so much change the patient, but disavow or minimize real parts of the patient that pose the greatest obstacles to change. In other words, sometimes the analyst wishes to minimize his sense of the patient's catastrophe. This may occur because of the analyst's disavowed identification with these parts of the patient that are visible but unseen by the analyst. In Bion's terms, in these moments the analyst is minimizing elements of what the patient has not been allowed to have; in turn, these denied elements are the capacities that would actually allow the patient to make greater use of the analyst. The analyst's wishes that the patient might circumvent these real and important experiences of which he was deprived are huge obstacles to the patient's growth and development during analysis. These fantasies of the analyst are essentially avoidant wishes that the patient be someone that the analyst might be able to better embrace or in some sense understand. These disavowed parts of the patient by the analyst may, at some point, be experienced by the patient and make the work of language development and translation particularly difficult. They form an additional force field, a kind of disturbance in the interpersonal field that interferes with the analyst's ability to help the patient to integrate split off and disavowed parts of the self. Often, however, the analyst is able to make sense of some of these processes of disavowal on his or her own, an activity that partly overlaps with what Strachey, Bion, and numerous Kleinian analysts would refer to as the process of metabolization.

I describe a session with a patient related to our efforts to find a language with which to say hello to the estranged parts of self. As is often the case, my language constantly threatened to enact and repeat old patterns that gave rise to his self-estrangement. There are special problems in finding a language for parts of another that are not necessarily welcomed or liked by the analyst. But, I present this moment to mostly demonstrate how the analyst's concerns or anticipation about the threat of repetition and disruption may be just as problematic as the actual disruption.

In particular, I hope to capture something about an atmosphere of potential transition, danger, and possibility that reside in both the patient and the analyst. Returning to Bion, it is difficult for the patient to learn a new exercise related to something from which we have been cheated. The language of interpretation and clinical discourse, interaction itself, always reminds us of what we have been cheated because that language points to the wishes and needs that our modes of self-cure help us to disavow. Sometimes, the analyst's anticipation of the patient's "catastrophe" interferes with the patient's nascent attempts to show the analyst the language that he or she is already developing.

ERICA

I felt fairly certain that it was a matter of time before I became one of the people who disappointed and enraged Erica. I had heard many stories over the first year of her analysis that involved a particular arc—Erica would either discover or cocreate a scenario in which someone would reveal himself to be overly critical, overly conventional, too rule bound, but usually downright harsh in Erica's view. She would feel a simultaneous sense of victimization and victory through these interactions. Many of these events would relate to people who would be critical of her parenting of her older child, Lewis, or they would be directly critical of Lewis.

By her own accounting, Erica did not like people very much. She had a successful career as an academic, but she avoided being seen as a resource to graduate students. She valued her well-cultivated reputation as someone interested in her own writing but who eschewed being asked to serve on dissertation committees. Similarly, her tendency toward being antiauthoritarian and impatient with colleagues ensured that she had few administrative demands. She laughed about these aspects of her reputation, but a sense of sadness was barely concealed by this laughter. She knew that she was a handful for others and for herself. In particular, she was hypervigilant to anyone telling her what to do. Erica was shocked when she was granted tenure at the university where she taught because she had believed that she had alienated two different department chairs with her refusal to engage in some of the shared duties of running an academic department.

Erica was married to a man 5 years her senior whom she felt that she "waited on" and supported emotionally. He was also a successful academic, but unlike Erica, he spent relatively little time caring for their two children, a son 8 years old and a daughter 5 years old. Erica was devoted to taking care of her children, particularly her son, Lewis. Lewis was, in Erica's words, "my project, my thing." Lewis had many behavioral problems with other children and authority figures, and Erica felt that she was Lewis's only defender. Erica's passion was for taking care of the children. It was Erica who took the children to school, did their homework with them, fed them, and arranged the details of their lives.

Being the "project" or thing of one's mother is a most complex matter. Erica's identity in part seemed to revolve around helping her son to feel good about himself and defending him from the criticism of others. Yet, Erica struggled with many people in the process because Lewis could be quite physically belligerent with other children and hostile to authority figures such as teachers and even the parents of other children. Erica was able at times to feel the need for Lewis to learn to control himself with other children and in school, but another part of her wanted Lewis to be able to be free of constraint, to live outside the law. It was difficult to determine the degree to which Erica was in conflict about these different wishes for Lewis or whether I was hoping that it would become a conflict for Erica.

Erica had also been a project of her father, and Erica was identified with her father in making Lewis her project. In both generations, the child had become an extension of the parent, a narcissistic appendage in which she or he exists as a source of affirmation, purpose, and vindication for the parent.

In contrast to Lewis, Annie, Erica's daughter, captured far less of her attention. She said that Annie did not seem to have as interesting a mind, and she did not seem to struggle as Lewis did. Annie craved to spend more time with her mother or to capture more of her attention but was rarely able to get much from Erica when Lewis was around. She was not her project, and as we began our work I experienced a desire to protect Annie from feelings of rejection by Erica. This wish to protect Annie may well have related to an identification with Annie—that I was also jealous that Erica's project with Lewis was more important than being curious about herself.

Erica's father had been a highly esteemed physician and well known in both the local and greater community in which he lived. Erica's father had died 5 years before Erica began her work with me. Her father was by all accounts a "scoundrel." Erica's parents divorced when she was 6 years old; the divorce was precipitated by a rather scandalous affair that her father had, and the community had learned about it. This was one of many affairs that her father had and that Erica and her older brother learned about from other children at school and from her mother. Her father was also known as a sadistic man who privately had contempt for many around him while maintaining a public persona that was affable and politically smooth. He was a "liberal" in his politics, but Erica knew him to be a man of bias and disregard for the rights of others. When Erica was a girl, her father would sometimes tell her in advance of a social situation in which he would manipulate someone else to get him to do what he wanted.

Erica had many complex memories of being with her father. She admired her father's status in the community and his power. She felt herself to be weak and unpopular with her peers and felt herself to be a "mama's girl." She felt attached to her mother but was the subject of her criticisms. Her mother was much closer to her older brother, and she felt that she was more appreciative of her brother's accomplishments in school despite the fact that she was a far better student. She felt in some ways more appreciated by her father than her mother, but as she entered adolescence she became disgusted and ashamed of her father. However, she had already been colonized by her father in a number of ways that were apparent in her adult life as both a wife and mother.

I focus on a particular clinical moment that exemplifies a sense of simultaneously felt dread (for her unconsciously held dread and for me it was conscious) and yet was a welcome development in analytic work. There was a complex disturbance in the intrapsychic field within Erica in which her various motivations and identifications were increasingly coming into conflict with one another. There was also a disturbance in the interpersonal field in which I was invited into a place in between the disconnected and dissociated parts of Erica.

As background, it is important to say that many hours were spent with Erica's stories about how family members, colleagues, and her children's teachers had not only let her down but also somehow cast aspersions on her or Lewis. She often felt that she was being unfairly vilified in her overly lax child rearing, but she took some pleasure in the scenario in which she was being berated by someone about not setting enough limits on Lewis. Erica also spoke about a fantasy of a young woman. She seemed to not be focused on actual sex but instead about being invited into her secrets. She wanted to be close to her as "one of the girls." She imagined trying to create contact with her but instead would make a nuisance of herself and always felt demeaned in these fantasized interactions.

It seemed to me that Erica was a woman who experienced a part of herself that was like her father, a person who was trying to seduce women and to bend the law in her parenting of Lewis. Yet, in her fantasized seductions she was also trying to be different from her father to the extent that she operated in an asexual position. She was also trying to find a way into the inner circle from which she felt excluded by her mother and brother. For Erica, part of a triadic context was organized around the mother–brother dyad, and she wanted to find a way in no matter what she had to do to accomplish this (e.g., Herzog, 2005). The other triad, between Erica and her parents, was compromised by Erica's father's rejection of her mother as well as the degraded way in which her father treated all women.

Erica equated Lewis with her father in that her father wished to manipulate people and then find the seam in which he would feel betrayed by them. In a sense, she knew that she would be betrayed because she wanted things for Lewis that no one could abide. Erica felt victimized by her sense that she could not be omnipotent, but she hid these wishes through a Trojan horse named Lewis. Erica wanted to vindicate her father particularly in relation to her own disgust and repulsion toward her father's behavior.

In a session about a year into her analysis, Erica shared in great detail the events of a morning that she spent with both her children. Her husband was away on this morning. Lewis had asked Erica to make him a favorite breakfast of pancakes, and Annie and Lewis had thought that it would be fun to help Erica prepare this breakfast. When they began the preparations, Lewis became testy and rude toward both Erica and Annie. He called Annie a name, and when Erica challenged Lewis about the way he had spoken to Annie, Lewis said something rude to Erica. Again, Erica told Lewis to stop speaking to both her and Annie in such a rude manner; Lewis became more rude, withdrew, and said that he no longer wanted to eat pancakes.

No matter how much Erica tried to speak to Lewis to get him to calm down and join them, Lewis became more and more rude and in Erica's words, "He was disrespecting me." Erica spoke to Lewis about it fairly calmly, and then at one point Lewis said to Erica, "I don't need you." Erica said to Lewis, "Who will take you to your music lessons and baseball games?" Lewis told her that his father would take him. Then, things quickly escalated, and Erica told Lewis that "I need an apology from you, right now." Lewis refused and then said that he was sorry in a very sarcastic way. Erica then more firmly said again with various kinds of threats that she needed an apology, and Lewis replied in a way that seemed sincere, "I'm sorry Mommy."

My reaction to this part of the telling of events over nearly the entire course of the hour was complicated. I was aware of feeling that it was relatively rare for Erica to tell me about helping and confronting Lewis with his rudeness toward others, including herself. I was curious about how Erica seemed to be upset about her own behavior with Lewis. I wondered to myself whether she felt as though she might be abandoning her project by setting limits with her son. In this sense, her project was to unconsciously preserve her father's grandiose needs and her own as continued or perpetuated through Lewis. She was responding, in part, like a good parent, a good limit-setting authority. While I had little doubt that sometimes Erica operated in this way in relation to Lewis, I thought that it was significant that she was now able to tell me more about it. Perhaps I was being asked to witness Erica's attempt to move from this more grandiose identification with Lewis to a role in which she was Lewis's mother.

Erica continued that usually threats hold little sway with Lewis, and that it was unusual for Lewis to be able to apologize. Erica said, "I felt like I was forcing him, fighting against this 8-year old." There was a long pause, and I asked Erica if she could say more about what this experience was like for her. Erica said, "I felt like I was being disrespected. What goes on in my head is that I take him around to all of these places, and that he's not treating me with respect. I mean I defend him everywhere with his coaches and teachers." I commented to Erica about how it seemed to me that she was feeling betrayed by Lewis. Erica associated more to her sense that she did feel betrayed, and that sometimes she anticipated with dread that Lewis would grow older and not need her anymore.

It was at this point in the hour that she relayed that when she was most exasperated by Lewis she had looked over at Annie and said, "Thank you, Annie, for not being a brat like Lewis." Then, she said to me, "This was one of the questionable things that I did that morning, and the other is that I began blaming Lewis for not keeping track of where he had put his gloves only to find that his gloves were in my car where I had put them. It wasn't even Lewis's fault. Later in the morning I apologized to Lewis and told him that I was being just as immature as he was by blaming him for something that he didn't do."

At this point in the hour, with only a few moments remaining, Erica stopped and shyly asked, "So, what's your reaction to the things that I said to Lewis? I was wondering what you might have said to him."

What interests me about this moment is how I was being invited into a very different kind of position with Erica that began to engage elements of conflict with these different aspects of self. Erica was expressing (not necessarily experiencing) a concern not only about what to do with Lewis but also about what to do with herself in managing feelings over which she felt little control. Perhaps she was asking me about what to do with her self, with her bad girl self who needs a talking to, not from a scoundrel father but from a loving father whom she admires.

What I was most aware of was that I felt that in supporting her efforts to teach Lewis, Erica would experience me as one of those who turned against Lewis or her. I also felt that she was trying to ask me to be more familiar to her as both a good and bad object. A part of Erica was asking me to advise her while also probably inviting me to find fault and to criticize her. I felt as though whatever I said would likely be hurtful to Erica, yet I wanted to say something. I was also struggling with many different kinds of feelings listening to Erica. I felt protective of Annie, who was being used as a pawn in Erica's angry way of pitting the children against each other. I felt protective of Lewis as well since Erica was ceding him far too much power. I sided with Erica's wish to confront her son's rudeness but felt that she needed to be more clear about her position, and that she was looking for Lewis's approval in ways that must be confusing for Lewis.

Yet, what I wanted most was to be able to say something to Erica about the many different complicated and intersecting points of conflict that Erica was showing. She was unconsciously identifying with Lewis's quest to be able to do as he wishes, yet consciously she was horrified by her son's behavior. In this moment of the question, I was more specially invited to consult on her parenting but also to potentially be one more person who was critical of Lewis and of Erica's parenting of Lewis. Erica was constantly trying to vindicate Lewis and, symbolically, her father in the face of Erica's own sense of disgust with Lewis and her father. She would be disappointed by any comment that would raise questions about the nature of her behavior with the children. Erica could only partly imagine something hopeful about renouncing her idealization of her father and son to find new and better possibilities in reality.

There are many questions that we might ask at this moment about what Erica was saying and doing. How might I take this question that Erica was asking and translate what it means to her in the real time of an analytic hour that was hearing its end? I might invite her to step back for a moment and try to consider what she was feeling as she asked me the question. I feared that this approach might invite intellectualization and compliance. Another might be to ask her further about how she felt about her own ways of dealing with the morning actions. This seems like a reasonable way to approach the question, but it does not address a particular register from which Erica had spoken—Erica has asked me something about my reaction to what she and her children have said or done. It was the first time in the analysis that she asked such a question. Was she seeking to find out about what a voice external to her unconscious scenarios might have to say?

Thinking about this moment later, I was most struck by Erica's capacity for a progressive regression to a wish for a mother or father who would have helped her to integrate her own sense of limits and benevolent authority.

I said to Erica that maybe I was being asked to side with either the part of her that wanted to be a different kind of parent than she had experienced or a part of her that was attached to (identified with) her father and that made Lewis into her father as well. I said that what she might be looking for in asking such a question—in effect, help with a reality in which it is necessary for Lewis and herself to feel aspects of both Erica's love and Erica's parental authority.

I also said to Erica that I'd want to try to help Lewis understand that I didn't like being with anyone who spoke to me in inconsiderate and hurtful ways, particularly someone whom I love so much. I wouldn't want to hurt him back, shame him, or pit the children against each other. However, if I found myself unable to get through to him then I'd also probably seek a way to let him know that his behavior was unacceptable.

Erica's immediate response to me was to say: "So the parent should make the child feel he's sorry when he's not?" Erica sounded sad as she said this and perhaps also slightly angry, as though I was forcing Lewis to act in a false way and submit to my authority. I had become one of the people I had anticipated becoming from the beginning of analysis—a critical authority slapping her down or slapping Lewis down. I pointed out to Erica that it seemed like what was available to her at this moment was a kind of dichotomous choice between either forcing Lewis into a false compliance or letting him do what he wanted, which was exasperating to Erica on this occasion. I told her that my goal would not be coercion but the goal of teaching Lewis something about struggling with his own wishes and limits. Erica's thoughts turned to how in some ways she felt she services both her husband and Lewis. She said that she thinks about her life as helping those around her, and that she always felt that she was the one to give in her relationships. As the hour ended, she became extremely sad as she fantasized about a time when Lewis would get older and not need her in the same way anymore. This sadness was new, and I felt as though she was communicating something to me about her old dependency on her father and Lewis and perhaps a new form of depending on me.

As our work developed, a pattern unfolded: When Erica became more aware of wishes to depend on me for guidance in a variety of areas, it often brought up a feeling that I would want to force her into abandoning her own position to fit in with what I or others wanted from her. Erica feared that I wanted her to comply with me and be a different person than she experienced herself to be. There were elements of this enacted dynamic going on between us through some of my interpretive work, which I take up in the second half of this chapter.

Erica's question to me in this hour was filled with complexity in terms of nuanced forms of conflict or proto-conflicts beginning to take shape as they are expressed in the analysis. The fact that Erica was feeling exasperated by Lewis's rudeness and disregard for others already bespeaks elements of conflict that were gradually becoming more conscious. It was becoming less easy for Erica to be simply identified with Lewis's and her father's quest for omnipotent control, particularly when Erica was the one who was also trying to help Lewis live with a reality that was something external to Lewis's and Erica's wishes for omnipotent control.

While it was not the first time that Erica had complained about Lewis's rudeness or his inability to respond to discipline, it was the first time that he had so directly invited me into the conflict. She was also feeling my anticipatory dread of taking up her identification and attachment to her father. Perhaps the help that Erica was asking for but was not yet conscious about was something along the lines of the following:

> Who do I have if I don't hold on to the attachment that I have to a father who acted in such rude and inconsiderate ways. I feel that I have to serve him and help him with his narcissistic needs. I don't know who I am or what I have without holding on to this attachment, and yet I don't want to any longer. I don't have a mother who is helping me enough with this. Will you be here for me if I let go of these other methods of self-cure and adaptation? Will you help me integrate reality about how people learn how to behave with each other? Will you help me with the catastrophe that went on with my father?

Erica was also moving into elements of what might be regarded as a newly expressed aspect of transference when she said: "So the parent should make the child feel he's sorry when he's not?" Erica was concerned that she or

I would wish to force Lewis into a kind of false-self compliance, and that Erica was experiencing me in the transference as someone forcing her into a kind of submission to my authority. Even if a part of Erica was trusting me in a new and different way to help her with Lewis's unruly behavior and to be a different kind of mother to her son, she was also unconsciously terrified that I would repeat with her her own experience with her father. This was a moment of welcome therapeutic regression in which unconscious repetition was being expressed and enacted. I had unwittingly stepped on Erica's toes, and it would take a long time to help her feel and integrate these various competing strategies intrinsic to her adaptation.

She was in a crisis in which she could feel the imperative to separate from her unconscious identification with the cruel and manipulative parts of her father. She felt this in the concretized anticipation that Lewis (symbolically, Erica's father) would leave her at some point. Erica was probably feeling this protean capacity to separate from her father and the accompanying fantasy of paternal power, partly in the context of feeling held by me in our work together. Erica was also likely feeling the parts of me that found it difficult to listen to some of her reluctance to take up her son's behavior in more consistent and less-ambivalent ways. She was also hearing my concerns about the way that she was capable of neglecting and using her daughter to advance her project with Lewis. We eventually talked a great deal about how her neglect of Annie repeated some of the ways that she had felt ignored by her own mother.

THE ANALYST'S FANTASIES ABOUT INTERPRETATION AND ANALYTIC PROCESS AS AID AND OBSTACLE

Some of what interests me about this moment of transition or disturbance in the field is how my anticipation of such a moment of potential rupture differed from the actual event and how it enacted psychic events going on between the two of us. In retrospect this is the moment and the process for which I'd been waiting; Erica allowed herself to ask a question of me about what she might need from me in current and developmental contexts.

So what was I dreading? I think that at a conscious level I wasn't sure about whether Erica could sustain her disappointment and anger with me enough to continue in the analytic process. While Erica had prematurely left many relationships, including a previous analysis with anger and disappointment about feeling coerced, she turned out to be able to sustain these experiences with me pretty well. To some extent she was in fact experiencing this kind of transference but she was much more able to work with it than I had imagined in my own ways of thinking about her "catastrophe."

I was surprised that in the following sessions Erica was not consciously expressive of anger toward me. Instead, she seemed to feel relieved that her struggle with Lewis was now a part of her analysis and that we could speak about it together. I brought her back to the moment in the hour previously discussed when she felt as though my imagined intervention made her feel a sense of concern that Lewis would feel criticized or that he would have to submit to her authority. Erica was in fact able to hold a number of different feelings about this moment including a sense of her identification with Lewis as someone who might feel coerced. Likely, part of my dread about becoming a bad object for Erica (a critical other who condemned her behavior) was that I was already feeling elements of criticism toward her that were quite difficult to integrate with feelings of affection and genuine curiosity that I experienced.

I tend to think that Erica's question to me reflected both her ability to usefully experience a kind of dependence on me in a new and different way about how to be a different kind of mother (and to have a different kind of father) as well as the ways that she experienced me as critical about her tendency to allow Lewis to be destructive to others and herself. With regard to the latter, Erica may have been allowing herself to feel the ways that I wanted to help her to stop holding on to Lewis as the parent who acted (like her father) with destructive, seductive impunity through her identification with her father.

My fantasy that Erica would feel betrayed and criticized by me in part reflected a wish to circumvent my actual feelings of criticism toward Erica. Within my fantasy, we wouldn't have to work on these feelings because she would leave. To some extent these fantasies of mine I think erased her— her conflicts, her struggle, our struggle, and my need to find her. As catastrophic as these fantasies were, they were fantasies of escape. This part of an enactment involved my wish to erase her as the person she was, something that her father did with impunity.

In some analyses that I have conducted and supervised I'm aware of behavior on the part of the analyst that may be clearly traced to trying to not become entangled as one of the bad objects in the patient's life. For example, sometimes analysts refer to the interpretation of transference and say something like, "interpreting it away." I didn't consciously try to curry favor with Erica but I was aware that I had some kind of fantasy of ruination about the analysis in which once I became one of these bad objects she would precipitously leave.

Another part of my anticipatory fantasies of hurting Erica through my criticism was based on wanting to erase my criticism toward her ways of relating to both children. While I was aware of feelings of criticism toward some of the ways that Erica spoke about her ways of treating the children, this feeling was less explicit and articulated than it sounds in writing this paper. In effect, I was partly enacting the wish that in our work we could circumvent the embedded ways in which Erica was still using Lewis as a repository for her unmetabolized wishes for omnipotence that she held on to through her unconscious equating of Lewis and her father. I was enacting a wish to bend the rules myself as an omnipotent analyst/father by not having to plow through this web of conflict. In so doing a part of my intervention involves also asking her to renounce or give up her fear of hurting Lewis and herself by integrating more realistic stances regarding the need for Lewis to be courteous and thoughtful toward others.

When Erica responded to my comment with a fear that she would be coercing Lewis into compliance, she was also communicating to me that I cannot or should not force her into compliance. This was the direction that our work went in as Erica began to feel more dependent on me. She feared that, like her father, I demanded her to be who I wanted her to be. But Erica's ability to hold and work with this complexity was far more developed than I initially imagined through my more catastrophic fantasy. Erica was also able to feel aspects of a maternal presence in me that were gratifying for her over time.

Erica was also partly attuned to and welcomed my own wishes to help her to help Lewis to self-regulate as well as my wishes for Erica to be able to separate more fully from her own father. I worked very hard in the "privacy" of my own mind (Cooper, 2008) to not push Erica into compliance; this involved being aware of some of my own magical wishes that interpretation would make her give up some of the most destructive aspects of her behavior. While I have no doubt as I said earlier that Erica was responding at some level to my own wishes for her to change, I also felt that it was important for me to work with some of my own sense of pressure about wanting her to change. At the same time, I began to develop more comfort in speaking with Erica about the ways that I thought that she was holding on to elements of her relationship with her father through her permissiveness toward Lewis.

Erica and I spent a great deal of time working with her feeling that her analysis was designed for her to submit to me and renounce her fight with the authority figures that she'd fought throughout her life. My work as an analyst was partly to struggle internally a great deal with how to help her see why she enacted her wishes to be different than her father (even as she acted like her father) as well as her wishes to hold on to Lewis as a way to preserve her father's narcissistic demands. Another part of my work was to find a way to verbalize the actual problematic patterns that I was observing with Erica's relationship with both children upon which I will elaborate. Erica and I became more comfortable together with the awareness that however we were together posed problems for her. She wanted me to help her with Lewis and to care, but she didn't want me to coerce her. We spent a great deal of time together in the ambiguity and complexity of feeling held and coerced.

For example, one of the subplots in this hour with Erica was the set of feelings I attached to some of the ways that Erica spoke to Annie and to Lewis. One of my greatest obstacles with Erica was a conscious fear that my reactions and developing language for understanding Erica's treatment of the children would be destructive to our relationship and thus to the analytic process. I was horrified by some of the ways in which Annie seemed to barely register for Erica and this obliteration seemed so difficult to talk about together. Perhaps it was unconsciously equated in my mind with screaming to her, "You daughter neglecter." Erica was not incapable of remorse and guilt about the ways in which Annie was less important to her than Lewis, but it didn't stop her from favoring Lewis and using Lewis as a repository for some of her own wishes and fantasies. If the analyst must find a language to speak to various parts of the patient, he must also overcome various sources of resistance that impede this process. It is in this process that the analyst is most likely to find his own "bad objects" (Davies, 2004; Russell, 1985).

Thus one side of my fear of my destructiveness toward Erica and the analytic process was an unconscious wish to eradicate or obliterate parts of Erica that I found repugnant in each of us.

I am often aware of a kind of continuum of fantasies that reside with the act of interpretation. I was aware of a wish (an absurd wish given the reality of character) that my comments to her about the children would somehow dissipate or perhaps even magically remove her dependence on Lewis and minimization of Annie. This fantasy of magical power through my words defended against both the reality of Erica's actual psychic position and once again enacted the omnipotence in the air that was being psychically traded between Erica's father, Erica, Lewis, and myself. Someone in the actual room and the representational space seemed to have to feel powerful and omnipotent whether it was a father whom Erica desperately needed; a son through whom Erica perpetuated elements of her attachment to her father; a son who vicariously held some of Erica's own wishes for power; or an analyst who, though his own magical power, might avoid the ominous sense of difficulty that lay ahead in negotiating an interpretive language with Erica.

In effect, I was partly enacting the wish that in our work we could circumvent the embedded ways in which Erica was still using Lewis as a repository for her unmetabolized wishes for omnipotence that she held on to through her unconscious equating of Lewis and her father. In so doing a part of my intervention involves also asking her to renounce or give up her fear of hurting Lewis and herself by integrating more realistic stances regarding the need for Lewis to be courteous and thoughtful toward others. It is also true that Erica's father hunger (Herzog, 2004; 2005) required her to hold on to her attachment to her father while trying to renounce it and shed it at the same time—an impossible psychic position to maintain and, at times, to help her to feel and integrate.

It is hardly surprising that the patient's attunement to some of the analyst's unconsciously held fantasies might overlap with some of the most problematic aspects of the patient's behavior. Nor is it surprising that the analyst's interpretive stance would be incorporated into elements of the transference. It is also not surprising that some of Erica's fantasies about me as a new and benevolent father overlapped with wishes that I held about how I might help Erica.

This process was aided a great deal by a growing appreciation of the degree to which Erica's motivation to treat Lewis as she did related to her deep attachment to her father. I became genuinely able to say to Erica when she would confront me about wanting her to change that this was true, not only as her analyst but that there were many problems for her in her current parenting—Lewis was her son and not her "project" if she was to help him integrate limits and Annie needed more of her. I was also able to point out that it was she who also wanted to change and that while frightening, sometimes it was easier to locate these wishes as residing exclusively in me. This comfort level with my own wishes for her to change was part of a gradually developing act of freedom (Symington, 1983) that led to a change in our field. I repeatedly pointed out to her that she was trying to discover if my help could be something other than coercion—that my actual wishes for her to change, that she perceived quite accurately, might be shared by us both. As a potentially new object, I constantly threatened to be a demanding father who was asking Erica to renounce her own life for his. She was increasingly able to see how her renunciation of her own life for Lewis's repeated this pattern. In the moment of the question to me: "What would you do?" Erica was beginning to feel the possibility of a language between us to negotiate these treacherous waters of repetition and newness. Stepping on toes became less painful as she embraced the possibility of new, albeit dangerous, play.

CONCLUSION

Analysts often hold curative fantasies (Ornstein, 1995) about their patients just as the patient often holds theories of pathogenesis (Goldberg, 1991). Analysts also sometimes hold catastrophic fantasies as well about how things might falter. In a realistic sense, the analyst wishes to use his formulations and words to help the patient to see something he hasn't seen or to develop a language for unconscious elements of his experience in the way that Loewald (1960) elaborated. The analyst is also trying to think about his own congruent and incongruent feelings about how patients prescribe particular kinds of object relations for us (e.g. Feldman, 1997). But there is often something more in the moment of interpretation. He sometimes wants more than will be realistically achieved and to some extent he may interfere with the development of a shared language through his own fantasies about how things will go.

These are examples of a failure on the analyst's part to achieve what Benjamin (2004) refers to as "the third in the one" or the moral third. I think of it as the analyst's ethical imagination. Despite what we call it, the analyst is trying to be thoughtful about what facilitates and interferes with understanding his patient's experience and its meaning. The analyst is also trying to reconcile what he wishes for regarding the patient and what the patient is saying about what he wants or feels is helpful. I agree with the "third in the one" or the analyst's "ethical imagination" as itself a dynamically complex process.

Benjamin (2004) suggests that the analyst can only soothe the patient or help him to regulate and integrate by maintaining a position of thirdness. Thirdness itself is comprised of dynamically complex feelings held by the analyst about ways that he is both empathic and insensitive to the patient's subjective experience. I am often in dynamic tension as interpreter between positions that Benjamin would describe as the third in the one and positions of complimentarity. Similarly, in my view Loewald's (1960) notion of the analyst's anticipation of the patient's psychic future is sometimes fraught with the analyst's anxiety about whether the future will have newness or instead will be limited by repetition.

Often we're not aware of the anticipatory elements of interpretation I have described and sometimes we should not be. I imagine that it would be crippling for the analyst to be preoccupied with his own wishes and fantasies each time he speaks. Yet there are times when it is extremely important to try to assess and translate these fantasies either to understand the patient or to help with the analyst's resistance to understanding the patient. To some extent the analyst wishes to make the patient into something that he is not—the real patient is abandoned in favor of constructing the imagined patient. The patient becomes an appendage to the analyst or a result of the analyst's omnipotent creation or Promethean fantasies (Winnicott, 1951; Bromberg, 1998; Cooper, 2007). In so doing, the analyst has lost a foot-hold in the part of the patient's adaptation that is required for self-regulation (e.g. Freud, 1914). The patient's fears of the most coercive aspects of externality may actually be confirmed by his realistic assessment of the analyst's need or wish for him to change.

The last thirty years of contemporary psychoanalytic writing from a variety of schools (e.g. Symington, 1984; Mitchell, 1997; Feldman, 1997; Smith, 2000; Parsons, 2006) has shown us that it is necessary for the analyst to discover his own obstacles that interfere with learning about his patient. It is also likely that the patient's read on the analyst's expectations and assumptions about how things will go is a part of most analyses, related to his read on the analyst's experience (e.g. Hoffman, 1983 Aron, 1991). As is true for so many patients, Erica's "read" was immediately incorporated into an old fantasy of being controlled by her father, an unconsciously held wish and terror. In my view, this problem once again marks the absurdity of "deciding between" various models of understanding transference. A patient who gets a read on the analyst (as emphasized in relational theory) will usually feed the "read" into an already forged internalized object relationship (as emphasized in Freudian and Kleinian theory).

I have suggested that at the time of the clinical moment that I have described, my "inner attitude" (Glover, 1937) reflected not only my wishes to help Erica but also in some ways to circumvent and obviate important parts of Erica that were difficult for me to see and experience with her. I needed to find parts of Erica's attachment to this father as more understandable (even perhaps loveable) in order for her to be able to use my interpretations to help in the integration of disparate parts of herself. The analyst's awareness of his ability to find parts of his patient that he also does not want to find helps transform and integrate the catastrophe of adaptive affliction into a felt part of the self. It makes the patient less a stranger to himself, the analyst less a stranger to the patient, and the analyst less a stranger to himself.

Chapter 6

Psychoanalytic process
Clinical and political dimensions*

In presenting a sense of how I see psychoanalytic process, there are clinical issues at stake, and of course, these matters also reside in the realms of political and social values and ethical ideals. I begin with the notion that while there is such a thing as nonanalytic versus analytic method, I have considerable doubt about the value of making distinctions between "psychoanalytic psychotherapy" and "psychoanalysis." Rather, I believe that what we call psychoanalytic process can be defined relatively simply.

A DEFINITION OF PSYCHOANALYTIC PROCESS

For me, psychoanalysis is the therapy through which the analyst *tries* to inspire and elicit the patient's interest and curiosity in his or her conscious and unconscious experience. What I aim to do as a psychoanalyst is probably best captured by Mitchell's (1997) notion of a process of self-reflective responsiveness. This process of responsiveness includes the attempt to examine the interaction and transference and always encompasses the patient's defenses as well as the patient's unconscious conflicts and affective states.

I think of psychoanalysis as the sustained dedication to elaborating the content and structure of the patient's inner life that includes both how it shapes interaction with others and how it is shaped through interaction with others, including the analyst. In analysis, the action itself of words and interpretations shapes and influences the nature of interaction between patient and analyst. We are never free of participation and observation. We are always trying to investigate this lack of freedom.

"Trying" is a key word. The patient's experience of growth is, I think, often tied to his or her experience of the analyst as "fallible" (Cooper, 1996) and "vulnerable" (Ehrenberg, 1992). An often-told story about Stravinsky,

---

* Portions of this chapter were presented, March 28, 2009, to commemorate the 75th anniversary of the Boston Psychoanalytic Society and Institute. The panel members were Lewis Aron, Henry Smith, Alan Pollack, and the author.

likely part truth and part folklore, was recounted by Mitchell (1997) in his brilliant discussion of the analyst's intentions. A violinist was rehearsing Stravinsky's recently completed violin concerto and became overwhelmed with frustration. The violinist stamped his foot down on the floor and yelled at Stravinsky: "I can't play this, nobody can." Stravinsky countered: "Of course, of course, nobody can play it. I was trying to capture the sound of someone trying to play it."

Many analyses begin with the hopes and fantasies that "the trying" in analysis will not be too trying. "Ships at a distance have every man's wishes on board" (Hurston, 1937, p. 73). Partly, the process of analysis is a process of getting closer to the ship and, through interpretation, trying to cultivate and revive the patient's imaginative capacities.

The patient's imaginative capacities are compromised by his various forms of conflict and dissociation. As Rycroft (1962) put it quite well: "The aim of psychoanalytic treatment is not primarily to make the unconscious conscious ... but to reestablish the connection between dissociated psychic functions so that the patient ceases to feel that there is an inherent antagonism between his imaginative and adaptive capacities." I would say that Rycroft gets at a large part of what we do, but I would include the notion of making the unconscious conscious.

Perhaps it could be stated that the violinist, patient, or analyst does not know yet to what extent the trying is an enlivening experience that helps to revive or integrate the patient's and analyst's imaginative capacities or a disillusioning one in terms of personal expectations for performance.

THE COUNTERTRANSFERENCE OF INDETERMINACY AND TRIAL

On the surface, it does not look good for psychoanalysis. Fewer students seek training, and many who do wish that their teachers had fewer theories and more certainty about understanding elements of therapeutic action. Yet, from my point of view it is a time of great possibility for psychoanalysis. No longer buoyed as much by the false knowledge claims about its pervasive efficacy across the spectrum of psychological disorders; no longer fueled too exclusively, too literally, and restrictively by the revolutionary creative genius of its progenitor at the beginning of the 20th century; and no longer as confined by the theoretical hegemony that has sometimes excluded and alienated psychoanalytic innovation, experimentation, and creativity, I think that psychoanalysis may really have a chance now.

Patients have a greater chance than in the past to know what they are getting and what they are not going to get. Having shed anachronistic claims to authority and knowledge, our clinical experience and the very history of psychoanalysis has given us a new kind of authority. Like a somewhat solipsistic adolescent, in the service of consolidating its hold on American psychiatry, psychoanalysis closed itself too quickly, unable to allow the ambiguities of its remarkable discoveries to unfold. As has been well documented by Jacoby (1983) and others, the medicalization of psychoanalysis and institutionalization of analysis through its journals and psychoanalytic institutes sometimes tended to constrict thought and technique rather than provide an ethic of thoughtful or disciplined experimentation (e.g., Kernberg, 1996).

Hardly the result of a desultory sequence of events, psychoanalysis has been humbled by patients who speak through their actions and decisions about how they want to receive help. There has been something profoundly symptomatic with psychoanalysis when so many of its patients come from those being trained to become therapists and analysts. Many within psychiatry have decisively rejected unproved technical precepts and what some cognitive scientists might refer to, unfairly, as the fetishization of the unconscious. Cognitive scientists cannot get rid of the unconscious.

It seems to me that the problems facing psychoanalysis as a profession relate to developing a comfortable position from which to learn. It is hoped that we are always oriented to learning from our patients. Tribal, interstice fighting between differing orientations has subsided a bit as a result of the interpenetration of theories.

What is called for in this time is an increased orientation toward learning more about how psychoanalysis can be helpful to patients. This involves many ways of integrating our authority about what we know with our modesty about what we do not know. In a sense, we all have to learn more about tolerating a kind of countertransference of indeterminacy. Indeterminacy relates to the fact that we have many theories and aspects of technique that have been elaborated but are no longer prescribed in the way that they were for earlier generations of psychoanalysts.

Psychoanalytic training is a kind of crucible for the countertransference of indeterminacy. We have a variety of theoretical choices, which for some candidates in training is exciting and invigorating, while for others it can be overwhelming and lead to a kind of crisis of choice. Many candidates and already trained analysts experience this range of feeling regarding choices. For people learning psychoanalysis, it is natural to want to know how to apply techniques generated from various theoretical orientations: "How do I know when to think about reverie as useful? When do I express something about my countertransference? I'm learning about shifts in affect and drive derivatives in my patient's associations, but the more I point these out to him the more I wonder if I enact the role of the teacher and father he says he never had. Shall I point this out to him, or will he learn more about these needs and wishes without my drawing his attention to that in our interaction?" Or, "I want to interpret what I see as transference, but the very act of interpreting it seems to involve an enactment of the kind he repeatedly engages in with his wife." Or, "She's searching for a developmentally interrupted kind of object responsiveness and yet pushing me away all the time, and if I point this out to her, I repeat the very experience she has told me about. Shall I share my dilemma with her or try to provide her with the kind of responsiveness she longs for despite my feeling of a lack of authentic engagement, a kind of ignoring of elements of my countertransference?"

The student of psychoanalysis today is confronted by so many important tools that psychoanalysts value and use in their theoretical and technical choices. While some current students feel overwhelmed by the number of choices, I believe that these choices of theory and technique, used in the service of thoughtful, disciplined experimentation, will lead psychoanalysts to have available to them a kind of posttribal approach to psychoanalysis. In this sense, the countertransference of indeterminacy is a new kind of unavoidable, potentially useful, and realistic approach to the contributions of so many psychoanalysts from so many different histories and cultures. Rather than a crisis in certainty, perhaps the countertransference of indeterminacy is the acknowledgment that many different lenses, individual personalities, and political beliefs have yielded a variety of observations about how people grow and change.

For analysts with a relational bent, there are at least a few imposing challenges. It is one thing to free oneself of technical constraint and theoretical hegemony, and it is quite another to offer new approaches to the analytic situation that can be learned and cultivated. There is a generational difference manifesting itself between teachers and students of relational theory. Students begin with the sense of valuing an ethic of disciplined experimentation. Disciplined experimentation suggests the analyst's continual commitment to appraising where he is, what the analyst and the patient are doing, and how the analyst has opened up or closed down the process of exploration within the analytic process. But, the question remains: Are there are a set of techniques, a body of techniques that students look for and to some extent need related to technical ideals and technical prohibitions—the dos and don'ts from which so many relational analysts recoil?

If relational theory is a kind of metatheory that I believe it is—that is, a theory that integrates elements of a number of other theories while providing some foundational principles—then it needs to be more clear about what and how it employs other theories. For example, relational theory has been relatively clear about foundational principles such as the notion of reciprocal influence, the notion that truth and meaning are negotiated, that we learn about the patient's unconscious mind through the experiences of the analyst, and the like. But, very few analysts who refer to themselves as relationally oriented really talk about the degree to which they make use of defense interpretation. More and more, I hear from students of relational theory that they do not really understand what relational theory stands for, what it teaches, how it conceptualizes the mind, and how it offers technical choices. I am increasingly sympathetic to these questions and complaints.

For myself, as an analyst trained classically yet also always drawn to the notion of the analytic situation as fundamentally a two-person field, there are elements of my approach that combine some different ideals. I am always listening for shifts in affects and ideas, unconscious fantasy, how a story is being told, what is being emphasized or left out, and in what sequence affects and ideas are being conveyed. I think of this partly as an analysis of defense. I cannot think of how someone experiences himself or presents himself without being keenly interested in what he or she does not experience or express about himself and why this is so.

I listen with the intent not only to follow the sequence of events that the patient lays out but also, specifically, where the patient is affectively located in whatever story the patient is relating. I listen to see if I can locate parts of the patient of which the patient may not be aware. I may feel parts of the patient that the patient does not feel or hear in the patient's language affects and ideas that are not consistent with what the patient is telling me he or she feels. In listening to the patient, I am also trying to locate myself in terms of both my inner experience vis-à-vis the patient's experience and my sense of how we are interacting with each other. Sometimes, I locate myself in relation to the patient by hearing, in some new way, what the patient is experiencing and observing about my participation.

This description of how I listen may be transposed into a set of technical ideals but not necessarily prescriptions. I believe that there are many forms of analytic listening that overlap between analysts from different schools. Each theory of technique offers ways of listening and engagement. What does this mean? Probably the best way for me to talk about how I work is by stepping back and trying to extrapolate a bit from what I try to do. My most important ideal is the one I have already mentioned—that for me psychoanalysis is the therapy through which the analyst *tries* to inspire and elicit the patient's interest and curiosity in his or her conscious and unconscious experience.

I believe in the well-described traditional psychoanalytic values of thinking about people as living with and struggling with conflict. Conflicts reside inside and are manifested and engaged within interpersonal relationships such as with the analyst. I think that the way patients engage with us as analysts, however, is special. The analyst is a special kind of listener, often an idealized listener, who aims not to impose himself too selfishly. But I do want to help, specifically by seeing if I can facilitate a person's curiosity about himself and what the person does and feels. This effort engages the patient with both his experiences of being helped and his dreadful and dreaded experiences of not being helped. My attention is always partly focused on this mode of participating in and trying to

observe these forms of engagement. I try to analyze these forms of idealization as much as I am able. It is obvious that the gratifying parts of
being idealized for both patient and analyst always mitigate how easily
I am able to see this idealization. I have become convinced that idealization of the analyst is at least as problematic as it is helpful, often more
problematic. In fact, I am concerned that Hoffman's (2009) most recent
work has become so skewed toward fighting the patient's internalized
hostile introjects that he is potentially depriving the patient of precious
opportunities to experience the analyst in complex ways, including as one
of these hostile introjects.

I aspire toward a kind of evenly hovering and evenly "roving" attention that is partly overlapping but also quite different from the evenly
hovering attention that Freud described. My felicitous term *roving*
incorporates many different dimensions of how my attention moves in
the clinical situation. Through the term, I am trying to accept the reality that my attention does rove, and that I try to pay attention to this
and to work with this to the best of my ability. My thoughts and feelings are moving back and forth between types of thinking, formulating,
and integrating what my patient is saying. My attention is also moving in and out of my own thoughts and feelings, which are sometimes,
although not always, clearly related to my patient's experience. I commit
always to try to ask how my thoughts and feelings may inform me about
my patient. The line between reverie and "my own stuff" is never completely clear and always worth asking myself about, as I tried to explore
in Chapter 3.

Disciplined listening is highly imperfect. However, like Freud's evenly
hovering attention, mine is partly focused on aspects of how the patient
expresses either wishes or prohibitions/condemnation or how the patient
titrates affects. My attention is focused on how the patient is struggling in
expressing and experiencing himself. It is rarely "even," although perhaps
it often "evens out" over time. Does the patient know something and not
want to know it? Is the patient unable to experience two different simultaneous feelings about himself or someone else? Is the patient ashamed to tell
me something? These are all experiences of self that involve the patient's
internal experience as it is expressed to me, the analyst. Did my female
patient make a slip by saying in reference to herself with me, "your son"
when she meant to say "your daughter" because she is beginning to allow
herself to express that she feels herself to be more of a man than a woman,
my son more than my daughter? The unconscious story about the past or
present told by the patient in the present is always told to the analyst. So, I
am always trying to determine where the rub is, whether it is a new statement of wish, of need, of conflict, of possibility. Where is the disturbance in
the field? Is it inside or something between us that I want to focus on with
the patient, or is it both?

My attention is often directed toward whether or how a problem, a conflict, a burr under the saddle as it were, is being expressed or not. Is it being experienced vividly or is it a diffuse experience? Is it being pushed away? I suppose that these kinds of questions are a kind of baseline form of listening for me. To me, the most important direction for relational theory to pursue at this point in clinical theory development is in the routine moments such as these. Relational theory has helpfully, if not exhaustively, explored moments of interpersonal crisis between patient and analyst. I think it remains to be seen whether there is a way to describe our technical ideals and actual methods without falling into prescription that dampens the unique factors confronting each dyad. I believe that a younger generation of analysts will have an easier time doing this because they are not fighting the demons that cry: "What you're doing isn't analysis." In some ways, the question of what is psychoanalytic is itself an old and somewhat anachronistic structure.

Many analysts from diverse theoretical backgrounds have suggested that each analytic relationship is unique (e.g., Ehrenberg, 1982; Epstein & Feiner, 1979; Schafer, 1983; Tronick, 2003). It is probably the case that there are many forms of therapeutic action, and that there must be unique forms given the particulars of each dyad. Part of what makes prescription so difficult is the particularity of each dyad. As Levenson (1991) put it: "One's response is only called for in a particular way by a particular patient and is responded to in a particular way with a particular patient" (p. 94).

PARTICIPATION, OBSERVATION, AND FREEDOM IN THE ANALYTIC SITUATION

While there are modes of participation and observation that offer the illusion of being distinct from each other for brief periods of time, there are many instances when the line between participation and observation is fused or blurry. One such instance occurs quite regularly for me when I am "working backward." I will find myself engaging with the patient in particular ways before I notice and ask myself why that might be the case or what it might mean.

For example, a supervisee describes a situation in which her patient, a talented graduate student, is prone to feel either bullied by her bosses or she becomes bullying, too pushy or unwilling to make compromises. She and her analyst have long been engaged in trying to investigate these matters. The patient was asked by her loving but rather immature parents as a child to in some ways take care of them by being a good girl in the ways that they wished for her to be. She has developed levels of idealization, gratitude, and reaction formation toward them and is threatened by the notion that analysis would throw her into an abyss of criticism and disappointment levied against her parents. Her father was prone to resolve interpersonal conflict with his colleagues through becoming quite angry and threatening, while her mother regressed to points of infantile victimization.

My supervisee's patient feared that in an upcoming meeting she will explode at her boss; more specifically, she feared that she will explode about what she regards as unfair negotiations. The patient pleaded with her analyst to help her figure out how to do something other than become overly compliant or angry and uncompromising. My supervisee had been staying close to her patient's affective experience. As I listened, I began having thoughts that the analyst's implicit stance was to try to be a kind of coach to the patient, guiding her through some new affective pathways and possibilities for resolving conflict.

At one point, my supervisee and I paused and asked the question of what was going on. The work was going well, and I had every reason to believe that her patient might indeed be finding new ways to deal with these complex affects. But, the interesting questions for us related to what was being enacted, who was being embodied, expressed, and taken in. Working backward, it seemed that the patient was allowing herself to usefully regress to a position in which she could rely on a parent or someone to help her resolve interpersonal negotiation and conflict without simply feeling that she was bullying or being bullied. She was asking her analyst to contain parts of her that felt explosive and felt overly passive and frightened. It was also clear that my supervisee might be avoiding, for now, the possibility that she would be one of those people with whom the patient would be embroiled in conflict.

Observation leads to new forms of participation and vice versa. Obviously, the very categories, dichotomous and circumscribed as they are defined, are woefully inadequate to describe the ways in which two minds interact. These minds are exploring the patient's historical storylines, which are in turn inhabited by objects with encoded affects. These affects appear in the analytic setting. The notion of working backward is, even as it is spoken, flawed with the illusion of linearity and a presumed figure ground relationship regarding how the analyst "should" work.

Rarely do these expectations about linearity fit with experience. I have been drawn to some of the ways that Ferro (2004) has noted some of the same phenomena that I am trying to describe about how we speak, when we speak, when we know what we want to say, and the like. He stated:

> This leads me to reflect on the analyst's mental functioning in terms of all the "noninterpretive" operations—for interpretation, whether saturated or unsaturated, is merely the last act in a series of processes of transformation and searching for meaning. When conducting supervision groups on clinical cases I increasingly find myself reversing the dictum "think before you speak" into "speak before you think," because one can then make contact with the dream-like functioning of

the mind, which can create more connections and meanings than any "reasoning." After all, our task is to discover a new and original meaning in "facts" that are in themselves silent. (p. 9)

This view of clinical process was also well captured by Paul Ricoeur's (1970) deliciously subversive and astute statement—that psychoanalysis is the hermeneutics of suspicion. Everything is worth questioning.

In my work, I have tried to develop what I think of as an ethic of disciplined experimentation different from the ethic of my psychoanalytic education, which was more focused on learning a body of technique. What was missing in learning a body of technique was the ideal of engaging our naturalistic ways of making use of ourselves as a way of learning more about the patient's conflicts, transference, and defense. Canestri (2006) and Fonagy (2006) each have described the value of moving to clinical practice from theory more than we have previously done. Fonagy emphasized that such innovations as play therapy grew out of clinical practice, not out of theory.

For example, I partly learn what I think from what I say, and one of the most interesting things about clinical work was discovering this for myself, long before reading the work of Ferro or many other analysts who have come to the same conclusion. In the early 1970s, Henry Kissinger, then secretary of state, was asked a question about his position on a particular matter, and he stated: "I don't know yet what I think because I haven't yet spoken on the matter." In this sense, thinking and speaking do not necessarily follow in consecutive order. Working backward may not be working backward at all. These observations also overlap with Stern's (1983) emphasis on the patient's and analyst's unformulated experience. An example of working backward follows.

My patient Zoe is examining more and more her pervasive anxiety, which gets in the way of taking care of issues in her life. She had neglected to pursue payments owed by her law clients for 6 months, depriving herself of a large sum of money that was owed to her. Furthermore, she was unable to look at a particular agreement with her legal firm that was important in renegotiating her contract. She describes how she gets diarrhea when she has to take care of such matters. Her associations go to a sense of shame about wanting to have sex with men when she feels most unable to take care of things such as reading her contracts. She feels humiliated that she would want to have sex under these circumstances and describes herself as pathetic. I began to imagine that Zoe would bring in the contract that she was struggling with for us to read together. I began to transpose this fantasy, this imagined scenario into a sense that Zoe seeks containment when she is anxious, and that sex is a way to feel contained while masochistically submitting to her father's authority. He claimed and still claims that he always knew what to do about all practical matters and encouraged Zoe and his two sons, all well into their 30s, to rely on him for his legal and practical advice. So, as I worked backward,

I felt myself having a fantasy of providing her containment but asking her to submit to my authority (e.g., she should bring the contract to me for me to advise her). As these feelings and thoughts worked over me, I associated to Zoe's mother, who also masochistically submitted to Zoe's father. I thought of how by containing my fantasy of having her bring in the contract I would be able to contain Zoe's father inside me. I was trying to control the force that would ask her to submit to his authority even though through the fantasy, I was unconsciously paternalistic and patronizing toward Zoe by dint of having the fantasy. But, my fantasies were about protecting her and containing her in some way that she was unable to do for herself. I thought more and more about Zoe's wish that her mother could have protected her from her father and provided a maternal model of control and composure regarding taking care of matters at home. Over time, I tried to convey some of these thoughts about Zoe's wishes to contain her feelings and "her shit" rather than explode with her shit through her somatic symptomology. We tried to look at how much she withdraws from parts of herself that might feel more enlivened to act on behalf of herself, and that part of the obstacle is dealing with her own anger toward her father and her own sense of his fragility. We also tried to examine how she is anxious and reluctant to use these internal resources because of an even greater wish that her mother or that I would protect her from her father's authority and demands.

I am aware that an example such as this reflects my own way of working, my own ethic of reconstructing from experience. The theoretical predilection and personality of the analyst are always potent factors in the analytic process. The interactive matrix of the analytic situation (Greenberg, 1995) places emphasis on the particular characteristics of the analyst that dictate how the analyst works—how he feels at ease, how the analyst has predilections to see conflict or not, what allows the analyst the privacy and sense of connection that he needs to think and feel. These individual characteristics are powerfully influential in determining the ways in which we observe and participate. Some of us have a tendency to speak first and listen to what we say later, while others are far more composed and deliberate in the ways that they observe and listen.

Some of the particular predilections of a very unique individual, Sigmund Freud, a man far more creative and intellectually bold and unconventional than most analysts who have followed, developed some particular technical principles that he found useful in the very early part of the 20th century— the early interactive matrix of psychoanalytic process between Sigmund Freud and some of his patients. These have been variously used to enormous benefit and probably destructiveness in the development of technique. In modeling ourselves after these particular idiosyncrasies, we have in part not only developed analytic technique but also likely restricted the creativity of many analysts. We are starting to integrate a greater sense of freedom as we explore psychoanalytic theory and technique.

As Steven Stern (2009) suggested, there has been a thread running through psychoanalytic theory, beginning with Ferenczi but explicitly highlighted by Winnicott, involving the value of freedom in the therapeutic action of psychoanalysis. I do not intend to conflate freedom with lack of discipline. Emancipation can be easily mistaken for simply being unbuttoned. Freedom has become extremely important in conceptualizing some dimensions of the analytic process—a freedom that takes into account spontaneity, appreciation of resilience and adaptation; freedom to unknow our formulations as patients and analysts, to speak without always knowing in advance how we would provide a more formal formulation; freedom to judiciously express elements of countertransference before fully understanding it; freedom from the myths of objectivity and neutrality; freedom for the analyst to change and be influenced by patients; and the freedom to learn from our patients.

Of course, in psychoanalysis, freedom is only made meaningful by structure, restraint, discipline, and frameworks related to the analyst's theory and personal preferences. While I do not emphasize the use of "extrinsic" criteria (e.g., Gill, 1984) such as frequency or recumbence for defining analytic process, this does not mean that each analytic dyad does not need a framework in which to work. At this point, it is well documented that many analysts discover that their patients want to increase frequency to the extent that the analytic process is already in motion as opposed to requiring a particular frequency to define it. Establishing a frame that is suitable to analyst and patient is a part of analytic work and a part of analytic negotiation as opposed to an extrinsic component that defines analytic work (e.g., Bass, 2007).

As analysts, we are making different kinds of formulations and interpretations with different patients engaged in an analytic process. If that analyst is helped by Bion's (1967) and Ogden's (1997a) emphasis on reverie; Kohut's (1969) notion of self-object function; Brenner's focus on compromise formation; Symington's focus on the analyst's act of freedom; Hoffman's, Mitchell's, and Smith's focus on enactment; Aron's appreciation of mutual engagement and reciprocal influence; Loewald's appreciation of futurity in interpretation; Winnicott's valorization of privacy; Harris's (2008) interest in the analyst's self-care as related to analytic process and outcome; Busch's (1993) interest in close process; Ogden's (1994a) and Benjamin's (2004) use of the third; Renik's illumination of the analyst's irreducible subjectivity; or my ideas about good enough impingement and interpretation, we are all engaged in an analytic process.

In observing, we are always committing ourselves to one line of thinking or one lens while foreclosing others (e.g., Bion, 1963; Britton, 1998). I make peace with the restrictions or lack of freedom in any theoretical by incorporating what I call the *pluralistic third*. The pluralistic third involves ways of consciously stepping back from clinical work to think about it from other perspectives. It involves using the cumulative knowledge of analysts to shed light on unconscious conflict and the nature of analytic interaction.

There is little doubt that our preconscious valued ways of observing and participating in an analytic process will also foreclose other possibilities. Theoretical choice should bring personal responsibility to consider the limitations of that approach as emphasized by colleagues from other positions.

REVISITING PSYCHOANALYSIS AND PSYCHOANALYTIC PSYCHOTHERAPY: THE POLITICS OF PSYCHOANALYTIC ENGAGEMENT AND A PROPOSED UNITY

Analysts have many ways of trying to speak to patients about the nature of their inner lives; about engendering curiosity; about looking at the interaction with their analyst and with others; and about viewing obvious but unseen dimensions of their actions, experience, and expressiveness. This list of things that we try to engender in our patients relates strictly to the intentions and activities of the analyst and does not say anything about the patient's responses to these interventions. These are matters of technique that reflect many different elements of analytic process, including the various dimensions of what Greenberg (1995) referred to as the "interactive matrix."

If we believe, as do I, that it is through the analyst's focus and intentions and what the analyst aims to engage his or her patient in examining that analytic process is best defined, then things become considerably more clear about what is psychoanalysis. Trying to differentiate what is analysis and what is not has been a fairly unsuccessful and unproductive process. I believe that in defining analysis as I have we can make some progress in parsing out what is at play clinically and politically in these matters. Stern's (2009) article examining extrinsic factors such as frequency and Aron's (2009) contribution to understanding some of the dynamic issues at play in the devaluation of what is regarded as psychodynamic therapy should also prove to be helpful in continuing to elaborate what we do when we do psychoanalysis.

Responding to the question of how to distinguish between psychoanalysis and psychotherapy, Winnicott (1965, p. 117) wrote: "Personally, I am not able to make this distinction. For me the question is: 'has the therapist had an analytic training or not?'"

Winnicott was trying to get at the high degree of overlap between therapy and analysis. Winnicott, like Gill a few decades later, was among the first psychoanalysts to propose disposing of differences between psychoanalytic therapy and analysis based on extrinsic factors such as frequency and recumbence. I have never found these extrinsic criteria a very compelling way to differentiate one therapy from another despite the fact that process is often changed by these factors; in general, I prefer to work at greater frequency. Earlier in Gill's career, he offered a great deal about what he regarded as the distinctions between therapy and analysis, but most of these were discarded by the end of his career.

I might have agreed with Winnicott's comment at the time. However, I would now say that focusing on the overlap between "psychoanalytic therapy" and analysis is missing the point. I believe that there is one psychoanalytic process defined by the analyst's intentions. I believe that we should dispense with these separate categories because if we define analytic process as based on the intentions of the psychoanalyst, then there is only one analytic process. This process will take many different forms and different structural arrangements. How we facilitate this process is what should be our focus in psychoanalytic institutes and in training and educating analysts to do their work. Each psychoanalytic process is different depending on the patient, the analyst, and the ways in which they work together.

There is also an apparent contradiction in Winnicott's statement when we take into consideration that in 1958, as is true today, many analytic institutes emphasized the differences between psychoanalytic therapy and analysis based on frequency and recumbence. So, in effect Winnicott was saying that since he saw no distinction between the two methods, students should train at institutes in which the difference is taught, and therefore someone would become an analyst. On one level, this statement seems mystifying to me except to the extent that Winnicott seemed to be implying that he wished not to enter into the political fracas that has burdened the development of psychoanalysis. One may also make the argument proposed by Stern (2009) that learning the psychoanalytic method with the greatest frequency possible is the best way to learn the method. I strongly agree with this statement even though I do not believe that the method is usefully defined by frequency.

Gill (1984, 1994) and Ehrenberg (1992) suggested that psychoanalysis is not defined by extrinsic factors such as frequency or recumbence. Gill (1994) made the following statement: "It is my view that the possibility of establishing an analytic situation exists no matter what the frequency" (p. 66). While I agree with Gill's position that frequency is not a defining criterion of analysis, I am also in disagreement with him about the particular way he argued how extrinsic factors in psychoanalysis are related to analytic process. Gill was asserting that analytic process is defined by whether the analyst is successful in engendering a particular type of process related to the patient's immersion or participation, and he was saying that this is not determined by extrinsic factors. It is easy to abandon the notion of focusing on the intentions of the analyst as exemplified in Gill's remarks. I know for example that I have said things before like, "I see some patients once or twice a week who develop more of an analytic process than some I see four or five times a week." What I usually mean by this is that there are some patients who are gifted at saying what comes to mind and exploring their inner lives no matter what the external circumstance. Yet, the problem with this idea is that again we are in the territory of reifying analytic process as opposed to defining analytic process through a focus on the intentions, aims, and actions of the analyst.

What is at play in some of the more idealized versions of defining *analytic process*, such as "immersion" and "deepening," is a valorization of particular forms of free association and transference experience. While I stongly value these aspects of analytic work with my patients, the patient's increased curiosity or a deepening of experience are not the hallmark of an analytic process. Instead, they are the desired outcome. I enjoy analytic work with patients who have high levels of curiosity, but this is different from defining analytic process as related to this capacity in the individual. Equally important to analytic process is the attempt to explore and analyze the reasons why someone is reluctant to be curious. Most analysts will say that one of the most breathtaking analytic developments is the patient's capacity to cultivate new levels of curiosity if the patient was previously unable to ask him- or herself and others questions.

This valuing of analytic process as central regardless of the structural arrangements that guide the work still bears substantial discussion despite the fact that for many it may seem like an anachronistic concern. This is a divisive issue for many analysts from diverse traditions, and there is value in the notion that analysts from different traditions might find ways to more productively speak about and debate their various biases about training and analytic process.

My sense is that for many younger analysts the rejection of extrinsic factors as defining analytic process is taken more for granted than actually a source of controversy. Yet, I can think of many objections to my argument for a unity of analytic therapies from some of my relationally oriented colleagues as well as from my more classically oriented colleagues. I will outline a few of these potential objections.

From a more relational perspective, some would be quick to point out that analytic process is negotiated. Psychoanalysis is an interaction and cannot be legislated by the intentions of one of its participants. Of course, the process of psychoanalysis involves constant negotiation. But, if two people agree to work together in an analysis, it seems fairly clear that the analyst will try to help a patient see all of the ways in which his or her psychic life is overdetermined and compromised by feelings and ideas that he or she might learn. These intentions within the analyst are diverse and of course vary across analysts, who are different as people from one another and who have been trained in different traditions. But, what remains is, again, the notion that psychoanalysts *try* to inspire and elicit the patient's interest and curiosity in the patient's conscious and unconscious experience. If you will, the definition of analysis as related to the intentions of the analyst is an area of asymmetry within the analytic pair.

Some might claim that what defines analysis as unique is that the frequency and recumbence provide an opportunity for free association that is different from the more conventional mode of verbal interaction in what has traditionally been called psychoanalytic therapy. These arguments are compelling in my own experience because frequency in particular is often quite conducive to greater opportunity for affective intensity and exploration. Generally, I prefer to work with patients as frequently as is possible, and often I find the couch helpful to the patient and me in a number of ways. My patients who come in four or five times a week are often able to associate and experience parts of their bodies and fantasy life in a way that I have not seen before with people who come in less frequently. But, I believe that the general intention to focus on illuminating aspects of the interaction, bodily experience, and the patient's inner conflicts, the patient's conscious and unconscious life, is the most important defining feature of analytic practice.

Central to my argument is the notion that while all analytic process is the same in relation to the analyst's general intention, this process will differ in terms of how the patient makes use of the process. There are differences in the type of reverie that I experience with patients who are lying down on the couch versus those sitting up. I am likely to make different interpretations to someone I will see the next day versus 5 days later. But, I believe that the general intention to focus on illuminating aspects of the interaction, inner conflict, and conscious and unconscious experience are the same regardless of frequency. Many analysts have the experience of the patient wanting to increase his or her amount of time in analysis if the patient becomes interested in how it works and if the patient is learning about him- or herself.

In the following case vignette of a patient seen once a week, I provide a brief glimpse of a session with Peter in which it was clear to us that his analysis had begun. Peter knew that he was moving to another city at the time of this session. We were meeting once a week for 6 months before he left Boston to move to a new city to continue his schooling. This session occurred about a month before he left. From the outset, I was trying to help Peter to examine his inner life, his conflicts, and at times our interaction. Were I not engaged in these attempts, I would not be predisposed to describe our process as an analytic process. It was also clear to me and Peter that were he to stay in Boston, he would have increased the frequency of our analytic process.

PETER

Peter was a 22-year-old man, the younger of two boys, who contacted me because he wanted to understand two tumultuous relationships in his life. One relationship was with his former roommate and closest friend and the other with his current girlfriend. In his relationship with his roommate Tom, he felt that Tom had become controlling and possessive of his time and flustered and jealous by the fact that Peter had other friendships. Peter ended the relationship feeling that his roommate was too controlling and dependent on him or maybe even sexually interested in him in ways that his roommate did not acknowledge or perhaps even know.

Peter felt that his girlfriend, Anna, also wanted things to revolve around her too much. He never felt her interest in him, and that he tended to take care of her and cater to her needs. Anna seemed to tune him out when he asked things of her, which in fact he rarely did. When he began meeting with me once a week, he wanted to understand how he had become involved in these two relationships. Peter was limited in funds, preventing him from coming in more frequently. Were he able, I would have suggested more frequent meetings from the outset of our work together.

Peter was very close to each of his parents. His mother doted over her younger son and was very interested in his achievements and supportive as well. His much older father was also curious about Peter, and they shared a number of interests in common. Peter felt that his parents were as "good as I can imagine parents being." Peter was a gifted student and athlete. He felt shy and unable to claim victory over his 2-year-older brother in sports and intellectual matters when victory was there to be claimed as they grew up. He adored his brother, who was a more flamboyant and expressive person. He also felt loved by his brother, who, as they grew older, encouraged Peter to be less shy. When Peter came to see me, he was feeling quite flummoxed by elements of his own inhibition as well as the turbulence of these two free-falling relationships.

PETER: I'm feeling freer to not make choices like I made with Tom and Anna [to comply with his former roommate and girlfriend]. It occurred to me that I thought I might tell you about something that I've never talked about. I've never told anyone except my father that I can't pee very easily in public. It started in adolescence, and I've noticed that it's been getting better recently. Then over the last month I've noticed that when I get stoned I can't pee. I do remember telling my father when it started to happen. I was in a movie theater with him, maybe we were seeing a play with my mother or something like that. I told him, and he was very reassuring, very nice to me. I think he said something like, "It happens. Just relax. It's no big deal."

COOPER: We've been talking about your feelings of inhibition around other people—that you can't speak so easily about what you need and maybe make choices of people who are sometimes content to have things focused around them. Maybe you were thinking about this situation with peeing because it represents a form of holding back.

PETER: I've always admired how I think it's in Norway, kids aren't clothed until they're five years old or so. Seems like such a good idea to me.

COOPER: To feel the encouragement to be yourself and not hold things back?

PETER: Right. But why when I'm high does this happen [smiling]. I find that so weird because I like getting high.

COOPER: Just a thought, but maybe it's a way for your mind or body to regulate the freedom that you have—to say it's not okay to be yourself too much. It also occurs to me that your attempt to tell me about this for the first time might involve your attempt to pee, to let something out that you're uncomfortable about.

PETER: Now I can only think of being with a woman who is mature, my equal, or more together than me. It's actually embarrassing to me that I wanted to be a kind of big brother to Anna.

COOPER: Why embarrassed?

PETER: I don't know. I mean I don't know so much about myself, so acting like I do seems so silly.

COOPER: I can imagine that your girlfriend and roommate were safe places to hide in a sense if it feels difficult to express yourself. Maybe you'd like to be more expressive for a change like your big brother.

This session continued in ways that were quite interesting and ended with Peter saying something along the lines like: "I really feel like we're getting somewhere." I felt the same way, and I immediately also felt a sense of sadness that I knew Peter and I were not going to be able to do this work together. Peter was getting extremely interested in his inner life, and I have no doubt that we would have met more frequently as his resources and time allowed were he to stay in Boston. I also have no doubt that we both felt that he was engaged in analytic work. I would have wanted to add time to our structure so that he could immerse himself in these feelings more deeply.

Peter was interested in the connections between his somatic symptoms and his affective experience. He was getting interested in the relationship with me and how it might reflect aspects of his relationship with his parents and others. He was also getting interested in the flow of his associative drift, for example, how his thoughts went from Norway, undressed children, and a fantasy of freedom after he discussed his own childhood expressions of inhibition as well as the current experience his own suppression of expressiveness when he was high.

I have little doubt that Peter's work with me would be quite different were we able to meet three to five times a week. I was sad thinking that we would not do that together. I could so easily imagine and remember how many young men and women who I have worked with and been moved by their discovery of their inner lives in analysis. But, I am also suspicious of the allure of pining away for a different structure that would allow us more time as a defense against thinking about what Peter was actually doing through analytic work. I think that analytic method is enhanced by not getting too focused on what it is not and instead thinking of psychoanalytic method as a unity that can be conducted in many different forms.

My work has always been influenced by Kris's (1982) methodological focus on the analyst's attempts to help the patient to say what is on his or her mind, including the wish not to say anything. I suspect that many would not agree with my notion that we have a unity of method that can be defined methodologically since I know that many would still retain a definition of analysis as requiring a certain minimum frequency of sessions per week. But, I would include Kris's intention to analyze the stops and starts of associations as related to the analyst's aims in conducting clinical work. Kris's (1982) focus on the patient's increased ability to free associate is a dimension of analytic process that most analysts would link with growth and a positive analytic outcome. It might include the patient's greater capacity to imagine, to think and feel with greater freedom and breadth, and to make links with different parts of him- or herself. Peter was learning about how to say what comes to mind, partly because what comes out of him was increasingly interesting. Of course, on the other side of that conflict was his fear that peeing will somehow not be good, and that he should suppress his feelings and thoughts. But, with regard to the issue of a unity of analytic method, I would only want to be evaluating my patient's ability to free associate as an outcome variable, if you will, related to therapeutic efficacy, not as a defining criterion of whether I have conducted an analytic process. The schizoid patient who is constrained and inhibited about a struggle to feel him- or herself as a real person or the analyst as a real person is in a process that is equally but differently analytic than the patient who associates relatively more freely. Sometimes when a patient can begin to say what comes to mind, our work is completed, not begun.

REFLECTIONS ON OUR HISTORY

Many historic discussions by Merton Gill (1984), Leo Stone (1961), and Robert Wallerstein (1989), to mention a few, have examined questions about what constitutes psychoanalytic process. Some of this discussion has focused on similarities and differences between so-called psychoanalytic psychotherapy and analysis. Traditionally, the differentiation between psychoanalysis and psychoanalytic therapy has been nearly exclusively organized around extrinsic criteria, and psychoanalysis has had the burden of maintaining these criteria without sufficient supporting evidence.

If we begin with the notion that there is a complex, dense unity called psychoanalytic process that can most readily and productively be defined through the intentions of the analyst, then whatever decisions are made regarding the extrinsic arrangements of psychoanalysis, frequency, recumbence, and the like will axiomatically be seen as part of everything else in the analytic process; these decisions will be part of what is enacted and the subject of the analyst's interpretive focus and understanding.

Some analysts never really get to compare the impact of extrinsic criteria in terms of their impact on the analytic process because they are not committed to the interpretation of unconscious process, of interaction, of conflict and defense in face-to-face arrangements or less-frequent sessions. When I began my analytic training, I was surprised to meet a number of teachers who did not really practice what they called psychoanalysis with the patients they saw only once or twice a week. This raised questions for me about how they would be able to determine the differences or similarities between the two treatment procedures. Since I had been trained to think about analytic process no matter what the extrinsic factors before I began analytic training, I had a different perspective than many of my senior colleagues.

It is necessary to think about what facilitates analytic work for the patient, but it is also important to think about what facilitates analytic work for the analyst. In some ways, we have all been subjected to and benefited from the particular idiosyncrasies of Sigmund Freud and perhaps been too oriented to making a "science" of a particular set of subjective preferences from the analyst's side of things. In the interactive matrix of analysis (e.g., Greenberg, 1995), many technical decisions may boil down to the preferences of the analyst, and extrinsic factors are among them.

The patient and the analyst need to create a productive and safe place to feel and think. Some patients feel that visually looking at the analyst is "too close," while others may feel too close when lying on the couch. I feel as if I need a place to feel and think, a place for reverie, and this is sometimes a significant factor in my suggesting the use of the couch. Where am I most free to think about my patient? For some patients, it is easier for me to be in one place or another to hold my attention. There are particular patients with whom I am more engaged when they are on the couch and definitely some with whom I am more engaged when they are sitting up. Thinking about how to govern and discipline our roving and potentially straying attention is an important matter but not one easily resolved through strictly geographical solutions (e.g., couch or vis-à-vis settings).

So, why do we keep asking the question of what makes something psychodynamic or the question of what is psychoanalysis? Why have our imaginations been so hampered in this regard? The idea of psychoanalysis, the discovery of the unconscious, has simply been too much to bear, its importance so gigantic that it has bred primitive, tribal proprietary instincts even from some of its most imaginative adherents. The collapse of theoretical hegemony has been unfolding since the 1980s. I think it is possible that the very understandable instincts to protect the integrity of psychoanalysis through maintaining narrow standards of technique and narrowly defined standards of training have also had a highly constrictive influence on its development.

This constriction has been enacted and expressed by maintaining sharp distinctions between psychoanalytic therapy and psychoanalysis. I find

Aron's (2009a, b) work that examines some of the reasons why these distinctions were maintained compelling, and I have suggested that his ideas are helpfully explicated through the work of Brickman (2003). Aron argued that psychoanalytic therapy was in some sense degraded and devalued in relation to psychoanalysis proper, not unlike the way we disavow and renounce degraded parts of ourselves. Brickman (2003) discussed about the ways in which Freud unconsciously held a kind of colonialist attitude toward the patient. From Brickman's perspective, the patient's inner life was "primitivized," while the colonialist psychoanalyst disavowed these parts of him- or herself as the analyst reformed and indoctrinated the patient. Brickman traced ways in which Freud's identity as a Jewish intellectual (equated in his time and place by many as being homosexual) was disavowed in this colonialist paradigm and located in the patient. Of course, this paradigm is not exhaustively explanatory since one of the unique gifts of psychoanalysis was Freud's ability for the first time to show us the primitive, elemental parts of all our personalities. Nevertheless, it seems to me that Brickman's perspective sheds light on the way in which psychoanalyts may have attempted to provide a more pure and detoxified analytic process as distinct from psychoanalytic psychotherapy. Aron (2009b) seems to have also reached this conclusion.

Collectively, we need to try to study the impact of various arrangements for conducting analytic work. This would make psychoanalytic institutes a far more inviting place for social work students, psychologists, and psychiatrists for whom psychoanalysis is currently an intriguing field, even if at the same time it has become increasingly seen as a failed experiment. Psychoanalysis has become too well lit, too visible as a therapy that made truth claims that were too large and too unsupported. We have a chance to create new experimentation and new discussions about what we do when we do psychoanalysis.

CONCLUSION

The more that I practice psychoanalysis, the more I find the terminology that we use in our accounts of therapeutic process are crude and overly schematic. The language cracks as it tries to hold the richness of actual clinical experience and observation. The language that I use in this book cracks again and again in the telling.

When I began to learn about psychoanalysis, I bristled when I heard explanations of therapeutic action that seemed either overly specific (e.g., the analysis and resolution of conflict) or too general (e.g., analysis as a corrective emotional experience). I was drawn to descriptions that were more precisely aimed at something about analyzing specific aspects of interaction and transference, defense and conflict. Now, I think of interpretation of transference and defense as something that I can deconstruct from trying to talk to a patient about what I am seeing and learning about the patient; it is what occurs along the way, not an end unto itself. The patient's experience of learning more about him- or herself, developing curiosity in the presence of another person, seems to me at the heart of therapeutic action.

It is all in the "presence," though, isn't it? While one part of the presence is to bear witness, so much of our presence relates to the ways in which we are inside elements of each other's minds and implicated, indeed embedded, in each other's experience. For example, a patient whom I discussed in Chapter 2, Leonard, was struggling to feel that he could be a specific person without feeling humiliated, too small, banal, and disappointed in himself. His expectations of himself were more heroic, taking residence on a panoramic scale and supported to a large extent by his considerable abilities. Leonard came on it one day in analysis when for some reason I mentioned his full name, and he was horrified. He associated to being in a line and the administrator needed to say his name aloud to page him to the ticket counter. Again, he was horrified. He then said, now a few months into his analysis, that he felt he had the "peculiar symptom of not wanting to be a person."

Leonard knows that I know about his particular, specific person, and he entrusts me with this knowledge. He knows that I have an understanding about why he needs his bird's-eye view of things. Leonard was upset by seeing traces of his person in daily life—his feces when he makes a bowel movement, the lipstick on a tissue in a wastebasket, saliva, and in general, hearing about his girlfriend's needs. Even worse are the glaring indications of vulnerability, such as his friend's guidebook sticking out of his pocket as they walk around a foreign city, which displays his friend's tourist status when Leonard is so familiar with the city. It disgusts and repels him.

In the analysis, Leonard has discovered that he is even uncomfortable hearing his name spoken aloud in various settings, despite the fact that he is a well-known person in his field and is required to make regular public appearances. In the analysis, he has been talking about his discomfort with his name being spoken and has begun to say his name aloud with me in various contexts as he talks about himself. He was horrified and humiliated when he said his name.

The structure of our interaction seemed to be that I was breaking the news to him gradually, carefully, but not always. Sometimes, I fell into a kind of engagement with Leonard in which I mentioned his full name to him in the context of our discussions about his anxiety, and to his horror, both feigned and real, he tried to bear the bad news of his existence as a real person. I say "feigned" because he had a sense of humor about his discomfort, so sometimes it almost seemed like he was responding to his name as does a child who wants to play up that he or she does not like a particular kind of food. This was a kind of play between us that was jointly negotiated. He would create a sentence in which the proper ending would be constructed by saying his name. For example, Leonard might say, "When I feel like I'm pathetic, I feel like I'm ____." I might end it by saying, "Leonard Smith."

Much was in play between Leonard and me in these interactions. I was interpreting something about his defenses against feeling his own self, his own vulnerability and needs, about which Leonard and I knew a great deal. At one level, I was containing his anxiety about saying his name and being the person he was. I conveyed to him the news with pleasure and approval about who he was and that he was a person. He knew that I knew that he was a person, and that I wanted him to be able to be his person.

I was also asserting things about myself. Was I envious of Leonard's achievements? Did I resent that I was the *shabbos goy* who first dirties himself with the knowledge that he and I were both real people? I had been entrusted with helping him feel like a real person, an actual person that had, for Leonard, an equivalence to being a pathetic anyone or nobody like me. Was our "joint" play related to competitive feelings that we may have experienced toward each other? I think so. As his analyst, I felt a commitment to help him to be his own person. I also felt a sense of caring for Leonard and admiration for him that made me want him to be a better integrated self. In effect, I was anticipating a psychic future for Leonard that he could not imagine himself through my interpretations. These interpretations accounted for his anachronistic and understandable adaptive stances that currently impeded growth.

At this point, it was costing Leonard more and more to try not to be a specific person. He was feeling in his analysis the cost of his well-honed "self-cure" (Khan, 1973) as much as anything else, and I was rubbing in that cost during our sessions. We were deeply implicated in each other's psychic lives in this form of analytic play. Leonard was gradually changing, but I had many questions about how and why that was happening.

I think that for Leonard what was helpful was his ability to let me be present with him through his shameful introduction to parts of himself that were anathema to him. In the language of psychoanalytic formulation, we detoxified and metabolized parts of his shameful self; we analyzed the parts of his sexual life in which sadomasochistic submission and wish to be controlled stood in for ways to hide his own wishes to control; Leonard felt with me an approving, full-bodied paternal presence in which he experienced an advocacy for being a person with a body and a name, in contrast to his loving, benevolent, but ethereal father. There was much more, and then there was the humbling wisdom of the cognitive scientist who would describe Leonard's analysis from the point of view of desensitization theory—he was becoming desensitized to his phobic reactions to being a person. At some level, this explanation is also compelling about what helped Leonard change.

Many explanations may be partly useful because at least temporarily they provide lighting for one explanation while the others move into the background. There is comfort in formulation both for our patients and for us in the face of uncertainty about the process. Spence's (1988) remarks are to some extent, unfortunately, still quite applicable today:

Theories are all comforting to the degree that they suggest that we know something about how and why treatment works. ... They comfort even more because they shield us from ignorance and from the knowledge that we have, at bottom, very little real understanding of the therapeutic process; a meager supply of facts, and almost nothing in the way of cumulative findings. (p. 190)

Psychoanalysts of various persuasions feel that they provide help, and in general I believe that they do, partly because through our presence and our interpretive engagement our patients are able to broaden their interior landscape, their experience of self and others through a variety of analytic approaches. We have, as Spence (1988) suggested, very few accumulated facts, but we do have accumulated experience. I suppose I have become more comfortable with the idea that I am a kind of psychic companion of sorts to the patient's journey, often welcome, sometimes decidedly not. I try to analyze the stops and starts, the invitations and withdrawal of invitations, and the ways that I see the patient's relationship to him- or herself undergoing constant change.

Many passages from Merleau-Ponty(1964) seem to capture some of the overwhelming complexity of intersubjective engagement that I attempt to describe. The following passage brought to my attention by Foehl (2008) tries to get at what it is like to touch another or be touched. What allows us to understand another person's experience or be understood? It is the point of intersection that Merleau-Ponty refers to as "intertwining" of two minds. The terminology of self and object, of projection and projective identification, new and old object, safe and dangerous, internal and external, transference and countertransference, and enactment are all woefully inadequate to help us observe and organize the range of experience that we confront in the clinical encounter:

It is the body and it alone, because it is a two-dimensional being [this means that as embodied we are both sensible *and* sentient] that can bring us to the things themselves [to participate in the world with others], which are themselves not flat beings, but beings in depth, inaccessible to a subject that would survey them from above, open to him alone that, if it be possible, would coexist with them in the same world ... if it touches and sees, this is not because it would have the visible before itself as objects: They are about it, they even enter into its enclosure, they are within it, they line its looks and its hands inside and outside. If it touches them and sees them, this is only because, being of their family, itself visible and tangible, it uses its own being as a means to participate in theirs, because the body belongs to the order of the things as the world is universal flesh. (pp. 136–137)

This is the border that psychoanalysis seeks to elaborate.

Infant researchers are also seeking to develop this language, although I think it fair to say that their illuminating creative work, like the work of clinicians, shows the limitations of language and linguistic categories in describing intersubjective experience. For example, Tronick (2003) described interaction that uses fresh and lively terminology to tell us about density and dimensionality, such as the term *thickness*. These notions of density and dimensionality seem superior to the dichotomies that clinicians usually use in both their clinical and theoretical descriptions partly because they are more affectively resonant with clinical experience. But, we have much to learn about how this density is created or changed.

Most of what we need to do now as psychoanalysts is to continue to describe how each of our therapeutic relationships is unique and how patient and analyst are constantly influencing the other. While it may seem quite indirectly related, I find Tronick's (2003) discussion of the application of Freeman's (1994) research on olfactory processes to understanding infant–mother interaction potentially quite relevant to helping us to think about the dynamic processes of interaction and influence in the analytic situation. Freeman demonstrated that the electroencephalographic (EEG) activation pattern for an odor in the olfactory cortex of the rabbit is different *each time* it is experienced. Different odors still produce activation patterns that are differentiated from one another. Most interesting, when a new odor is introduced, the organization of all of the individual EEG patterns of the previously experienced odors and the overall olfactory cortical pattern are changed. Freeman found no fixed patterns or prototypes.

Tronick (2001) suggests that "relational activation patterns" are also constantly changing. The mother–infant relationship has tremendous thickness and importance because of the size and frequency of its occurrence with the infant. But, its influence on other interactions is constantly changing because it is changing. Each interaction is experienced as different with each instance, and each interaction creates a level of change and instability in the organization of interactions.

A psychoanalytic focus on a particular metaphor of a stable relationship with mother is probably not only inaccurate but also not very useful. Tronik (2003) suggests that the cocreative model of relationships can explain "how the mother–infant relationship and other relationships can influence other relationships without the infant–mother relationship or any other relationship becoming fixed or the form of its influence becoming fixed" (p. 48).

It is of course a leap to describe the relevance of olfactory selection patterns in rabbits to understanding relational patterns in human infants and mothers. It is also a leap to understand the relevance of infant–mother relational patterns to adults, a leap that psychoanalysts have in large measure always taken for granted. But, I do think that the paradigm of how to think about the dynamic relationships of internalized dyadic interactions to one another is important, as is the relationship between new interaction and internalized and encoded patterns of interaction (e.g., Seligman, 2005). With all due respect to the refractoriness of character and the power of transference, we may well have minimized how each interaction within the dyad has an impact on the way that previous interactions are encoded. One way that the work of researchers on infants has relevance to psychoanalysts is to help us take very seriously how each interaction within the analytic dyad is unique. This means that, in addition to our focus on repetition within the transference, encoded introjects, and embedded unconscious fantasy, we may need to consider much more than ever that interactions between patient and analyst are unique. There is something that is probably always new even though it is hard to see through the conspicuous experience of what is familiar about the patient and about the interaction.

What does this mean? It might mean that when the analyst is interpreting something that he or she thinks that he or she has seen or said before, it may not be repetitive for the patient. In fact, it may be new for the patient in ways that the analyst is unable to see or has defensively truncated. It also means that if the patient says that it is old hat or something that has been said before, it is always worth the analyst seeing this as a defensive construction that minimizes the ways that patient and analyst may be in some new form of interaction.

The field of nonlinear dynamics also offers a great deal of hope in understanding much more of intersubjective experience to the extent that it specializes in emergent, unpredictable, spontaneous, idiosyncratic, or discontinuous parts of nature. Marks-Tarlow (1999, 2009) suggests that fractal boundaries between inner and outer worlds "help to ground the intersubjective thicket and to avoid the endless recursion of the mutual gaze" (2008, p. 22). Marks-Tarlow uses the term *interobjective* to describe a level of open boundary between self and world. Interobjectivity implies a level of reality as it exists at the boundaries of social observation.

This model may help us with the problems related to understanding at the border of how what we interpret is experienced by the patient just as what we experience as analysts contains elements of the dynamics that the analyst is trying to illuminate for the patient.

There is little doubt, however, that intersubjective experience and interaction are too thick and too dense to effectively delineate at this point, and yet this is what our clinical articles try to do. If anything, the psychic firmament is expanding, not narrowing, as psychoanalysis develops. Perhaps we are letting go of our illusions about categorizing and describing very small parts of this firmament. When will psychoanalysts have a way to get at Merleau-Ponty's philosophical attempts to describe the dense "chiasm" or intertwining of two subjectivities? Is it folly to think that we will?

Chapter 7

Good enough vulnerability, victimization, and responsibility

Why one- and two-person models need one another*

In many psychoanalyses, the metaphorical experience of victimization is and should be relevant. No matter how respectful of the patient's psychic reality, any perspective outside that of the patient's urges the patient into challenging and potentially scary new ways of feeling or seeing things. The analyst, like the Greek messenger, is delivering elements of an unwelcome message and participating in the dismantling of an earlier adaptation that the patient recognizes as a familiar form of selfhood. This external imposition of otherness occurs even when the patient feels met and understood in new and partly welcome ways. New moments of meaning bring new challenges.

One of filmmaker Ingmar Bergman's gifts was the way he let the camera linger on those moments in which parents hurt children through their limitations. In these moments, we can see these events register on the child's face. We are present at the creation of memories of painful influence, memories that will have enduring impact. As analysts, we are privileged to bear witness to the registration of new and therapeutic experiences, but we also participate in the repetition and enactment of painful experiences along the way. Just as analysis engenders growth and new experience, it also potentiates our participation in the universal victimization of intimate relationships between children and parents, romantic partners, and of course, patient and analyst.

Freedom is, of course, an illusion. Psychoanalysis is such a radically bold and ultimately indigestible idea because it shows us how understanding this clinical "fact" is about as close to freedom as we are going to get. Psychoanalysis was probably only ever popular to the extent that the general public did not fully grasp this painful truth; most of us only fully understand this after analysis. In fact, we might not have tried it if we had understood this at the outset. Given that the truth about tyranny and restriction in psychic life is so difficult to bear, psychoanalysis in part needs to be understood as set against this painful backdrop.

---

* Portions of this chapter appeared in *Contemporary Psychoanalysis*, 43, 621–637, 2007. Reprinted with permission.

Freud (1909) elaborated on how the patient is always subject to experiencing his illness and even the gains made by analysis in the service of resistance to deeper exploration and change. Thus, the patient will always feel a potential for a kind of existential victimization (e.g., Curtis, 1990) in response to the analyst's efforts to help. This is likely what Freud had in mind when he remarked wryly to Ferenczi, "We may treat a neurotic any way we like, he always treats himself psychotherapeutically, that is to say, with transferences" (1909, p. 55). The implication here is that the patient will gratefully accept help and change on this basis but, out of anxiety associated with becoming aware of warded-off material, will use these gains as resistance to deeper exploration. From a Freudian perspective, even the ways that the patient may feel understood and cared for will not fully account for the impact that the patient's unconscious will have on his or her attempts to remain in the familiar positions he or she has secured in relation to unconscious conflict.

Like many analysts, I find this observation quite useful and essential to understanding a patient's conflicts and a patient's reluctance to change. Yet, part of the reason that I believe that a two-person model is essential in combination with these perspectives is not just that we can never understand one mind without understanding two or the mind in interaction with another mind. Another essential reason that we need a two-person model is that the truth is too much for any one person, patient or analyst, to bear. Patients are helped by knowing and feeling that the analyst is also struggling to deal with this condition of human life. This awareness is not achieved through the analyst's disclosure but through a sensibility that reveals the analyst's attunement to the patient's read on all matters, including the analyst. It is also revealed in what Mitchell (1997) referred to as the analyst's self-reflective participation. While the responsibilities for bearing affect fall squarely on the shoulders of the analyst, there are many aspects of mutual containment (Cooper, 1998a) in the analytic situation.

Thus, one of the universals of the analytic situation is that all of us are victims of our own psychologies as well as those of our parents. We aim through analytic work to help the patient cope with and take responsibility for the consequences of his previous, current, and future experience. But, we know that we are limited in this matter (e.g., Russell, 1985). Psychoanalysis helps us make sense not only of our responsibilities but also of our limitations in being able to do so. We are all vulnerable to various degrees of victimization when we feel that our responsibilities are too much to bear. Some of us feel so victimized that achievement of responsibility is only conceivable after analytic work.

Russell (1985) wrote that it would be far easier to work therapeutically if the patient were the only one who repeated. He stated (1985):

However, the ... treatment experience forces us to widen our [awareness], to recognize that there are parts of ourselves, even more than our patients, that we do not yet understand. Some experiences are so scorching, some feelings so frightening or painful, that, at whatever cost, the patient will know far more about it than we do. They do not need us to know that we do not know. The most important source of resistance in the treatment process is the therapist's resistance to what the patient feels. (p. 15)

Bromberg (1995) described Mary Shelley's character Victor Frankenstein as depicting the way the Promethean needs of a parent can impose on, victimize, and punish the next generation. Victor Frankenstein's son was truly victimized by his father's inability to integrate his own very human and inevitable darkness into his nature. The son is the object of his father's passionate and human wish for Promethean potential and capacity. Caught in his father's life goal, he has been tragically prevented from experiencing being human and is instead the victim of what Bromberg referred to as his father's "creationship" rather than their relationship.

We analysts are constantly dealing with the quandary of Dr. Frankenstein and his son. We are attempting to help a person integrate parts of the self that he is unable to experience. Yet, the patient's sense of life is bound by what is familiar and what has been adaptive in coping with the circumstances of his early life and of his experiences with the analyst. We know that we cannot change people through our own urges toward creationship or through our own wishes to change our patients. Yet, we must try to understand and interpret to help create different psychic possibilities for our patients (Loewald, 1960) or what I have previously called a new "psychic future" (Cooper, 1997).

In fact, our own allegiance to a particular orientation or set of beliefs involves aspects of "creationship" that must, by definition, not only enlighten our patients but also impose prescribed meaning on them (Britton, 1998; Britton & Steiner, 1994; Cooper, 1996). Our general theory about psychoanalysis and our specific theory about the patient always contain something about the analyst's actual model for understanding as well as the helplessness and futility of how far this model will go. Bion's (1958) familiar statement—that the patient hopes through analysis for a mechanism of which the patient has been deprived and the analyst's countertransference is an experience of this catastrophe and the realization about his limitations in helping with it—is what I am trying to elaborate.

The analyst is in some ways victimizing the patient through a provision of structure that ultimately cannot replace the mechanism of which the patient has been deprived just as the analyst is making a provision that is the best he or she can offer to help the patient bear his or her psychic burdens.

Patients are also victimized by their analysts' personalities, which take us in particular directions during analytic work (Cooper, 2000a, 2004a; Josephs, 2003; Mendelsohn, 2002; Slochower, 2003). Some of us are pushier than others, in the words of Bromberg (1995), "more emphatic than empathic." Others of us are less likely to be emphatic but may fail our patients through our reluctance to negotiate or traverse the difficult process of integrating various parts of self. Interpretation often involves what I call "good enough impingement" (Cooper, 2000a).

Within the therapeutic process, there are intrinsic aspects of masochism, surrender, and even victimization for the analytic patient. Aspects of the patient's masochism or victimization emerge in the context of analytic regression. Yet, there are some aspects of surrender that reside not only in the context of regression but also in the act of asking patients to surrender to the parameters of analysis. These include the asymmetry inherent in the patient's free associating and the analyst's not-free associating as well as in the intrinsic elements of erotic masochism in the analytic situation (i.e., the ways in which expressions of love occur with no place to go with regard to sexual contact) and the limits of psychoanalysis as a process organized around language.

Some of a patient's surrender is related to the analyst's hopes, some to aspects of the analyst's "hatred" (in the Winnicottian sense of hatred of the patient), that is, the analyst's distinction from the patient, which requires the analyst to introduce the patient to a methodology. In my view, this separation is part of the meaning of Bion's (1963) aphorism for the analytic method: "We're both in this alone." The analyst's hopes by definition ignore the reality of the analyst's limitations in addressing the catastrophe about that which the patient feels deprived of having been able to get—the mechanism of which he is deprived. The patient surrenders to the idea that it is enough to know (which of course during the analysis it often is not) that the analyst sees and feels this catastrophe—a catastrophe about which the analyst is simultaneously interested in helping the patient to solve and unable to do so in a way that the analyst wishes he would be able to achieve.

Some of these aspects of therapeutic process are also present for the analyst, although in a much less regressive context. The patient has the opportunity to express feelings of vulnerability and need to the analyst. While the analyst may experience some of this vulnerability toward the patient, he is generally not encouraged to express these feelings in a direct way, even if the analyst is an analyst who judiciously uses analyst disclosure. That said, there are aspects of erotic masochism that the analyst also experiences, including his restraint, surrender, and feelings of loss.

Analysts are vulnerable in all kinds of ways to their patients (e.g., Ehrenberg, 1992). An analyst wishes for improvement in his patients, no matter how much the analyst tries not to "cure" or to impose his need for the improvement (e.g., Caper, 1992) on them. Analysts are also vulnerable in the degree to which they are implicated in the transference and depend on the patient to help them make sense of what the patient is saying and feeling regarding the transference. Most experienced analysts have had at least once the devastating experience of vulnerability with a patient who loses a sense of the capacity to hold transference complexity and multiple views of reality. When these capacities are compromised, it is easy to blame the analyst and to feel a profound disappointment that can doom analysis to a premature conclusion.

We are understandably so used to focusing on the patient's experience of the asymmetrical aspects of the analytic situation that it may seem outrageous to consider aspects of the analyst as victim. Yet, a number of analysts have successfully rendered us pictures of how analysis can move toward interpreting the unconscious tyranny that the patient's conflicts hold on the analyst (e.g., Ghent, 1990; Searles, 1979; Symington, 1983).

What are the responsibilities of the patient? These are to try to understand and absorb expanding levels of awareness about himself. The patient is trying to gain a greater sense of responsibility about what he imposes on other people and his analyst in interactions. To me, this capacity for responsibility is the hallmark of the achievement of the depressive position. The patient may come to understand what he requires of those around him, and sometimes even how he burdens others, including the analyst, with his feelings, fantasies, and attributions. In my view, this realization is a part of the patient's achievement of the depressive position when it is not a form of compliance and submission. For example, when patients feel the implications of their negative transference in a deep and heartfelt way, they also see a particular kind of reality—a reality that the patient may be in some ways projecting elements of an internalized representation on to the analyst. The more that they come to see these projections, the more they come to see realistically the ways in which the analyst is trying to bear or contain these projected experiences. It is always extraordinarily moving for me when a patient comes to deeply feel how he has been harsh or even brutal in assessment of others or of me. It is also moving when the patient comes to see how he has been afraid of asking for things, another kind of burdening of the other.

It is also true that if the patient cannot feel that the analyst is vulnerable to the "realness" of the patient's experience, then the patient cannot engage in the regressive play of analytic work. The analyst's vulnerability is not conveyed to the patient through words or expression of fear. It is conveyed through a willingness to investigate and be interested in what the patient is saying, no matter how the analyst is implicated. One of the problems that many analysts have is a difficulty with feeling vulnerable and engaged while maintaining separateness. This may take the form of trying not to feel enough vulnerability for engagement or not enough separation to engage the patient's mind and emotions as separate from the analyst's feelings and mind. If we take seriously the patient's reality, the patient's way of seeing things, then the analyst's "good enough" vulnerability can be experienced and used by the patient.

It is the analyst's responsibility to take the patient's psychic reality seriously, even when the analyst sees this psychic reality as overdetermined by many factors under consideration in the analytic process. This is the implication of Gill's (1982) seminal contribution to the understanding of transference as potentially related to the patient's experience of the relationship. It is difficult for some younger analysts to consider how much transference was conceptualized, prior to Gill's work, as completely unrelated to the patient's experience of the relationship. But in my view, the analyst has to have the courage not only to value the patient's experience but also to engage in curiosity about the complexity of the patient's experience. Again, one- and two-person psychologies can be complementary to one another in thinking about the myriad manifestations of transference, such as thinking about transference as potentially completely unconscious or as something that the patient experiences more consciously.

The confluence of conscious and unconscious experience goes to the heart of one of the most fundamentally misunderstood problems in how we conceptualize thinking about separate minds or, in Caper's (1997) terminology, "a mind of one's own." I am better able to think about the patient's mind by thinking at once about the nature of unconscious conflict in the context of an interaction with me. The continuum of factors related to the interpersonal context of analysis—the notion of mutual influence, the attention to the patient's perceptions of the analyst, the elements of mutual containment—do not imply a lack of attention to the idea that both patient and analyst have separate minds. For me, attention to these elements of interpersonal engagement does not imply a minimization of interest in unconscious fantasy as one of the essential areas of exploration in analytic work.

When the patient is not helped to see his or her internalized experience, such as in the failure of the analyst to hold projections and to put them into focus, the patient is victimized in a highly problematic way. Naturally, some of these failures are inevitable. The analyst cannot in some absolute way hold all negative and positive affects and put them into focus for the patient. However, when the analyst is unwilling to contain enough of the patient's experiences to point out what they are and where they come from, or if the analyst is so reactive to them that he or she cannot make sense of them in more routine ways, the patient is genuinely victimized by the analyst. In my view, good enough experiences of being "victimized" by the analyst's failures in these ways involve the patient's continued sense of the analyst's efforts to understand, even in the context of failure. But obviously, good enough can only be determined by the patient or through the patient and analyst negotiating what is good enough rather than by the analyst alone.

The patient is also often victimized by enactments with the analyst that the analyst does not help the patient understand. If the analyst cannot acknowledge his own participation and help the patient understand what has gone on between them, the patient has been hurt in some way, at least temporarily, within the analytic process. I agree with many analysts who have stated that a great deal of the analyst's work on his or her own participation can be done privately and silently (e.g., Ogden, 1997a) and does not necessarily need to be done with the patient. But, it is often quite productive to do this work with the patient. I often find that I am more successful in understanding these enactments when I speak directly with the patient about what has gone on, or is going on, within our work.

Good enough forms of victimization occur against a background of normative containment, with the analyst's failures, and it is hoped are more the exception than the rule. These failures are more likely to occur in the context of heightened affect on the part of the patient or times when the analyst is unsuccessful at pointing out the patient's intense need to hold on to internalized experiences. But, good enough participation on the part of the analyst means that the analyst is always paying attention to mutual levels of containment.

CONSIDERING THE PATIENT'S AND THE ANALYST'S VULNERABILITY, VICTIMIZATION, AND RESPONSIBILITY

The following case is offered as an example to explore the argument that our patients often benefit from our unique gifts for analytic work, just as they are sometimes victimized by elements of who we are as individuals. As patient and analyst get to "know" each other well, the analyst can feel misunderstood and victimized by the patient. Often, the two processes of victimization and growth are inextricably related to one another. In this clinical example, I attend particularly to aspects of the analyst's self-reflection and accountability.

PAUL

Paul, at age 29, was in his third year of analysis at the time of this brief vignette. He had begun analysis after his wife of 3 years had left him "for another man." Paul partly blamed himself for his wife's departure because he felt that she was correct in feeling ignored by him. Paul was an environmental activist with a background in political science, history, and environmental science. He was dedicated to social change and threw himself into his work. His wife had admired those aspects of Paul but grew resentful about his devotion to his work. She felt that, to the extent that she asked for more from him, he saw her as selfish and small-minded. When she left, she told him that she wanted him to have balls—"the kind of balls that don't involve standing up for others but the kind of balls that involve standing up for you and for me." She said, during one argument, "I want someone who wants to spend time with me and fuck me and can tell me that and tell himself that."

While Paul initially felt blamed and victimized by his wife and angry with her for becoming involved with another man, by this point in the analysis he was increasingly seeing her point of view. Several of his employees had complained to Paul that he was often judgmental about the limits of their own dedication to their work. They observed hours that were consistent with their contract and felt that Paul was contemptuous toward them for not being more dedicated and spending more time at work. Paul had difficulty setting limits on his own involvement. He was running a program and had many opportunities to delegate work but quite consciously felt reluctant to do so.

The oldest of three siblings, Paul had grown up in an extremely advantaged family. Paul's mother was an attorney who worked part time and was a devoted mother. He experienced her as involved in his pursuits and interests although not particularly warm or engaged with him. She did not seem to laugh with him, and he felt that he could not pull her out of whatever she was doing. Paul's father, also an attorney by training, had developed a large real estate business that extended to various regions in the United States and later Europe. By the time that Paul was 12, he had gone from idealizing his father to feeling massively disillusioned with him because of his business dealings. Paul's father talked to him about how important it was always to have the upper hand and to think about one's self-interest. While Paul experienced his father as dedicated to his family and to Paul's mother, he began to see his father as an extremely selfish and, to some extent, dishonest person.

By the time that Paul was 16, he had become interested in social causes, particularly environmental interests, and left-leaning lobbyist groups. He felt supported by his parents in his interests and in most of who he was as a person. But quietly, and somewhat secretly, he also felt a kind of revulsion toward his father and did not know what to do with the feelings of guilt and disloyalty this engendered. As a parent who was interested in Paul and his siblings, Paul felt that his father was unassailable. As a person and as a man to identify with, his father repulsed him.

During the analysis, Paul and I had come to see how much he had been taken up with proving to himself that he was not his father. He wanted to be honest and responsible and to help others. But, in our work he learned that to be close to his wife and to take care of her in the way that she wished, and to take care of their children were they to have children, was impossible for Paul. It was impossible because he felt that if he were to love his wife and family he would be acting like his father—he would be loving a self-serving corporation while ignoring the fate of others who were less fortunate. His wife tired of this corporate ideal. She resented Paul's unstated demands that she renounce her needs for love and attention in order to be a good wife. Paul was also running up against his own strong wishes to subvert time to his own needs.

Paul sometimes asked me to reschedule his thrice-weekly sessions because of various meetings. I always felt that he was responsible about making his appointments and that he exercised care and restraint about how often he would ask—in other words, something had to be important for him to ask. Most of the time, I was able to reschedule, although not always. I also conveyed to him that I would do whatever I could to change his set times if we could find other set times that would be more convenient for him. I always found it interesting that Paul seemed to appreciate my willingness to reschedule if I could, but that he was never angry or disappointed when I could not. Further, he never expressed feelings about my own self-interest becoming a focus. I think that he felt me to be someone who appreciated his interest in other people and social causes and who cared about and admired him. Perhaps it borrowed from the way that he felt loved and admired by both his parents.

At the time of this vignette, Paul had met a new woman with whom he was very much enjoying spending time. She reminded him of his mother in certain ways. She was quite bright and accomplished, but also, like his mother, more materialistic than his former wife or any of his former girlfriends. She wanted him to be finished with work by 6 o'clock and spend time with her. He was trying to oblige, partly by asking his workers to attend evening meetings for him, which they were willing to do, but he was struggling with his guilt and self-loathing about delegating work.

At the same time, I noticed that Paul had begun asking me far more often to reschedule his appointments, and I began to feel quite differently about the rescheduling. He seemed to be impatient about the demands of our schedule and irritated with my suggestions for rescheduling. I was also feeling that he was no longer holding up his end of the bargain—that our appointment times were pretty well fixed, and that it would be better to try to make an overall change in our regular set times if, in fact, they were so frequently inconvenient for him. When I returned his phone calls about rescheduling or tried to talk about it with him during our sessions, I would feel a mild sense of irritation and sense that something was going on that we needed to examine.

The content of his sessions at this point in the analysis revolved around Paul's awareness of his needs to be heroic and to attain a different kind of success than his father had, one that was not only based on self-interest. Around this time, he reported a dream in which he was at his high school reunion with a group of the "popular girls." During his actual high school career, he had been critical of this group, but in his dream he was not. However, in his dream he was being criticized by a boy who was both his friend and a friend of the girls. In his associations, it became clear that the girls represented something about his seemingly more conventional and personal concerns, like wanting to be a good boyfriend. He wanted to be less concerned with his work and more available to his girlfriend, but this also made him feel passive, superficial, and less masculine. In some way, his self-interest, including wanting to attend better to his girlfriend, seemed superficial.

After a few weeks of more frequent requests (with some instances of my being able to reschedule and some not), I asked Paul if he agreed that he was asking to reschedule more frequently. Uncharacteristically, Paul became suddenly very angry and said that I was "being a rigid asshole." He said, "I'm trying to be in a relationship with Lisa, I'm trying to delegate to the kids [those who worked for him] to help me out, and I'm trying to balance a hundred things at once. All you care about is your stupid schedule, your little world here in the office." Afterward, he was a bit taken aback by his outburst. First, he laughed nervously and then calmed down, but he maintained that I was asking too much of him, and that Lisa was asking too much of him. He continued to claim that I was being rigid as he elaborated on his feeling that too much was being asked of him, and as he did so, he began getting angry and loud again.

I could feel the interpretive direction that I needed to take, but I was also irritated. I did not want to be irritated because I knew that Paul was in a tough spot, beginning to feel the confluence of a series of conflicts that he could not integrate or reconcile. But, I felt insulted and devalued. I began thinking to myself within a formulation that went like this (not a vocabulary with which I speak to patients): "I know that you're locating in me some of the feelings that you have for your father, which are changing slowly because you're not acting on them. Instead of behaving as though your girlfriend is a bad person for wanting more of you and constantly enacting your antifather identification through overwork and depriving those whom you love, you're actually feeling how difficult it is to be your father's son. Your father loved you and you loved him, and you've kept an unconscious attachment to him through some of your actions no matter how much you consciously rejected him. You have to risk finding out whether you are able to give more to your girlfriend, to the people who need you, without becoming the selfish and dishonest guy that you sometimes feel your father was. Meanwhile, you're asking me to hold all the feelings of being the selfish man/father so that you can feel okay about trying on this new identification and new self."

Despite my thinking along these lines, the first thing that came out of my mouth, unfortunately, was, "You're right. I care about my stupid schedule and my little world here. It may be stupid, but it's my little world." He was taken aback not only by my voice being more firm than usual but also by his own language, which he heard back from me. At that point, I veered us into some of the interpretations that I had been thinking about (as mentioned). I told him that I thought that he was trying to feel okay about also having his "own stupid little world" without feeling like a bad guy. Indeed, he was trying on some new and scary ways of relating to his girlfriend and colleagues, and he wanted me to absorb some of his old and antiquated adaptive behaviors, like going out of his way to take things on for others. If he was not going to be a saint, then I had better be. I told him that I thought he was experiencing my self-interest in ways that were like his father's and that disappointed him, just as he was trying to be devoted to his girlfriend (expressing his self-interest to be with family) without feeling that he was immoral in his dislike for his father. Could he be self-interested and caring, and could I?

For a period of a few months, Paul and I were stuck, and this interpretive direction went nowhere. Whenever I asked him if it had been difficult for him to hear my more disregulated state, my outburst, he insisted that it was not. Paul said that he liked that I was more real, and that he felt more trusting of me somehow in that state. However, he said that he also felt mistrust because of my rigidity. When Paul asked me to reschedule appointments, which I was sometimes able to do, I continued to ask him to go into more detail about the reasons and the context for his requests, and I was sometimes able to do so. I always felt that I needed to ask about the circumstances because I thought that we had to understand the ways that Paul's neurotic compromises were becoming condensed and organized in some of our scheduling conflicts. From my perspective, Paul could not let himself enter into the illusory and symbolic realm within which I was interpreting some of his projections onto me. He seemed to agree that he was trying to give up his counteridentification with his father and experimenting with giving more to his girlfriend without feeling like this was an act of selfishness. But, he also felt that he was being victimized by his honesty and attempts to change, particularly by trying to give more to those he loved. He was telling me straight up about his needs for rescheduling, and to boot, some of these requests were so that he could accomplish some of the behavioral goals that he had hoped for—to give more to those he loved.

Eventually, Paul began to feel that he was asking me to accommodate him in part to see if I would care about him and go out of my way for him. He also began to link his sense of his father's self-interest with mine. At the same time, he continued to struggle with feeling abandoned by me, seeing me as not wanting to support him in his attempts at change. This struggle and feelings related to the struggle became an important part of our work together for a long time. During this period, it seemed to me that Paul felt that I was either helping him by frequently rescheduling or getting in his way because of my own self-interest. Further, he was now seeing me as more like his father, as having organized my ethics around my business. He would get better despite me.

Paul said that he was disappointed in me, and that I was not the kind of person that he had thought I was. I felt a kind of ingratitude, not unlike what a parent sometimes feels about his young adult children. The parent is glad that they have the freedom to feel disappointed by the parent in the ways that they do, but it does not always feel fair. At times, I felt a kind of can't win quality to the work with Paul. If I do not always reschedule because I see his request as an enactment of his wish for me to assume his old identity as the antifather, I disappoint him. I always have to accommodate him, and for now at least, Paul did not see what interpreting rather than enacting this had to do with his growth. If I did accommodate blindly, then I did not fulfill my clinical obligations—and it was not in my nature to do so anyway.

The binary aspect of these moments of clinical impasse are familiar to most analysts (e.g., Benjamin, 2004; Cooper, 1998b; Ghent, 1990; Searles, 1979). Often, such moments boil down to elements of victimization by parental figures that are being enacted in the transference-countertransference impasse. They are moments of impasse because they are essential adaptations and counteridentifications, such as Paul's, which may appear masochistic to him during particular stages of analytic experience. These moments are related to what Chasseguet-Smirgel (1985) termed the patient's method of "self-cure." She applied this idea to her notions of perversion, as attempts to push forward the frontiers of what is possible and to unsettle reality. Patients feel victimized by the idea of giving up parts of themselves that have been their best ways of coping and adapting that they have felt so far. Freud (1918) beautifully captured this idea in the Wolf Man: "Any position of the libido which he had once taken up was obstinately defended by him from fear of what he would lose by giving it up and from distrust of the probability of a complete substitute being offered by the new position that was in view" (p. 115). This is also what Curtis (1990) was referring to in discussing the existential victimization that many patients feel during the process of analysis.

The patient feels what I call the "perverse hopes" (Cooper, 2000b) related to his or her adaptation at these times. The hopes are perverse in that they represent unconsciously stultifying parts of adaptation that the patient clings to for a sense of safety and, perhaps, hope. Interpersonally, this binary experience translates into the notion that I was either for or against Paul in his omnipotent relation to time and his perverse hopes to keep up his antifather identification cause—if he was going to dismantle his self-cure in the service of working in the analysis, I must be willing to assume his previous identity and take on his ethos of self-sacrifice without question or demand.

In some analyses, the analyst feels victimized by the patient's ingratitude. He or she may feel caught in between irreconcilable positions within the patient's mind and experience. In Winnicottian (Winnicott, 1962) terms, the analyst, on the one hand, functions as an environment/mother, holding the contradictory experiences that allow the patient gradually to experience unconscious and enacted conflicts previously unable to be experienced. At the same time, the analyst is simultaneously the recipient of an object transference that is directly at odds with these types of holding and containment. For example, with Paul, as I held his nascent and terrifying experiences of his trying to be good to his girlfriend and risking his dreaded identificatory elements with his father, I also became his father—the executive of a sketchy corporation with self-serving corporate ideals. Previously, in essence, I held a compromise formation for Paul in which he would try to be with his girlfriend more frequently while not feeling too much like his father. In a sense, then, the victimization that occurred when I spoke to him defensively was a simple concretization and enactment of a more complex demand that I was making of Paul.

Paul's attempts to relinquish his counteridentification with his father allowed him, or at least was concomitant with his ability, to work with me as his bad, disappointing father. If he relinquished this counteridentification, then I had better be a supportive father, not the self-interested father who had disappointed him. While there are many dimensions to the analyst's sense of victimization, this postoedipal, or transference shift, quality is among the most difficult. The patient has been able to shift into some important place, in Paul's case into trying on aspects of his self-interest. Rather than being grateful, he became concrete and unable to realize that *some* of the experiences that he was attributing to me were projections. For this moment, he could not work in a realm of illusory play with me as his father but instead became convinced that I was actually obstructing his changes; it was difficult to play analytically with the possibility that both were true.

It is also true that in my own way I was concretizing elements of the interaction. When I became irritated, I was in some way losing my appreciation of how difficult these circumstances, internal and external, were for Paul. In that sense, I was an obstruction to his attempted changes. Paul was both repeating something with me about his old experience of feeling his father's self-interest and feeling the real ways in which I was not giving myself over to my work with Paul. My outburst and irritation concretized a dreaded conviction that Paul had about me and his analysis. Rather than contain my own irritation with Paul's devaluation, I responded from within a realm of conscious negotiation. Another analyst might very well have been able to respond to Paul's devaluation of my small world with a more contained statement: "It is small for many reasons to you. You want my world to be large enough to be able to meet you and accommodate to you in a way that you haven't felt before. You're also worried that my world being small means that I'm like your father, and you don't want to be like us in that way. And yet you know that if you take care of yourself and your girlfriend, it might be small like us."

My failures in containment are almost always helpful to me in trying to understand experiences of which I was previously unable to metabolize or make sense. The ways in which I try to make sense of these failures with patients are moments when we are able to take what is inside the mind of the patient and inside my mind and work together in creating a new language comprised of two minds trying to understand one another.

Paul was in a process that involved moving from feelings of victimization to vulnerability. What interests me most in this very small part of Paul's analysis is that for Paul it was my responsibility to inhabit aspects of his father (a paternal transference) as well as aspects of his old and familiar behaviors (going out of my way to accommodate as he did for so long) for him to explore changes. In my moment of protesting, I failed to interpret how much he needed me to fulfill these roles.

Freud (1920) suggested the ego is a "frontier creature" that lives between the internal and external worlds. From an interpersonal point of view, the analyst at these times becomes a lonely frontier creature. The analyst loses his or her fellow frontier creature in the patient's mind and is subjected to the patient's most rigid beliefs. The analyst is victim of the patient's self-protective creationship and is not, in Britton's (1998) terms, able to find the patient's "vulnerable knowledge." The analyst has victimized the patient by encouraging the patient to experience previously sequestered self-states and to relinquish previously overdeveloped cover stories.

VICTIMIZATION AS COMPROMISE FORMATION AND DEFENSE WITHIN THE PATIENT AND ANALYST

The following vignette from my work with Mark occurred during my training after about 2 years of his analysis. In an earlier discussion of this work (Cooper, 2007c), I discussed how Mark figured into my own training analysis. While I touch on this interesting, somewhat parallel, process, first I focus on the various kinds of experiences of victimization and vulnerability that Mark and I struggled with together.

MARK

Mark was a very obsessional and anxious man who felt that he was making little money as a young physician and was besieged with debts incurred by his wife and three young children. I recognized some of these feelings in my own life. Mark asked me to see him very early in the morning (he complained that 7 A.M. was too late because he needed to get to the office), and he guardedly agreed to a very low fee. I was eager to work with Mark both because I thought that he could really use analysis and because I wanted to begin doing analytic work. So, in some sense, through no fault of Mark's, I felt that he had me over a barrel.

Mark, a supervised case, was a challenging patient. He had a very powerful paternal transference in which he wished me to be a father who would be strong in the face of his mother's perceived bossiness, rather than compliant and passive. Mark had felt that his mother dominated his father, and as a child he often longed for his father to act "more like a man." Even more complex and painful for Mark, his father died when he was 16 years old. During a year of his father's decline, Mark felt guilty about his anger toward his father's weakness. Thus, his father's illness concretized a psychological experience that he had been having about his father since he had been about 10 years old.

While Mark admired what he regarded as my strength and relative lack of inhibition about work, he was also threatened by the meaning of his analysis as an act of autonomy and freedom vis-à-vis his mother. He avoided telling his mother about his analysis. Mark's domineering female boss occupied his thoughts and feelings during the analysis at this point. He felt that, like his mother, his boss at his medical practice regarded him as a good boy, but that he had to do what she wished to win her favor. His passivity in the face of his mother's domineering attitude was formidable, as were his wishes for me to be his strong father and command him, as his mother did. His defenses were highly obsessional, often stripping away his own emotional participation in what he was discussing. It seemed to me that Mark felt that he and I both experienced ourselves as going along with conditions that were difficult and as something externally demanded of us. Mark felt helpless and victimized by his mother's assertiveness and by his wife's as well. He longed for me to bestow strength on him, but he only knew how to get that through passivity and compliance with me, a pose that involved him depending yet again on a strong person who would tell him what to do.

I had often talked about Mark in my own analysis as a very likable man who at times presented challenging analytic work. In some ways, I described feeling a bit victimized by Mark, as if something was being extracted from me. I (Cooper, 2007c) have previously taken up my analyst's resistance or reluctance to exploring my sense of feeling victimized by this particular patient in a clinical moment in my own analysis. I do not recount that story in detail now except to say that at one point we laughed together quite hysterically about the ways that I felt tortured by my patient's particular versions of obsessionality. One day, while I was complaining to my analyst about how early in the morning that I saw Mark and how little I was paid, I told him about how we had agreed to a very, very small fee increase after a few years of work. My analyst started laughing fairly uncontrollably, which was quite uncharacteristic of him. In that moment, I think that he was laughing about the ways in which I felt that I was being victimized by Mark in order to take care of him. It was necessary to try to translate this sense of victimization into the very real and anxiety-producing feelings about the demands that the patients (Mark and I) wanted to make on our analysts.

My intention in writing about this moment several years ago was to show how that laughter was important to deconstruct and interpret in terms of what I was expressing to him about me. In other words, a moment of patient (me) victimization needed to be translated into the language of interpretation.

In a sense, Mark and I were becoming victims of deprivation by each other. Mark wanted so much more from me than he was receiving by way of paternal love and protection. I eventually wanted more appreciation from him for my various sacrifices of time and money. We both felt deprived. I was unconsciously identifying with Mark's sense of deprivation, which was also being enacted in the realistic logistics of the analytic situation—Mark had asked for very early hours and an extremely low fee as a control patient. While I wanted to work with him and begin my analytic work, I also soon realized that the terms of the project were challenging for me.

I want to take up why I felt so victimized by Mark and what was involved in trying to find ways to examine our interaction together. As the analysis unfolded, it seemed to become what I might call a kind of "oy vey chamber"—a place where Mark had the freedom to describe how besieged he felt by his mother. His sense of himself as a small boy without a father was palpable. He often cried about his sense of inadequacy and helplessness. In many ways, I felt that all I could do at these moments was receive Mark's pain and try to help him bear his sense of aloneness and smallness in the face of adult challenges that he felt woefully inadequate to face.

I believe that my countertransference fear was unwittingly hurting Mark through my presence as an adult and particularly as a vital, aggressive person. In other words, I felt that the analysis itself might become another source of failure for him—a place with a set of demands involving using analysis to help him grow. Mark would feel that he was again in over his head and besieged with his limited ability to cope with an adult world. In my compromised position of passively (and privately) complaining about our work, I was disarming myself. No longer equipped with interpretive understanding and hope about the analytic project, I also was a child being asked to do the work (being an analyst) of an adult. Countertransference victimization became a useful compromise between being a demanding mother or wife and withdrawing altogether and abandoning the project.

When two men feel themselves to be disarmed and inadequate together that there is often something related to castration at play. I think that Mark felt that if he had the penis he wanted to have, and that he did not feel his father had, that he would be placing himself in various kinds of danger. He feared hurting his father and not being the kind of man that his mother wanted him to be—a compliant man. In some ways, I equated my own power as destructive and hurtful, perhaps castrating, to Mark. Somehow, we both needed to find a way to be alive and to have a voice.

My dilemma as Mark's analyst related to having to continually ask why different psychic realities seemed so incompatible. Why did empathizing with Mark's genuine sense of isolation and abandonment—related to both his father's death and his sense of his father's paternal inadequacy while he was alive—prevent me from working with Mark's avoidance to challenging himself? Why did I feel I needed to give Mark a pass on challenges and to avoid taking up his unconscious creation of failed scenarios?

Clearly, I was afraid of becoming a "bad" object for Mark in the sense of reproducing his experiences of inadequacy with his mother. Yet, in my own withdrawal from him into passive victimization, I was enacting being a genuinely bad object. I needed to risk using some of my negative counter-transference about Mark's sense of victimization and passivity.

Ironically, what I was resisting was a level of therapeutic vulnerability that I had equated with the risk of being hurtful to my patient. This is indeed an almost perverse irony of clinical work and one that is easily lost in discussions about what vulnerability means. In psychoanalytic work, the analyst is sometimes most vulnerable when able to risk facilitating the patient's broadest experiences of him or her, including those that are "negative." While Hoffman (2009) has usefully suggested that psychoanalysts are not expressive enough about their "passion in the countertransference," I am struck by how his examples involved the passion of positive transference and countertransference. Hoffman correctly turned our attention to potential ways that we may inhibit ourselves in fighting the patient's hostile introjects. He was right that analysts are vulnerable to the extent that they let themselves feel how much they care about their patients and how much damage has been inflicted by the patient's important caretakers. But for me, one of the most difficult and important kinds of therapeutic vulnerability also relates to offering patients the opportunity to feel what they need to feel toward their analyst. It was easier for me either to pity or to feel victimized by Mark than it was to make sense of my passionate positive and negative countertransference experiences.

Is the analyst vulnerable enough in combating hostile objects in the patient's life? The analyst needs to be quite vulnerable in allowing the patient to experience the analyst as a hostile introject or a part of his internal saboteurs. Hoffman's point is well taken, but it requires of us enormous responsibility to preserve the analytic situation as a place to experience the analyst in a wide ranging way.

I began to show Mark something about a set of unconscious fantasies that I believed he held about the analysis. These fantasies related to how he felt that in the analysis he would have the father he needed—a father who understood that he felt overwhelmed with the tasks of adult life and his own fatherhood and who would help him with these tasks. Mark was essentially waiting for this to happen. None of this was new. We had been talking for a long time about how much Mark wanted this to happen, but these interventions were more than that, essentially me saying to Mark: "You know, I'm not kidding. This is what you really want." Mark began laughing about this interpretive direction with remarks like: "You mean, you're not going to help me do that?" Ironically, of course, that is exactly the area in which I hoped to help him. I wanted to help him feel that he could be a man and a father rather than exclusively a boy and a son.

In fact, Mark was able to work with this interpretive direction quite successfully. He spent a great deal of time in regressive fantasies about wanting to be cared for by me, often wishing that I would be a father who would stand up to his mother and protect him from her. It was very painful for Mark to experience these feelings and fantasies and very moving for us both. But, this regression involved Mark and I at work in his analysis. We had begun to extract ourselves from the compromise formation of victim privately competing for who had it worse. Mark was finally able to surrender to a level of vulnerability that allowed him to laugh and to express something that he had previously been unable to express.

We had also been able to move, together, from our mutually held experiences of victimization into positions of vulnerability and responsibility. The analyst needs to be able to surrender (Ghent, 1990) to his feelings of vulnerability about potentially hurting his or her patient, essentially the analyst's fears about his hostility toward the patient along with his fears of becoming the object of the patient's hostility.

DISCUSSION

Ghent's (1990) seminal article on masochism and surrender poses the question of how we as analysts play out roles of masochism and surrender in our work. One of the implications that emerged from Ghent's article is that we have institutionalized elements of victimization in the conduct of analytic work. Historically, some of the most absolute versions of containment or neutrality may have implicitly held highly unrealistic ideals for analysts to achieve, minimizing the analyst's real levels of vulnerability. More recently, Harris (2008) suggested various forms of resistance that analysts display in relation to self-care along with their vulnerability for heroic action and identifications.

The analyst is responsible for not pretending to achieve unrealistic positions. But, I believe that any "brand" of analysis can fail to live up to this obligation. While the classical ideal of asceticism or neutrality fails to take responsibility for the complexity of the analyst's broad and diverse countertransference experience, I have concerns that analysts of any persuasion, including relational analysts, may fail to take responsibility through abuse of expressive authority. Passionate devotion to the truth in a psychoanalytic context requires the analyst to investigate both the patient's experience of the analyst and his own experience. This is not achieved through either exclamations of what a patient should be doing or feeling or by ascetic positions of neutrality.

In my view, responsibility resides in a dedication to exploring and understanding a patient's complex experience so that the patient can take action. Part of our responsibility in this process resides in our accepting the profound limitations of what we are able to do in that regard. It is not only that we cannot make a choice for another person but also that sometimes it is only after a great deal of time that we can even get a clear read on what the patient wants or how the patient's conflicts are determining his or her decision. Sometimes, the patient idealizes the analyst as having certainty or clarity in relation to these decisions when the patient does not. This fantasy may involve the wish for a caring and knowing parent. At other times, it may involve projected parts of the patient that the patient is uncomfortable feeling more directly, such as a fear of personal authority. These are just some of the many reasons that I link elements of the analyst's responsibility with the analysis of these idealizations.

Often, in clinical case conferences, particularly difficult points of impasse or stultification in the analytic process are presented. As the analyst presents material, the melody may be playing a tune related to the specifics of the patient's life, history, and particular form of transference. But, there is often a background overtone that is highly expressive of frustration, sometimes even a sense of victimization: "I feel as if anything I say to this patient is rejected. I feel that I'm nothing. She won't invest in coming more often." Or, "No matter how often I try to get him to look at the transference, it goes nowhere." Or, "He won't increase his fee, and I feel exploited."

When we get comfortable with our supervisors or our colleagues in study groups, we are often more likely to allow ourselves to express raw, undistilled emotions related to feeling helpless and victimized. Those feelings can sometimes build up, particularly if they evoke guilt. After all, the analyst is a helper. How can it be legitimate to feel victimized by a patient? But, when all is said and done, this is a very human relationship, and often in the private mind of the analyst there is self-reproach, blame, anger, and sometimes even a sense of victimization in response to difficult points in the analytic process. Even those who are most likely to blame themselves are in the realm of victimization—self-victimization. This self-blame is the other side of blaming another.

The line between the patient's and analyst's vulnerability and sense of victimization is thin and often fluctuates on a moment-to-moment basis. "I hate it when my husband treats me like this," alternates with "I know that I make him act this way." "My son drives me crazy when he behaves like this," seamlessly moves into "He's like me; I know that I've somehow taught him to act like this."

Instances of analysts externalizing levels of responsibility on to the patient are far more common than we realize. I am always interested in those instances when a supervisee feels burdened by the transference, unable to follow the threads of what is adaptive for the patient in maintaining the perceptions and experiences that the patient is conveying to the analyst. I find that often in these circumstances the analyst wants the patient to yield to the analyst's interpretations to provide affirmation of the analyst. Often, what the analyst overlooks are particular forms of defense that are being conveyed by the patient, defenses that the analyst is unable to see or to verbalize. Mark's persistent efforts to express his long-standing wishes for strong paternal support became burdensome to me because of my own refusal to take responsibility for the role I would play in disappointing him. To some extent, I wished that he would change so that I would not have to continue analyzing his feelings and fantasies that I could not fulfill.

Sometimes, these examples occur in relatively routine clinical moments. For example, the patient may speak in ways that the analyst regards as relatively superficial or as hard to follow. The analyst may be unable to understand that the patient wants the analyst to know what he or she is saying without having to say it more explicitly. The patient wants the analyst to understand even though the patient may not be able to articulate or even fully understand what he or she is trying to communicate. The analyst may, in these instances, want the patient to be "more clear" or to provide associations that are easier to follow rather than pointing out the modes of communication that are being conveyed. These include the patient's defensive movements, which protect the patient's wishes to be understood without having to articulate anything. The analyst's experience of victimization are in these moments a source of resistance, and the outcome is a kind of barely conscious form of blaming the patient for not being the way that the analyst wishes the patient to be.

What is this sense of victimization that the analyst is more likely to express in the context of dialogue with colleagues? At these moments, it is as if the analyst is surrendering to the wish for someone else to be the responsible one in analyzing what is going on. The analyst is asking for holding for himself. The analyst does not want to continue bearing the responsibility for understanding the patient's psychology, for bearing his or her pain and compromise formations. Or, the analyst feels inadequate because he or she feels unable to bear the responsibility. Often, the analyst literally explains to the supervisor or group, "I find it unbearable." The analyst feels victimized by his side of the asymmetrical relationship, victimized by having to interpret, having to provide a level of ego functioning that the patient cannot provide, or to find a place for his participation/observation when this is hard to find. The supervisor or case consultant needs to find a way to explore what seems unbearable or might make it bearable. How might the analyst convey something to the patient that the patient needs to hear or bear in a different way?

Coen (2002) has written cogently about the analyst's wish to regress under those circumstances, when responsibility for interpretation seems unbearable. The analyst is likely to view some forms of mutual regression as involving retreat from having to bear hope for the patient and responsibility for continuing to keep on an interpretive trajectory. Echoing Racker (1968) and Searles (1979), Coen understands that this sense of regression and what I call victimization can sometimes turn into something progressive. He states: "Unless we can feel our own willingness to remain stuck in negative, regressive relatedness, we cannot offer our patients the potential to become unstuck, and to move forward with us toward something more separate, differentiated, and loving" (p. 152).

There are also many forms of countertransference reluctance that do not allow the analyst to enter into the patient's transference world or, on the analyst's side, its regressive counterpart. Such reluctance sometimes takes the form of the analyst's failure to play in the illusory realm of developmentally based versions of victimization, a failure that to some extent occurred when I defended my small world to Paul or when I was too absorbed in my identification with Mark. In the small world moment, I failed to enter into this aggressive realm of play with Paul and instead chose to defend my world and interpret something more immediately, thus risking the foreclosure of this form of play. I view these moments as failures in the analyst's "ethical imagination." These also overlap with a failure in what Benjamin (2004) has referred to as "the moral third." I was unable to surrender to aspects of victimization in the service of transference play until Paul's projections and attributions became less harsh.

The language of victimization requires an imaginative ethic, one that captures an aspect of the analyst's honesty about the vulnerability involved in offering oneself up for transference play. It requires responsibility not only as a helper but also as a potential inflicter of pain in the process of helping. It is the imperfect and evolving language of analyst and patient as frontier creatures.

Chapter 8

The new bad object and the therapeutic action of psychoanalysis*

An analytic lens sharpens and magnifies the way in which newness usually carries with it elements of the old. Hope itself, in psychoanalysis, is born of the constant tug between our emphasis on understanding the shackles of the past and the notion that a new experience might emerge. Traditional psychoanalytic understandings of newness rarely refer to actual capabilities that appear anew. Instead, newness often includes emergent emotional and cognitive reworkings of experience. Such reworkings may be visible only to the subject (patient, analyst, or both) who is seeing and feeling something in a different way.

Psychoanalysis has probably minimized how often newness occurs in the psychoanalytic process. The concept of newness itself may intrinsically imply something more dramatic when, in fact, newness in psychoanalysis is often quite subtle. The more accustomed to its subtlety we become, the greater our capacity to appreciate how breathtaking and moving it is when it occurs. I have been influenced by Tronick's (e.g., 2002) work in pointing to the frequency with which new behaviors are occurring in infant–mother interactions during development as well. Our models based on the repetition of constructed maternal–infant interaction have, I fear, kept us often from understanding the subtle shifts and nuance that patients are expressing with great consistency.

To be sure, much of new experience in analysis involves a reworking of a past relational experience or relational configuration. As emphasized by Winnicott (1974), it is often the case that a patient's conscious dread of the future is not really about what will be but is instead about whatever enslavement has already happened. This simultaneously adaptive and maladaptive function of our mechanism to transform unmetabolized past experience into dreaded future experience is well explored in Tom Perrotta's novel *Little Children* (2006). The suburban post-9/11 town is in terror of a local pedophile. This terror, in some ways, relates to the transformation

* Portions of this chapter appeared in *Psychoanalytic Dialogues, 14,* 527–553, 2004. Reprinted with permission. Portions were also delivered as the Keynote address to the American Psychological Association, Division 39, Minneapolis, 2003.

of unmetabolized aspects of the recent terrorist attack on neighboring Manhattan. The community is terrified of a pedophile not only because of the damage that he could do but also because he has become a magnet for the unmetabolized experiences that have already occurred. They direct and transform their diffuse fears of passive and ambiguous threat into an active, focused target.

Many of us as patients are often like the sole surviving Japanese soldier holding down an island in the South Pacific, fighting a war that is long over without knowing it. A patient's awareness that the war is over sometimes involves a reconfiguration of the past, reflective of the therapeutic action of psychoanalysis. It is partially described by the process of grieving, but there is an additional element, something active that is both transformed and transforming, some new way of thinking about and experiencing what happened and how we can imagine ourselves in the future. This experience has been well articulated by Joseph (1989):

> I think that we need to make links for our patients from the transfer-ence to the past in order to help to build a sense of their own continuity and individuality, to achieve some detachment, and thus to help to free them from their earlier and more distorted sense of the past. About these issues many problems arise, theoretical and technical. ... But what we can do, by tracing the movement and conflict within the transference, is bring alive again feelings within a relationship that have been deeply defended against or only fleetingly experienced, and we enable them to get firmer roots in the transference. We are not completely new objects, but, I think, greatly strengthened objects, because stronger and deeper emotions have been worked through in the transference. (p. 173)

Despite the shackles placed on the new by the old, psychoanalytic writers have been turning from elucidation of how the past informs the present to include more about how newness, albeit often subtle newness, emerges in the present. Having mined for so long the examination of ways in which experience is overdetermined by the straightjacket of repe-tition, psychoanalysts since 1980 or so have been exploring whether new-ness can be decontaminated of some of its most derogatory implications. Newness is often associated with circumvention of resistance or psycho-analytic cure through love; there is now more opportunity for discussing aspects of newness that have always been present but less articulated and documented.

New experience is a part of each analysis that has gone anywhere. Each analyst is a person the patient gets to know in some ways, and the patient must contend with the analyst's personality, strengths, and limitations, which may be similar to or different from early important others in the patient's life (Racker, 1968; Searles, 1979). The interpretive assumption that the patient's experience of the analyst's psychology (his goodness or badness) exclusively involves the evocation of past experience creates a shackle for the patient and the analyst. Psychoanalysis as a method of treatment allows us to lay claim to the complexity and ambiguity (although not the complete accuracy) of events. Of course, in analysis we achieve hope and freedom through reworking the past, which is elegantly explored in the tradition of classical psychoanalysis. Cognitive neuroscientists have shown us that this expression of the past often occurs through implicit and associative memory—that is, the evocation of affective memory as expressed through attitude, action, and enactment. But, we hope that the patient will get a chance to love, reject, or release some of his shackles prospectively and with someone he or she has felt helped him. Ideally, a modicum of psychic choice replaces psychic inevitability.

There is always something new from the analyst's side, and it is some of this newness that I explore in this chapter. Some of the potential therapeutic action and potential harm is related to the patient's experience of the analyst as a new bad object. At the heart of what I refer to as the patient's experience of the new bad object are the patient's and analyst's ongoing capacities for bearing and tolerating a loving connection in the face of disappointment, aggression, and hostility. I am deeply influenced by Searles's (1979) descriptions of the patient's efforts to drive the therapist crazy to find parts of the self; I am also influenced by Davies's (2004, p. 713) more recent descriptions of "the patient's and the analyst's unconscious need to seek out, find, and provoke the very worst that the other can be." Mendelsohn (2002) has also suggested that the analyst must notice the destructive impact that he contributes and that he must own. Accompanying this awareness is the potential that the analyst's guilt may induce the analyst to look for his own badness and, in turn, to tame and homogenize the analytic experience into a bland amalgam in which the patient feels that the analyst, fearfully, never laid a glove on him.

Paul Russell (1985), as much as any analysts I can recall, noted the analyst's inevitable limitations in understanding his patient. It is in the uniqueness of these limitations, for each patient/analyst dyad, where "new badness" partly resides.

I will trace some theoretical notions of hope and the concept of the new object in American psychoanalysis and then review some clinical work that examines new badness in the context of these theoretical observations.

A NOTE ON SOME SUBTLE FORMS OF THE ANALYST AS A NEW BAD OBJECT

There are many instances when I am working as an analyst when I think about the ways in which the analyst is a new object, old and new. This chapter addresses some theoretical obstacles to thinking about the analyst as a new bad object and I provide an intensive discussion of some analytic work.

There are many subtle instances of how this concept may come into play for the analyst as he thinks about enactment and analytic process. Consider for a moment the patient I presented in Chapter 5, Erica. I described some of my anticipatory fantasies about how I imagined that her analysis might proceed. Some of these fantasies were catastrophic, focusing on how she might feel criticized by me as I tried to interpret some of her needs to allow her son to act in some of the unruly and hurtful ways to others that had been her father's custom—that is, that Erica equated her son Lewis with her father and unconsciously tried to permit some of their noxious behavior even as she was repulsed by it in each of them.

In that discussion I described how some of my internal work as an analyst involved working with some of my omnipotent and grandiose fantasies that we might circumvent that process—that I would provide interpretations of her identification that would be easily integrated or that we might not even have to go through that process at all. As I became aware of these kinds of fantasies I realized that in some ways I was conducting myself like Erica's grandiose and exploitative father, being an analyst who would achieve the results that I wished for without going through the work with my patient that would be necessary in order to achieve a different kind of integration of her experience.

It is these kinds of feelings and thoughts about the analysis, these kinds of ways of thinking about the analyst's participation with his patient that I have in mind when I think about the analyst as a new bad object. Naturally, the analyst who is working with this set of feelings is a new good object too. I am doing my job as engaging in self-reflective participation as an analyst. I am working hard to try to understand Erica's conflicts and struggles, her adaptation and the nature of her transference to me. However I am also becoming aware of ways that I repeat old patterns of those whom she has loved (my omnipotent fantasies that render her unimportant except as an extension of my analytic wishes). I am a new bad object in that the forms of newness, which are problematic for both of us, are occurring in the very unique context of analysis and with me as a particular person. Many analysts would not experience these particular kinds of grandiose or omnipotent fantasies about the fate of interpretation. I am a unique, new bad object within the particular anticipatory fantasies that I hold about her analysis. I am a new good object, if you will, as I try to reflect on my participation with Erica.

When I lose interest in what my patient is saying and struggle to be engaged relative to how I was previously listening, I try to think about how this new form of engagement is similar to and different from the patient's internalized object world that I have understood. How does my inhibition in listening repeat or represent something new in response to the patient.

Even as these patterns are easily traceable to earlier object experience there is always something new, something unique to me as a person and to the unique setting of analysis that is worth understanding.

I rarely verbalize these stops and starts regarding my listening and how they might reflect on my participation as a new object, good or bad. But I do try to make very active use of these reflections in analyzing the patient's relational experience with me and with himself, his conflicts and defenses.

For example, when I become more bored with a patient, Phoebe, I realize that she has moved away from a set of longings that she had been expressing about what she wished for from her father long ago and her husband now. She feels loved by each of them but not well known. "Why don't they need to know things about me? Why are they content to just know the first two or three sentences about my day, my experiences, my projects? She switches topics to something at work, and I find that I'm having a hard time listening. I don't feel curious any longer about what she is saying. At one level, Phoebe has defensively moved away from her desires and longings into a kind of isolation of affect. She has moved to safer terrain, a zero sum game in which she asks for little and expects little in return. I am aware of this defense operating within her. I am also aware that I have become in reality more like the internal object experience that is familiar to her. Phoebe is unconsciously reducing the discrepancy between the internalized object and her interpersonal object/analyst (e.g., Feldman, 1997). I am a new bad object (like the old object who isn't that interested in her) but in the unique ways in which I am her analyst with a job description that includes trying to listen and be thoughtful about it. I am recovering from my withdrawal and being the best that I can be by reflecting on these processes.

In my attempt to reflect on my participation I think of a kind of updated version of Loewald's (1960) new object concept. Loewald placed great stock in the analyst's ability to be more objective than the patient about understanding the patient's conflicts. I believe that analysts who provide contemporary perspectives about the ubiquity of enactment (e.g., Mitchell, 1997; Smith, 2000) and the analyst's participation in the patient's conflicts either as a recruited object (e.g., Feldman, 1997) or a self-reflective object (e.g., Mitchell, 1997) are in effect suggesting that the best that we can do is to try very hard to understand the meaning of these enactments. In this sense these views share with Loewald the tremendously therapeutic value for the patient of having a "partner in thought" (Stern, 2009) and a partner in enactment, as it were—hopefully a partner who is able to have more reliable and regulated observational capacity than the patient at least for considerable periods of time. It is one thing to suggest that the analyst is not "objective" in contrast to Loewald's (1960) epistemological position. It is another, however, to hope that the analyst is generally more steady in his ability to observe as he participates with the patient and less prone to dysregulation and to being buffeted by the patient's conflicts than is the patient.

I find it very useful to employ Parson's (2006) concept of the analyst's coun-tertransference to method as an inroad into my participation as a new object. Often as I think about the particular line of interpretation I am taking or feel inhibited about taking, I am able to see elements of my newness and how it repeats elements of old object experience. It is also a part of transference as a total situation (Joseph, 1989). In Joseph's paper she describes a case confer-ence in which the analyst and her colleagues were particularly inhibited in thinking about a particular patient, in a sense bereft of formulations. Joseph beautifully illustrates the analyst's capacity to use this countertransference experience to illuminate the nature of repetition (old and new bad object par-ticipation). It is in the illumination and examination that we are always pro-viding the best that we have. Perhaps the only thing as good is our capacity to participate, to try to immerse ourselves in our patient's experience and even get lost at times, that precedes our ability to think about our participation.

THE ANATOMY OF HOPE AND THE CONCEPT OF NEWNESS

I view the concept of hope as providing a kind of experiential background or context for conceptualizing newness in psychoanalytic process. In a sense, Freud corporealized hope, conceptualizing the body and its biological sub-strate with the metaphor of drive. For Freud, hope for new experience lay in the attempt at consciousness and the capacity to partially tame instinctual pressure. A variety of psychoanalytic perspectives, including the relational (Aron & Anderson, 1998) and Kleinian (Steiner, 1993) approaches, keep the body "in mind."

It is not surprising that a criticism of the importance of hope in analytic theory or practice is that it can seem as if what is being valorized is a kind of conscious, Pollyannaish emphasis on our good intentions—a positive transference-countertransference in which patient and analyst are saying, in effect, "Gee willickers, let's work hard together to figure out why you envy everyone who tries to make contact with you. Let's just change that silly pat-tern." Hope, in this context, represents a kind of monotonal, simplistic ear-nestness—a zealotry and forced willfulness to circumvent conflict. It suggests that newness be declared by fiat. This hope lacks genitalia. It is, of course, utter foolishness because it turns a blind eye to destructiveness, allowing the language of the envious or hateful parts of self to die out. In its own way, it is a kind of defiance except that it kills softly a part of the self that is in the way—a loss that is consigned to the category of collateral damage in a just war.

In contrast to this overoptimistic view of hope, Searles (1979) wrote:

> The realm of hope seems to us a last repository of such innate good-ness as human beings possess. One of the harshest maturational tasks

the individual must accomplish, to become truly adult, is to realize and accept that hope is impure in two vast ways: First, it is not unitary in nature but multifarious and permeated with ambivalence and conflict ... and second, many of these hopes are devoted not to loving, but rather to destructive ends. (p. 479)

The naïve forms of hope are also too focused on aggression/badness as extended to patient and analyst. Iago is among the worst bad objects of all time, yet the story of *Othello* is hardly a story simply about a psychopath. Intense love such as experienced by Desdemona and Othello makes them vulnerable to hateful stories of betrayal and loss created by Iago. He is indeed the vile and depraved part of us all. Bob Dylan put it well: "All men's conscience is vile and depraved. You cannot depend on it to be your guide when it's you, who must keep it satisfied" ("Man in the Long Black Coat," *Oh Mercy*, 1989).

Hope, in my view, lies substantially in the effort for the patient to experience and work with the analyst as a new bad object as well as a new good object in psychoanalytic process. In theoretical terms that integrate some of our most important contributions, here is what I can best summarize: For hope to occur, one's old objects must (in the Winnicottian sense) survive reconfiguration after mourning; they must (in a Kleinian sense) be mourned again and brought back to life as internal objects that are eligible for a kind of internal object use. Sometimes, the parts of self and one's objects are externalized and dissociated, inhabiting realms of the analyst's self and object world, just as reciprocally the patient locates parts of himself by discovering aspects of the analyst's experience inside the self. Finally, through a process of negotiation, the experiences of self are reconfigured in a postrevolutionary state. (It is no wonder we need hope.)

Given this daunting therapeutic task, the closest that I can come to characterizing my ideal clinical stance is that I am hopeful but not necessarily optimistic. Whereas optimism can be general, blind, or obliterating of the demands and uncertainty of pain and challenge, hope can have built-in terror and a sobering awareness of the challenge.

THE NEW OBJECT AND THE FAMILY OF AMERICAN PSYCHOANALYSIS

It has been said, with some degree of accuracy, that hope is the national religion of the United States. With the immigration of many European analysts that began in 1936, Anna Freud's ego psychology and its accompanying logic of hope were a perfect fit with much that is American. At the heart of both the American ideal and the ideal of ego psychology were the power to tame the irrational with the rational and the hope of doing so.

Even if many of our American founders came from cultural and intellectual aristocracy, at the core of the Constitution is a democratic ideal and a hope—that everyone can have choice or agency in working toward rational goals. These founding fathers were not Pollyannaish. John Adams, like the later Sigmund Freud and Harold Searles, had little faith in the goodwill of people, which is why he insisted on a system of government that includes checks and balances. Newness does not necessarily represent goodness. In a sense, ego psychologists viewed the tripartite structure as a kind of built-in check-and-balance system.

For example, Loewald's (1960) new object analyst was a rational observer capable of being less distorting than the patient. For Loewald, the new object derives power and newness from the analyst's capacity to metabolize conflictual elements of the patient's experience. Loewald suggests that relational pathways could become unclogged or could be purged of negative affective, plaque through analytic interpretation—the appeal to the rational.

Following Sigmund Freud's death, Anna Freud and American ego psychology became, in a sense, the oldest "child" in a family headed by the progenitor of the family business of psychoanalysis. As such, ego psychologists worked within the basic structure of the family—innovating, but honoring the parents at all times, especially by holding to many of the basic tenets of drive theory.

During this period when ego psychology held sway in the United States, hope and the notion of the analyst as a new good object lay substantially in the analyst's and patient's ability to work with a kind of unobjectionable positive transference and countertransference. The new object experience, embedded in the notion of the therapeutic alliance, came to represent the part of the patient that could trust the analyst even in the context of negative transference. Kleinian and Lacanian analysts roundly criticized the (1960s) concept of therapeutic alliance as one more American gadget that could slice, dice, and dilute the radical nature of transference and the unconscious. I agree with this critique of the concept of therapeutic alliance. The ego psychological theory of psychoanalytic technique did not emphasize the analyst's strong affect or participation with the patient— the analyst's envy, competitiveness, hostility, and especially erotic countertransference—except to see it as a resistance to the treatment.

In a sense, then, ego psychology minimized the rich and dense opportunities for understanding our patients afforded through analysis of the countertransference. Loewald's (1960) view of the analyst as a new object focused instead on the analyst's special abilities for objectivity and maturity in relation to the regressive position of the patient. For Loewald, newness largely resides in the unobjectionable positive transference and countertransference in providing to the patient the analyst's auxiliary ego functions.

The unobjectionable negative countertransference was explored without naming within Kleinian theory in understanding aspects of projective identification. In Kleinian and contemporary Kleinian theory, hope lies in the patient's augmented capacity to integrate aggression in the form of envy and hatred and to move from a paranoid position to a depressive position. In this model, the analyst's countertransference is seen as exclusively unconscious and reactive to the patient's unconscious fantasies and conflicts, privileging a unidirectional rather than a bidirectional mode of influence between the patient and analyst. The analyst becomes a new object to the extent that he engages in an introjective counteridentification in response to the patient's projections as the host of internalized objects within the patient is detoxified and transformed.

In contemporary Kleinian theory, the analyst is seen as also making his own contribution to the projective identification process. For example, Feldman (1997) notes that importance of the fit between the patient's proscribed object relations and the analyst's predilection to receive particular proscriptions. The analyst may be new in terms of how effectively he is able to show the patient how he tries to minimize the discrepancy between internalized object relations and his experience of the analyst.

In an exceptional way in the history of psychoanalytic theory, Fairbairn (1952) emphasized how the new object analyst threatens the old object attachment. In other words, he began to conceptualize how a patient could associate the analyst with newness and badness. For Fairbairn, getting a ticket to be admitted as a new object to begin with was almost impossible, as if the psychic inner world was usually all sold out to season ticket holders. Fairbairn also knew that the new object experience does not usually help a patient change through one-trial learning. Unfortunately, the deck is stacked against us as people and as analysts because trauma does sometimes occur in one-trial learning. Fairbairn realized that new experience often either is not experienced as new because the old colors the new or, if it is seen as new, is questioned or feared because it threatens the old object attachment.

Although Fairbairn was unique among theorists in his ability to conceptualize the new object as bad, he did not explore the analyst as a subject. Instead, the new object analyst was a kind of composite of representational parts, but it did not breathe in the here and now. In fact, the here and now, for Fairbairn, was essentially platonic in nature—an illusion, a derivative form without a reality sign.

In the late 1970s and early 1980s, Kohut's self-psychology put forth a definition of the new object as a selfobject function that does not interfere with the patient's experience of the analyst as a part of the self. In so doing, the patient meets an empathic other where there had not been such a presence in childhood. The patient has a kind of innate, internalized capacity to resume development when disappointment had earlier been stultifying. Kohut's (1984) posthumously published book referred to this innate capacity as "the innate vigor of the self," and he equated this capacity with defense itself. Since pathology was conceptualized as a premature experience of otherness, therapeutic action relates to less-disruptive otherness. Kohut referred to a tolerable dose of otherness (as the selfobject function) versus an overdose of otherness or newness. The patient is speaking to the classical analyst as though she is the waitress in the movie *Five Easy Pieces*: "I'll have the chicken salad sandwich; hold the newness [or otherness]" (Rafelson, 1970). Newness for Kohut is seen as a new opportunity for growth but growth that is facilitated by a lack of external impingement. In some ways, Kohut's actual recommendations for analytic posture were as provocative and threatening to many psychoanalysts as had been Alexander's suggestions for analytic posturing.

From Feldman's (1997) perspective, the analysis of a selfobject function is nothing but a kind of enactment of a collusive relational engagement. The analyst fails to provide external observation of the patient's unconscious fantasies, wishes, and conflicts. From a Kleinian perspective, newness actually derives from the patient's experience of the analyst's observations. From a relational perspective, the opportunity for newness partly derives from the patient's experience of the analyst's subjectivity, an experience minimized in the selfobject function.

The conceptualization of the analyst as subject promoted by many theorists within relational theory set the stage for considering the new object as potentially bad in a therapeutic or growth-enhancing way. No longer was the mother a receptive blob, an animate but single-dimensional breast; instead, she became a complex person, a center of subjectivity with needs of her own and, significantly, limits of her own that inevitably impinge on the patient. In elaborating Winnicott's focus on hatred as expressed in the infant's subjective reaction to the separation between child and mother, Benjamin (1988) suggested that the mother's subjectivity and the child's will inevitably and "hopefully" clash. Recent infant researchers such as Beebe (2000) and Tronick (2001) have elaborated the degree to which newness is an important part of infant–mother interactions. These become the developmental underpinning or prototype for what I (Cooper, 2000) have previously referred to as good enough impingement.

During the mid-1980s—influenced by the traditions of object relations theory, interpersonal theory, and even some of the silently radical aspects of ego psychology—along came a fiery, American younger sibling. Broadly referred to as relational theory, the newcomer suggested that, whether we like it or not, as a human being the analyst will experience and express aspects of himself in the conduct of clinical work. In working with and learning about these forms of expressiveness, part of our newness became conceptualized as another road to understanding unknown, unintegrated, and disavowed part of our patients.

Part of the early work of relational theory in the United States involved a critique of ego psychology's approach to the new object concept. The epistemological critique of the approach of ego psychology to the new object is well documented (Hoffman, 1991; Stern, 1992). Briefly, the problem with the notion of the analyst as a nondistorting, objective influence is that it is epistemologically naive and even more naive regarding the humanness of the analyst. Enactment, as a concept, became a way for relational theory to incorporate an understanding of both the analyst's fallibility and potential to become a new object as he is scripted and scripting plot lines related to the unfolding of the patient's unconscious. We cannot ever stay entirely outside the conflict, but once we get in there, we can do our best to make sense of it with our patients.

Relational theory was also unmistakably American. It has explored the boundaries of democracy in the analytic situation, regarding both epistemological certainty and authenticity. Oliver Wendell Holmes and his metaphysical club colleagues (Menand, 2001) championed the notion of valuing uncertainty. The notion of experiment is at the heart of the American hope; as Holmes put it, "Every social interest should have its chance" (p. 67). Broadly conceived, the relational model puts forward the notion that experimentation as an intellectual and clinical ideal must occur if we are to help our patients grow as well as to help us, as psychoanalysts, to learn. The valuing of experimentation in relational theory is embedded in the notion that countertransference expressiveness can sometimes be used interpretively to forward the patient's integration of affective experience.

Although much about the family of psychoanalytic theory and technique has involved broad divergence, until recently most psychoanalytic theories of technique, to the extent that they have focused on the analyst as a new object, have tended to equate oldness with the bad and with danger, while equating newness with good experience and safety. In an important article on neutrality, Greenberg (1986) asserted that too much danger or too much safety meant that analysis could not fly. Although Greenberg posited that a useful tension must exist between danger and safety and between oldness and newness, there is a tilt toward conceptualizing oldness as dangerous and bad and newness as more safe and generally positive. In his last work, on love, Mitchell (2002) questioned these assumptions about oldness and newness by asserting that oldness and familiarity can sometimes be constructed to protect against the danger of potential newness in the old and familiar.

THE NEW BAD OBJECT

The notion of the need for the patient to integrate experiences of the analyst as good and bad is hardly a new idea; many analysts have experienced how often a patient's trust is expressed at least as much in the opportunity to experience the negative transference as it is in the experience of the positive. Mendelsohn (2002) wrote cogently about what he referred to as the "analyst's bad-enough participation" (p. 331). Davies (2004) described the complexity of a clinical situation in which the task of articulating and tolerating the patient's experience of her as bad (withholding and cruel) was arduous and involved Davies's own needs at times—not only to try to articulate the patient's affects but, as well, to try to hold, contain, and detoxify those affects. In some previous work (Cooper, 2000a, 2000b, 2008), I have tried to introduce concepts such as good enough impingement and good enough retaliation to explicate our inevitable participation as limited, and therefore sometimes as bad, objects.

Both Freudian and Kleinian analysis have held quite useful purchase on the idea that a patient may gain a great deal through experiencing the analyst as both a loving and a disappointing object. A primary element of the analyst's new badness resides in the degree to which the analyst is unable to fulfill and gratify elements of the patient's fantasies about the analyst. I agree with Feldman (1997) that the patient exerts efforts to reduce the difference between internalized object relation and the analyst's observed behavior. New elements of "goodness" such as understanding will thus require repudiation or attempts to make the analyst bad in an old and familiar way.

Yet, despite the classical emphasis on the therapeutic value of the patient's broad object experience of the analyst, including positive and negative transference, there is less emphasis for considering the patient's experience of the analyst as a *new* bad object and its contributions to the therapeutic action of psychoanalysis. In particular, what is not discussed is the analyst's inevitable versus pathological participation as a new bad object that is distinct from although overlapping with the evocation of bad historical objects in the transference. I am interested in how we participate in old and new ways both in terms of the patient's experience of us and with regard to the analyst's own experience.

New badness or bad newness is sometimes conveyed in the patient's experience of the analyst's selfhood, which for periods of time will experientially overlap with elements of the transference. Sometimes, the new badness includes experiences of the analyst's limitation and the limitations of analysis as a therapy, but it may also include aspects of the analyst's aliveness, excitement, greed, sexuality, envy, love, and the like, which impinge on the patient through the patient's experience, through unconscious fantasy, and through enactment. There is a constant dialectic in analytic work between the analyst's need to change (Slavin & Kriegman, 1998) and to extend the boundaries of his or her selfhood to meet the patient and the reality that, from an analytic perspective, the analyst is intrinsically limited in his or her ability to enter another's and still be an interpretive object. Part of the patient's sense of newness has to come from experiencing aspects of the analyst as a person like the patient who is trying to change but sometimes unable, perhaps sometimes even unwilling, to change (with a deep dedication to understanding the impact of his or her limitations on the patient), just as the patient needs to experience the analyst as an agent of change.

I begin my clinical discussion of the topic of the analyst as a new bad object with the major caveat that there is something decidedly reductive about our tendency to conceptualize our participation with the categories of good and bad because most experience is neither exclusively good nor exclusively bad. It may be a remnant of Freud's dual-drive theory, which categorized human motivation as either libidinal or aggressive. Nevertheless, I have reluctantly decided to judiciously use these dominant metaphors throughout this chapter and the book. I hope that the content may help us build new ways of transcending this dichotomous approach to describing complex, multifarious affective experience as well as analytic participation.

JONATHAN

For important reasons, Jonathan always felt that he had to take care of those he loved. But, he felt that he was bad and would be criticized if he asked more directly for more support. Despite his close relationship with his wife and three daughters, he questioned whether it was acceptable for him to realize his considerable intellectual potential and to enjoy more of his financial privilege. Jonathan had grown up in a wealthy family, with high-achieving parents. His mother appreciated the privilege that she now enjoyed (which contrasted with her middle-class upbringing). Quick to condemn the bourgeois values of many around her, she was also highly contemptuous of her husband, Jonathan's father, who was a successful businessman and intellectually sophisticated but never the great man that she had hoped he would become.

Despite considerable academic success, Jonathan felt inhibited in his work, often feeling superior to and critical of successful others around him. We both understood this inhibition as related to his wishes to please his mother by not asking or demanding too much attention from others. It was significant that he had witnessed his mother's contempt for his father's successes and, in a kind of compromise, had determined that he would be more likely to receive her approbation if he did not try too hard to achieve success. As a result, he was made miserable by both his inhibition and his envy of others. When he felt critical and envious of others around him, he felt as though he was colonized or controlled by his mother.

Jonathan had experienced me in several distinct ways during the analysis prior to the vignettes I discuss here. I was often experienced as a father who was present for him and loved him in a way that he had not felt with his father. He viewed his father as loving but rarely home, well intentioned but emotionally clueless and absent. In the first few years of analysis, I was also viewed partially as a defective father who worked hard but never met with both his mother's and his own standards of intellectual excellence. As the analysis progressed, I was a successful peer whom he envied, but one who was maybe not as bright, discriminating, and talented as he. Jonathan was always horrified by my annual request for a small fee increase, his budget allowing. But, he was predictably horrified and vaguely intrigued by what he regarded as my unabashed ability to make this request without discomfort. Jonathan and his wife lived on their combined incomes as well as money provided to them by his wife's inheritance, which made a very small yearly increase quite affordable for him.

As the analysis progressed, Jonathan referred repeatedly (and with no small degree of playfulness) to my greed. During the early parts of analysis, we both understood how much he wished me to love him without demands of my own. Later, I began to take it up saying: "We know how much you don't allow yourself to consider whether you might be greedy, too. You know that you do everything possible not to ask for what you might need or even to consider it, except after you feel terribly resentful about giving everything and then feeling gypped."

Deconstructing this routine clinical moment, I would say that a part of what I was doing in playfully accepting his attribution of greed (not disingenuously submitting to his attribution) was holding an affect that was anathema for Jonathan—holding, containing, detoxifying the affect and then putting it back on the table between us for him to consider repossessing or owning it in a way that he never had before. Jonathan had to defensively locate in me—his analyst and his fallen father—all such desires, lest he be shot down or abandoned by his mother for having desires and strivings of his own. Because these projections were familiar to Jonathan and had been usefully interpreted over repeated instances, combined with a shoe-that-fits feeling for me about his attributions, I felt that it was worth aiming for developing a new language and a new form of interpretive play.

I think that it is valuable for the analyst to be willing to play with these routine constructions and attributed affect in a way that adds to the patient's understanding of its historical antecedents. The analyst has to take responsibility for aspects of the attribution, which feel real, with the risk of feeling misunderstood or misconstrued and dissociated for periods of time. The analyst enters a kind of transitional space, similar to what Ghent (1990) referred to as the analyst's expression of a willingness to surrender. Moreover, the analyst has to know that his or her burden is not only holding all of the badness, but also being burdened by knowing that the patient is sometimes right in what is perceived about the analyst. I am a new bad object to the extent that I am expressing parts of Jonathan that scare him, that will bring bad consequences, while he takes the role of his critical mother. Although there is similarity with Racker's (1968) and Sandler's (1976) notions of the complementary roles, what is different is the notion of the analyst as actually playing parts of wished-for or new aspects of self that were seen as bad and dangerous (and still are).

To be sure, my expression of self-interest included a resonance, for him, of aspects of his parents (i.e., the old bad objects) that were also highly neglectful and self-absorbed. His mother's anxiety and self-absorption could often make her oblivious to the unique talents and gifts of her son. His father often attempted to minimize his wife's anxiety and her prone-ness to criticism of both him and Jonathan, leaving Jonathan feeling alone. Undoubtedly, my so-called greed resonated for him not only with this parental neglect, but also with some of his own fears of becoming his fallen father, who was punished for showing his strivings and desires. But, our own psychologies are an important part of being a new bad object as well. One analyst might have brought to the patient's attention this issue in advance—that Jonathan would be likely to feel hurt or upset about my wish to increase the fee. I was more direct or even blunt. Perhaps it could be said that I was greedy.

It is interesting to think about how some analysts avoid being perceived as bad objects, while others are at risk for what might be regarded as libidi-nizing badness. I think of Muhammad Ali's awareness of our fascination with badness in the early 1960s. Ali's celebration of himself as a "bad" man was so appealing, in part, because it provided permission for the cel-ebration of selfhood, particularly striking in a man whose forbearers were slaves. Jonathan's awareness and ascriptions of this routine moment felt partially familiar or real, to me, but in a way that I did not feel was bad. While I did not feel that I was libidinizing badness, I was not predisposed to do things to avoid his experiences of me as greedy, demanding, or self-interested as long as I felt that I was acting responsibly and ethically.

To be sure, different analysts have different levels of tolerance for their patient's positive and negative transferences and our own positive and neg-ative countertransference experience. I often feel extremely admiring of my patients as they are able to explore the depths of their sadness, anger, envy, greed, and competitive feelings that are stimulated through our work and sometimes their experiences directly with me. It is important to emphasize the analyst's awareness of how some transference attributions are more congruent for us than others in terms of trying to gain purchase of our blind spots.

My new badness played out in some very complicated ways later in the analysis. As Jonathan began working more actively and needing to travel, he was confronted with my vacation absence policy, which he had known about for many years but had not experienced previously. My patients are charged for work-related missed sessions unless we can reschedule or I can fill their appointment times. Jonathan had to travel to another city on busi-ness for a week and was charged because we could not reschedule. He was furious, questioning how I could support his increased ability to work and yet make him literally pay the price for it. In a previous treatment, he had been told that he was charged because it was as if he were renting time. As we explored his fury about a policy of which he had been made aware at the beginning of treatment, we were able to understand at an even deeper level how much he desperately needed me to support his work self, which he had felt was so precariously held. He felt that I was lording it over him. I told Jonathan that he felt abandoned by me with a policy that was so reflective of my self-interest. (I realize that many analysts do not have similar policies about missed sessions related to work—again, this is an aspect of my person with which the patient is asked to contend.) I told Jonathan that if I stopped charging him for these missed sessions, we would have two problems. The first, I said, related to my wish to be paid more. The second would be that I might be doing something that had been painful for him—I would have to stop myself from working in the way that I wished to ingratiate myself or be loved by him. At this moment, his conscious hope lay less in integrating more about his ancient wishes for a more supportive father and more in talking me out of this selfish, greedy policy in the present. If I would not change my policy for him, it meant that I really did not care about him and his problems related to work.

Jonathan struggled with fears that I was really a bad guy and would not bend for anyone. He told me about a fantasy of going to get a consultation with one of my close colleagues to get the straight dope on me. This fantasy, offered with some degree of playful humor, was one that we explored in depth. He wanted to hurt me, and he was aware that his mother could be depended on to cut his father down; he also wanted to offload his devaluation of me onto her. I wondered with him if he was making a new attempt to constitute his own opinion about me that might run counter to his mother's views. For Jonathan, that would mean really being bad. "New" in this framework equaled "emergent," a re-created old object, self-organized into a new configuration—a subject not only of desire but also of self-definition. In turn, this effort at constituting a new view of a paternal figure ran the risk of his becoming a new bad object to his mother, one that he had always dreaded becoming. Jonathan agreed that he was afraid of threatening his mother. He also associated his consultation fantasy with a tearing down of the frame of analytic work, defying the constraints that he felt were binding him. He would become, at last, a "bad mother _____"—a subject of transformational desire. He was struggling to accept the psychic possibility that I could simultaneously care about him a great deal and have self-interest. To put it still another way, I conveyed to him that there was a sense of hope in his learning about and tolerating my own needs. It was at this point that, at times (not always), Jonathan could really experience the pain he felt about his neglectful father and let me be a source of support to him in his current life.

With Jonathan's increased ability to work (which fortunately brought him into conflict with my absence policy) and his attempt to more independently constitute a new view of me, the line between me as a new bad object and him as a new self endangered by his mother became fuzzier. He could not completely locate greed in me because he decided that his work took priority over our work together. He also could not take quite as seriously his adaptation involving becoming his critical mother toward me (the old bad object), which he displayed in his somewhat playful attitude toward the consultation with my colleague. He was also beginning to feel excited about his own potential self, simultaneously preferring to deed all greed and aspiration to me.

What made Jonathan feel more hopeful, at this point in the analysis, was our discussion about whether and how to reconcile two feelings that he held about how I felt about him, that in turn seemed in conflict with one another: my love for him and my self-interest. He was begging to know and feel the limits of my love and the experience of me as a person with needs of my own without feeling murdered himself. His new experience came in hating and loving me at this point. In a sense, Jonathan was free to challenge or be destructive to the one he loved because the one he loved (in the present) could not love him the way he wanted to be loved. This act of freedom is caricatured beautifully in the film *Punch-Drunk Love* (Anderson, 2002) when the central male and female characters (both of whom are loving individuals with barely concealed, seething anger) are in bed and intoxicated with each other. She tells him, as she kisses him lovingly, that he is so adorable that she wants to tear his cheek off; he tells her that he would like to take a sledgehammer to her head, while he is tenderly looking into her eyes and kissing her softly. Finding someone whom they love allows them, in a caricatured way, to experience their pent-up rage about the limits they have encountered with themselves, others and will no doubt encounter with each other in the future. Infatuation seems to mean never having to say you are an old bad object—at least for a fleeting moment in time. Nostalgia means never having to say that you were an old bad self or object.

Six months after Jonathan and I dealt with the absence policy issue, a much less routine incident occurred. I was making an overnight business trip to another city. Jonathan had a morning appointment the next day, and I was fairly confident that I would be back in time for it, but I asked how I could contact him if I was not going to make it. I conveyed to him that this was a very unlikely possibility.

Why did I mention it at all? Should I have contained that possibility and not burdened him with it? Was I trying too much to protect him from being surprised if I needed to cancel? Was I doing the opposite by putting my work life—the active, uninhibited (in his construction) part of my self—in his face and rubbing his face in it to boot? Was I being greedy, as we had constructed earlier in the analysis—keeping the appointment while running the risk of having to cancel? In informing him of this possibility, I did not feel that I was trying to protect him by being different from his parents and letting him know that I had him in mind, but the thought did occur to me. And, when I asked how to reach him, he got very upset. If anything, he felt that I did not have him in mind at all. He wanted just to cancel the appointment in advance because that would be less painful than my having to abruptly cancel this session, especially when my 3-week summer vacation was coming up shortly. I told him that I did not want to cancel the appointment because it was highly unlikely that I would not be back. I felt that I did not want to create an analytic reality in which disappointment could be avoided. I asked him if he felt that I was putting my active or professional self in his face in a way that made him angry. He kind of laughed at this point and said, "No more than usual." But, he was quite angry, and initially I had the sense that he had not really been able to give voice to what caused his anger.

There are at least a few cogent questions about my approach that can be raised here. Had I decided to cancel the appointment in advance to avoid his disappointment, it would not mean that (in general) he would no longer have the opportunity for disappointment. It was clear, in this interaction, that although I was trying to mitigate disappointment, I was also potentially creating a sense of abandonment. And, of all things, it was (from his point of view) my professional life that created the whole scheduling problem at the beginning.

Initially, I felt a stubborn resistance to listening and thinking about what he was saying and feeling. Of course, he felt abandoned by me. How could I not get that? I felt that I was understanding this better, but Jonathan could sense that I did not entirely see it or feel it that way, which was also quite true. This sequence of my disappointing him by my insensitivity (from his point of view), and my feeling as though he wished me to create an analytic space devoid of disappointment, remained with us for quite a while. Fortunately, he could often experience my efforts to see and understand things through his eyes, even if he felt that I failed.

After much effort to explore his feelings, Jonathan agreed to meet at the regular time but was still somewhat angry with me for not canceling the appointment. More important, he felt that he had to acclimate himself too much to people whom he loved. I feared imposing myself too much on him but hoped that something potentially useful was taking place. (In the end, my plane arrived on time, and I was able to keep our appointment.)

I think that it was increasingly bothering me that Jonathan wanted his analysis to provide him with a haven from his relentless sense of disappointment by those close to him. He was angry and felt persecuted by all the people in his life that he felt were free to use themselves in ways that he felt inhibited from doing, and he wished us also to withdraw from our aggressive and desirous aspects of self. He also hated himself for his inhibitions and his envy. In a way, I think that I began unwittingly to inoculate him with a small dose of the dreaded bacteria or disease—he was experiencing my self-interest and apparent lack of inhibition and equating it with a sense of abandoning him. I was doing it with a very strong message to him that had been given from the beginning: "I'm going to be as responsible and available to this process as I am able to be, but I don't think that the fundamental change regarding your anger will be achieved through other people accommodating to your inhibitions."

This vaccination metaphor is slightly different from the way in which projective identification is usually conceived because although some of the "bacteria" came from disowned parts of Jonathan, some of the bacteria came from me. It is even a bit different from the descriptions of the analyst's participation in the projective identification process (e.g., Feldman, 1997). By more explicitly locating them in both patient and analyst, there is sometimes a possibility that the analyst will become less persecutory, with less of a sense of being on the outside looking in and more of a sense of looking with the patient. Davies (2004, 2005) has illustrated that what can be transforming for the patient is the ability, over time, to connect with the analyst's bad internalized experience. In Davies' case, aspects of the analyst's self-loathing helped to reduce the patient's shame in further integrating that which she experienced as hateful in herself. Davies' ability to refrain from reflexively locating her bad objects in the patient seemed to allow this process to occur.

It is of interest that Kleinians have for many years illustrated how the interpretation of projective identification allows the patient to gradually locate and examine bad parts of the self that have been previously warded off or denied. In addition to the location and detoxification of parts of the self in the analyst, there are new experiences of the analyst's inner life with which the patient contends, just as many of the analyst's experiences are responsive to aspects of the patient's inner life. Grotstein's (2005) work discussed the process of projective transidentification, which involves the analyst's projection of unconscious fantasy as well as the patient's projections. But, from a Kleinian point of view, almost any acknowledgment or disclosure on the part of the analyst (regardless of the aim of the interpretation or content) symbolically constitutes an act of merger and fails to honor the separateness of the patient and analyst. I think that this restrictive view of interpretations employing expressive aspects of countertransference minimizes how the analyst's ability to communicate aspects of his subjective survival can, in turn, help the patient to find new words with which to represent experience.

One cannot say anything simple or fixed about the notion of the analyst verbalizing some of his own bad experiences for the patient to consider and digest. It can be a source of failed projective identification interpretation. It can easily also involve enactments related to repetition of parental demands for children to absorb and metabolize elements of the parents' unintegrated experience. But, I also have found that sometimes when the analyst locates his bad experiences for the patient to differentiate from the patient's bad experience that the patient's capacity to modify his persecutory and self-hating elements is augmented. This analytic activity is another form of what Gill (1979) referred to as "an interpersonal experience with the analyst which is more beneficent than the transference experience" (p. 179).

I want to emphasize that, by characterizing this experience as a kind of vaccination, I am obviously not talking about a planned experiment. I was not consciously introducing a manipulative series of events so that we could deal more fully with his experience of abandonment. What transpired really grew out of particular aspects of the ways in which our personalities intersected, including aspects of my self-interest. When my two sons were young boys, we saw the film *Ace Ventura: Pet Detective* (Robinson & Shadyac, 1994) many times, and it became a source of quotes for years to come. One of the funnier lines relates to what I am discussing. We would say it when we fell into something that worked out, but that we did not plan. After clumsily falling into some important information while solving the mystery of a missing pet dolphin, Ace Ventura says, "Unconscious, exactly as I planned"—an apt way to describe the process of looking at an enactment and trying to make sense of it, albeit with thinly veiled, retrospective omnipotence on the part of the analyst.

What began happening between us was interesting. As this pattern (in which Jonathan's access to his anger and envy toward me for what he construed as my relative freedom to work) recurred, he became closer to his wife, less envious of her, and less prone to devaluing her. He felt as though he was giving up on me. This brought sadness for Jonathan, but we examined how what he was giving up on was his wish that I would change in the way that he wished. He did not want to continue expecting me to give him love by renouncing my interests and career. Was this a good thing, he wondered? He did not know, and I did not know. He felt now that his unconscious plan to paint me as a professional failure (as he viewed himself), or to wish me to fail, was lame and unconvincing. But, he did also still feel envious of me and abandoned by my work—even if part of my work was helping him to become freer. Was he realizing that his legitimate needs to be protected and special were beyond my psychic capacities, or was there something he was mourning about his experience with his parents that really needed to be mourned?

To my way of thinking, his giving up on me was not just a defensive withdrawal from particular kinds of punitive wishes toward me. He was also withdrawing from a fantasy based on the perverse and omnipotent hope that if I could suppress my active self, he would feel loved and less envious and angry. I was now a new bad object, experienced more directly and less through the precariously held wish that he could omnipotently control me. Now, it seemed that we were dealing with a different level, a more basic level of desiring that related to his wishes to be seen and mirrored by his parents as the person he could be, not for his complex inhibitions and masochistic plea for love through relinquishment. With regard to the scripted plot in his family for psychic survival, Jonathan was now breaking in a new plot line—that of being able to be bad himself rather than continuing to suppress his desire, need, and greed or pretending that I did not also feel these things. I think it is fair to say that, in some ways, I had wanted Jonathan to be able to be bad, as defined by his willingness to not obey the family rules. In Symington's (1983) terms, Jonathan was reworking the "corporate ideal" that he had learned within his family.

As Jonathan felt his inhibitions more directly and with less anger and hatred toward me, he seemed to enjoy recruiting my support for his achievements. His struggles with work now seemed to more clearly involve struggles to actually try. He would become frustrated, in stops and starts, but he could try. We began to have more fun together and to joke about how he wanted my pity but hated wanting my pity. Other possibilities for love beyond ritualistic masochistic/submissive scenarios now seemed possible. At one point, when he was complaining about the stops and starts in a work project in which he was making some progress, he quoted a line that Dr. Evil said to his complaining son in *Austin Powers: International Man of Mystery* (Todd, Moore, Todd, Myers, & Roach, 2001): "Got an issue, get a tissue." I countered by telling him that I had recently heard someone say, in mocking empathy (really, in contempt) for someone who was complaining: "Cry me a river." We laughed together about his feeling at that moment about not wanting me to sympathize as much with the fearful side of him. I suggested, and he agreed, that maybe I could be Dr. Evil without his feeling so hurt.

Of course, Jonathan's ability to use me as a source of support and encouragement for his work could be seen as his movement into an identification with the aggressor—he could not get what he wanted from me, so he joined forces with me in a false way. But, it did not feel that way to either of us. I was Dr. Evil, or to put it another way, I was the new bad object who had (through our enactments and interpretations of the process) given him psychic permission to get out of the miserable oedipal compromise in which he had wasted so much time. Dr. Evil is also the antilibidinal counterforce to the hyperlibidinal Austin Powers. Taken together as a single self, they comprise the multifarious nature of hope—sex, fun, and play countered by greed, hatred, and domination for domination's sake. It had taken Jonathan a long time to let me help with his ability to work and play and to laugh about it and to let me be a more playful form of evil, a complex self and analyst to him with good/bad and bad/good, caring and greedy parts. (And of course, this is a very small and partial view of a complex and lengthy piece of analytic work.)

DISCUSSION

In some very interesting ways, society at large plays with the concept of badness as a construction. In the 1960s and early 1970s, it was common to hear the word *bad* used in conjunction with attributes of coolness, competence, excitement, and appeal. Similarly, the term *phat* emerged more recently, a term used often by white suburbanite teenagers pretending to be something other than what they are. What is phat? Like bad, it has the audacity to suggest that the ultimate goodness and coolness of someone or something transcends the usual conception of what is fat or bad. When a patient experiences us as bad, often the analysis has deepened. A level of trust has been achieved so that the patient can look and allow himself or herself to see the analyst as an influencing person—to be sure, as a person engaged in analyzing the patient and someone who is known only very partially, but whose personal attributes are always coming through and are now safer to explore.

These expressions or experiences of the analyst's personal attributes or selfhood (or "selfishnesshood") represent one of the most dangerous points in analysis. It is the point at which the analyst has to determine whether he is not seeing something about what the patient needs or how the patient needs the analyst to change versus a determination that the patient needs to try to integrate something about limitation. It is where new hope, through new integration of reality, including acknowledging the reality of the analyst's limitations, can be fostered. Or, it is where the patient's needs or hopes for the analyst to understand experience or to change can be truncated.

It is interesting that many schools of analytic thought have been able to understand the patient's experience of negative transference related to various kinds of limitations, frustrations, and losses, but the line between these frustrations and those related to iatrogenic experiences of anonymity in the analytic arrangement can be blurry. There is also a vivid difference between the analyst as bad at a distance, in the there-and-then or historical transference, versus the analyst as bad, up close in the here and now. At the very least, in trying to understand and contain some parts of the patient's part-selves or representations, the analyst cannot always be able to understand in other ways or to contain other parts of the patient's part-selves or representational world. To me, this conceptualization allows us to move out of the somewhat bland and even avuncular conceptualizations of the analyst as a new object. It takes us beyond the general and blurry meaning of the "unobjectionable good" new object. It brings badness into the more humanized, potentially loving, struggling, and resistant aspects of the analytic situation.

A logical question is, Does this conceptualization of the new bad object in some ways libidinize badness or potentially valorize aspects of a sadomasochistic relationship? My aim is not to valorize badness but instead to acknowledge that badness, destructiveness, and even hatred are often inte-grated into love. In fact, some of the most destructive kinds of love that analyst and patient enact are often born of a wish to exclude sadistic or angry and hateful aspects of the therapeutic relationship. So, in response to the question concerning the new bad object, it is important to emphasize that theory should provide a modicum of compatibility with the limits of the analyst—the person we are capable of being as an analyst. These destructive or bad elements of the analyst's deep participation are intrinsic to a process that helps us to integrate what we know about ourselves and that our patients feel sometimes, in part because we have helped them to feel these parts of themselves, us, and others. At some points in analysis, these parts are also expressive of the patient's experience of my limits and the limits of analysis. There is a profound level of depth to analytic work, bravery, and risk when a patient trusts enough to explore the limits of that analyst's responsiveness on multiple levels of development and experience.

I think it is important to ask why so many analysts are in some ways trained to be more comfortable with unobjectionable positive transference-countertransference than what I call *objectionable positive transference-countertransference*. For example, it has become more rare to think of idealization as defensive, a backlash from the pre-Kohut days when it was always regarded as defensive. My guess is that, understandably, we fear the analyst's narcissism or self-interest because it is a potential threat to the analytic situation. But, it is also essential to understand the patient's and analyst's sometimes malignant efforts to pretend that it is not there. As analysts, we have sometimes had an implicitly enacted heroic fantasy about ourselves—an idealized view or expectation that we can always be good. The paradox is that ownership of one's failings and limitations, or being clear regarding self-interest, can be (but is not always) an act of com-mitment to the work in the form of a painful acceptance of separateness between analyst and patient. A paradox related to this separateness is that it can make for some of the deepest kinds of intimacy. For the patient, the loss of hope is sometimes associated with parental wishes and needs that preempted the expression of his needs. A patient is often relieved to find in the collaboration and interpersonal context of analysis a place for parts of the self that had been interrupted or sequestered in the context of paren-tal disappointment or narcissistic needs. It can also be a relief to experi-ence aspects of the analyst's needs and person—and even, I daresay, some aspects of his narcissism, which can be felt as less toxic and more playful and loving. Of course, the really bad and destructive aspects of the ana-lyst's narcissism are often unconscious and are unconsciously enacted.

This is where traditional notions of neutrality can sometimes implicitly contain a persecutory attitude toward the analyst's own bad parts; these parts are not permitted access to the relationship, which in turn the patient experiences as a rejection or a foreclosure of getting to know himself through the analyst. At the same time, it is also a time in which psychoanalysts of all theoretical orientations, but especially those who describe themselves as relational, need to consider that countertransference expression requires thoughtful restraint. We must always ask at least two questions— what might I say that advances the patient's understanding of himself and what is the meaning for the patient of what I have already said. Relational practitioners are just as vulnerable to want heroic and unrealistic wishes about the analytic experience as analysts of other persuasions.

Among the many issues that contemporary theorists have tried to redress as the children of the 1960s that many of them are, it is hardly an accident that the therapeutic aspects of countertransference expressiveness have been emphasized. Now, a generation of analysts has moved into a new stage of development regarding the American psychoanalytic family. At an important sociologic level, the notion of the new bad object, emerging conceptually within our body of theory, involves the recognition by a generation of baby-boomer therapists that our task is to help our patients explore the multifarious nature of hope in psychoanalysis, engaging in the "goodness of badness" with curiosity and a modicum of grace.

Chapter 9

Franz Alexander's corrective emotional experience reconsidered*

In response to the 75th anniversary of the *Psychoanalytic Quarterly*, the journal that published Franz Alexander's original manuscript dealing with the corrective emotional experience, I was asked to write an article that examined Alexander's (1950) paper in light of developments in contemporary psychoanalysis. It provided me with a chance to look, more than 50 years after its publication, at one of the quirkiest and odd articles in the history of the psychoanalytic literature.

In this chapter, I examine again what Alexander did and why it still has relevance for psychoanalysts today. I believe that he has been massively misunderstood, with some people giving him far too much credit for the actual content of his work and others minimizing the creativity and forcefulness of his efforts. My central argument is that Alexander's notion of corrective emotional experience has become a kind of generalized version of phobic dread and defense regarding noninterpretive factors in psychoanalytic work. This is ironic since his focus was exclusively on interpretation, a fact that nearly all psychoanalysts do not really know because at this point his work has become iconic rather than actually studied.

I think that Alexander's article and his ideas are still quite valuable to us, although I suggest that we retire the particular term *corrective emotional experience* from any current way of explaining the many emotional and cognitive elements that factor into our patients' growth in the analytic process. It is a term so historically embedded in a rationalist/positivist tradition and has been so misunderstood that it seems to me a problematic way to describe clinical process. In fact, I suggest that its continued use serves as a kind of defensive devaluation for analysts—a way to disavow and degrade important factors in clinical process that were naively and grandiosely misapplied by Alexander. Moving toward greater accountability while abandoning the project of analyzing the refractory nature of unconscious

---

* Portions of this chapter appeared in *Psychoanalytic Quarterly*, 76, 1085–1102, 2007. Reprinted with permission.

fantasy and transference, Alexander's proposals defy easy categorization in the history of psychoanalytic thinking.

To explore Alexander's contribution to psychoanalysis and my thesis about the problematic nature of the corrective emotional experience term, in this chapter I examine some of the issues that Alexander tackled, however unsuccessfully. Alexander's attempt to address the increasing length of analysis and potential regression for analytic patients was extraordinarily important in the history of psychoanalysis. I also believe that we have not fully understood our own dismissal of his ideas, and that in trying to understand this dismissal we might further the conversation about concepts like nonspecific factors and new object experience that exist in varying schools of psychoanalytic thought.

A FUNDAMENTAL MISUNDERSTANDING

Part of what has interested me in our response to Alexander's work is that there has been a fundamental misunderstanding about his article. Alexander's attempt to provide a corrective emotional experience has been largely associated with the analyst's attempt to become a "good object," which has very little to do with what Alexander was discussing. Instead, he attempted through a proposed radical objectivism and a minimization of both the patient's unconscious experience (transference) and the analyst's unconscious experience (countertransference) to construct a new object experience that was fundamentally different from (not better than) what the patient experienced during childhood. While misguided in many respects, it is still interesting that analysts have systematically misunderstood this basic tenet of Alexander's work.

While there are some valuable ideas in Alexander's original article, it is because of this fundamental misunderstanding that I have a strong preference for completely discarding the language of corrective emotional experience. The term itself is embedded in the language of the rational, objective tactician with almost a complete neglect and lack of respect for the unconscious experience of the patient. I discuss in this chapter the ways in which the term *corrective* seems ill suited to describe the analytic process. The term has also become so identified with an obliteration of the analytic frame that I suggest that we entirely abandon the corrective emotional experience term. But, before discarding his terminology I suggest that we further understand it and further examine the forces that Alexander was trying to address.

Alexander was holding at once many contradictory positions within his clinical stance and, as well, within his understanding of so-called classical analytic technique. I would like to focus on what he might have been announcing to contemporary analytic technique and how we need to find ways to incorporate explaining avenues of analytic change that are not exclusively explained through analysis of unconscious conflict. But, to do it I would like to briefly summarize the contradictions in his original article.

More than any other analyst before him or after, Alexander was a believer in the notion of the analyst as a rational tactician. He believed that the analyst could decide in advance what was problematic for the patient in the patient's transference to his or her parents, others, and the analyst. He believed that the analyst could devise an alternative stance to counteract the patient's tendency to erect particular transferences. Never before or since was the analyst so focused on the ability for the analyst's conscious stance and behavior to overcome the patient's unconscious experience. To me, this is part of the disaster of Alexander's contribution. He minimized the notion that the patient's unconscious will constantly devise new ways to express transference phenomena. Moreover, Alexander had little means to understand that the analyst would also be unconsciously contributing to the enactment of these scenarios. To be sure, Alexander was not alone in failing to grasp the patient's ability to recruit the analyst in unconscious enactment of his or her conflicts. Sandler (1976) called attention to this capacity within the patient more than 20 years after Alexander's publication. Analysts were not aware of what would later be developed by relational analysts, namely, the notion that the analytic framework was fundamentally intersubjective and mutually influencing, and that it was necessary to consider the engagement of two unconscious minds in interaction with one another.

Alexander's effort did, however implicitly, grasp problems in psychoanalytic technique that no one had been able to articulate. He, too, did not grasp them, but he did struggle with problems that became a focus in the next 50 years of analytic technique. He did grasp in some way, however concretely, that analysis that only involves old experience and repetition will go nowhere. Greenberg (1986) and I (Cooper & Levit, 1998) have previously described how if analysis has too much old and the absence of newness it is unlikely to facilitate growth. If it is aiming to provide newness—that is, by avoiding the possibility of repetition—it is also doomed to failure and superficiality. Alexander's belief that the analyst could consciously and rationally decide what would be a facilitating alternative to the patient's transference and experience of his parents was an extremely grandiose idea. But, in a remarkably sophisticated way, he accurately referred to the traditional analyst's stance as a posture, no more or less specifically chosen than the one he was choosing.

While Alexander's is a radical criticism of classical analytic technique, it became a familiar point that was to be made by Merton Gill, Irwin Hoffman, and dozens of other psychoanalytic writers since 1980. Essentially, Alexander was calling attention to all of psychoanalysis that traditional approaches had consistently minimized the analyst's unconscious engagement and participation with his patient, and that one could not, through fiat, not participate. What was grandiose was Alexander's belief that he had somehow developed a way to circumvent that participation in a way that provided shorter and more effective analysis than any other approaches. At least the posture of Freudian technique could be justified by providing a setting for the analysis of unconscious conflict, no matter how problematic that stance is seen by analysts of various persuasions.

I believe that if we forget about Alexander's notorious and problematic language and antianalytic attitudes that informed his approach we can reduce his contribution to important questions for contemporary analysts. How does analysis facilitate and foster change? What are the factors that contribute to therapeutic action? And, how can we or can we discuss the notion of helping patients without violating the radical intentions of the psychoanalytic project—to deeply understand a unique person, both his or her conscious ideas and experience and his or her unconscious experience? In the analytic undertaking, the patient will understand parts of his or her experience that were not necessarily knowable without the presence of the analyst or, if not knowable, not easily integrated.

AN INTRODUCTION TO ALEXANDER'S IDEAS

Franz Alexander's notorious introduction of the term *corrective emotional experience* carried with it directions to analysts to explicitly manipulate the transference. In one fell swoop, Alexander proposed a radical revision of the concept of the neutral analyst. Alexander, the first candidate at the Berlin Institute and the first person to be named professor of psychoanalysis in the United States, aimed to provide a briefer and more efficient form of analysis. Perhaps more than any writer in the psychoanalytic literature, he believed in the analyst's rational and conscious capacities to conquer countertransference obstruction and to "know" in advance what would most facilitate a workable level of transference intensity.

In light of contemporary developments in psychoanalytic theory, Alexander is a most complex theorist and practitioner. While his work has sometimes been associated with largely nonspecific factors, especially naïve expressions of support related to growth in the analytic situation, in fact the corrective emotional experience, as Alexander introduced the term, has very little relationship to these characterizations. Instead, Alexander's modifications in technique grew out of a claim for technical rationality, analytic authority, affect titration, and transference regulation that distinguished it from all other forms of analysis.

Alexander's suggestions for manipulation of transference reflect his extraordinary confidence in the analyst's technical rationality (Hoffman, 1991), an unusual degree of epistemological certainty and a revised version of both analytic neutrality and the blank screen concepts. Alexander also proposed an expanded role for the analyst as a new object and recommended a method aimed to manipulate the transference at optimal levels to titrate regression and accomplish briefer work.

I suggest that his wishes to shorten analysis were at odds with emerging contributions from British object relations theory and American ego psychology that elaborated elements of the analyst's newness without manipulation of transference (Fairbairn, 1952; Gill, 1979; Kohut, 1984; Loewald, 1960; Winnicott, 1963). It is interesting to consider whether psychoanalysis has developed ways for the analyst to modify and titrate transference intensity that were influenced by some of Alexander's more extreme and concrete recommendations. Finally, I explore how his original proposals have been distorted by subsequent generations of psychoanalysts by conflating his corrective emotional experience with "being a good object."

One of my first reactions to reading Alexander's (1950) article "Analysis of the Therapeutic Factors in Psychoanalytic Treatment" was one of surprise that it was published in a psychoanalytic journal at all. While there is much in it with which I and countless others dispute about the use of manipulation of transference, it is to the credit of the *Psychoanalytic Quarterly* that it was published, and that there was room in our journals for a provocative critique of our methods, including the length of analytic treatment (which was far shorter in 1950 than it is today) and how we analyze transference and defense. The *Quarterly* seems to have honored Alexander's stated aims in the article: "This presentation is based on the premise that much in our therapeutic procedure is still empirical, and that many of the processes which take place in patients during psychoanalysis are not yet fully understood" (p. 481). Alexander wanted to examine a variety of factors related to therapeutic action, including frequency and the relative importance of parallel experiences in life, issues that are still worthy of our exploration to understand some of this thinking as transitional to later theorists.

ALEXANDER'S TECHNICAL AMBITION

Alexander can be viewed as a practitioner who valorized the analyst's capacity to rationally determine, and predetermine at that, what was appropriate for any given patient. Quite apart from the dubious wisdom of manipulating the transference at all, Alexander seemed to minimize how difficult it is to determine what kind of a corrective emotional experience might be useful or required by a particular patient. In fact, in the most detailed case example in his article, Alexander came on his discovery of how to manipulate the transference with his patient by accident in what in contemporary terms we might refer to as an *enactment*. He found himself expressing some irrepressible feelings—what Mitchell (1988) referred to as an "outburst"—which in retrospect he might have avoided with a different stance and attitude toward his patient. He viewed this discovery as accidental and regrettable in many ways, preferring instead to focus on our requirements to know in advance the appropriate position that we should occupy—usually a position that is in maximal contrast with the neurotogenic parent.

Most schools of analysis have their own views of enactment. Each in different ways and to varying degrees suggests that the analyst can learn to find interpretive positions that might shed light on these forms of interaction rather than establish in advance technical prescriptions and manipulations that will prevent enactment. Naturally, the classical emphasis on neutrality is partly a way to minimize the degree to which enactments can become derailing. But increasingly, in most schools of analytic thought, analytic authority is derived more from the notion of the analyst as a learner rather than exclusively as a teacher.

An even more profound problem and one that seems strikingly outside the realm of any kind of psychoanalytic perspective is Alexander's failure to take into account the patient's experiential and psychic reality in responding to the analyst's efforts to provide a corrective emotional experience. In other words, Alexander failed to account for the distinct possibility that a patient might not necessarily experience the analyst's targeted manipulated behavior (explicitly chosen to contrast with the parental behavior) as a corrective emotional experience. Alexander offered very little related to tracking the patient's experience or perspective, which I imagine may have not been uncommon during his era. Nevertheless, his hyptertrophied sense of the analyst's objectivity in constructing a therapeutic stance in contrast with the neurotogenic parental behavior might make him even less likely than others to examine the patient's experience. In light of much of contemporary theory related to enactment, naturally Alexander had little means to appreciate that his efforts to manipulate the transference for "optimal" intensity might very well unconsciously repeat experiences of earlier caretakers.

Alexander is no less optimistic, ambitious, or technically rational about manipulating transference intensity through frequency, an important subtext for his 1950 article. He believed that the transference could be modified and titrated by reducing the frequency of interviews whenever the transference neurosis became too intense. He also believed that it is through the analyst's behavior of reducing the frequency of sessions that unnoticed hidden gratification of dependent needs could be made more conscious. Thus, he agrees with Ferenczi (1988, p. 197) that frustrating the patient by "denying the patient just that satisfaction which he most intensively desires" will produce the most pertinent unconscious material.

Again, Alexander positioned himself as one who can predetermine what satisfaction the patient most actively desires as opposed to viewing this desire as the project itself of analysis and one that both patient and analyst learn about over the course of analysis. He is preemptively circumscribing the analytic project, thus ensuring its relative brevity.

Alexander repeatedly makes reference to that group of patients who become pathologically dependent on the analyst. He seems particularly interested in avoiding what Balint (1968) termed "malignant regression" abetted by determining the most optimal counterposed analytic behavior to contrast with the old object. He seems relatively less aware of the problem from the other side—that of truncating the possibility for useful, adaptive regression and exploration. It could very well be that Alexander is address-ing a group of patients for whom the standard analytic procedure did lead to levels of transference that interfered in unwieldy ways for the patient and analyst. His approach is not to modify toward the goal of supporting the patient's ego functions through ego-supportive measures of clarification but instead to propose an entirely different form of analytic conduct that assumes a kind of postured persona. This presumes both that the analyst can know in advance what this is and that the patient can experience it in the way that Alexander deemed most useful. He minimized the complexity and diversity of the patient's experience in the analytic framework.

The longest and most complex case illustration is one that is truly remark-able in light of much of contemporary analysis that examines the inevitabil-ity of enactment. Alexander presented a case of a young male college student who had been heavily indulged by his father and who was inhibited in work, slovenly in his dress, and particularly slothful in his work habits. He com-plained that his father never loved him. The patient "did everything to make himself disagreeable." He usually arrived unwashed, often was critical, and paid a very low fee. One day, Alexander spoke to him impatiently, and the patient demanded to confirm his sense that Alexander disliked him and had expressed impatience with him. Alexander directly acknowledged some of these feelings and suggested to him that he wanted to prove that his father and Alexander disliked him, justifying his hostility and self-destructive behavior. This marked a dramatic change in the patient and the analysis. Alexander (1950) argues that "the case is noteworthy because of the dynam-ics of the patient's remarkable improvement which was induced not by the usual understanding objective attitude of the analyst but by an involuntary display of his irritation" (p. 490). He goes on to say:

> My point is that the knowledge of the early interpersonal attitudes which contributed to a patient's neurosis can help the analyst to assume intentionally a kind of attitude which is conducive to provoking the kind of emotional experience in the patient which is suited to undo the pathogenic effect of the original parental attitude. (p. 490)

Many contemporary analysts from various points of view would regard this example as illustrative of enactment. They would argue that something about the patient engaged the analyst in a form of role responsiveness (Sandler, 1976) or projective identification in which the analyst acted out a particular type of old object behavior and interpreted the patient's evacuation and enactment of uncomfortable adaptive mechanisms for regulating depressive affect or self-states, and that the analyst was able to show the patient the earlier roots of these affects. The patient could allow the analyst's interpretive function to be used as a kind of new object experience. The analyst's behavior was not predicted or known in advance. Yet, Alexander (1950) suggested that were he able to do so, in other words, were he able to "replace his spontaneous countertransference reactions with attitudes which are consciously planned and adopted according to the dynamic exigencies of the therapeutic situation" (p. 491), an optimal level of transference intensity would guide successful and shorter treatment.

What is so striking is that Alexander (1950), more than any analyst I have encountered, believed in the value and power of the analyst's ability to be objective and neutral, paradoxically through the construction of the corrective emotional experience. He believed that "within the framework of the objective atmosphere of the psychoanalytic situation, there is sufficient opportunity for replacing the spontaneous countertransference reactions with well-defined and designed attitudes which facilitate the patient's own emotional reorientation" (p. 492). Here, Alexander abandoned almost any notion of the countertransference as an intrinsically unconscious phenomenon.

ALEXANDER'S MODEL OF CORRECTIVE EMOTIONAL EXPERIENCE RETOLD: DISENTANGLING CORRECTIVE EMOTIONAL EXPERIENCE FROM TRANSFERENCE MANIPULATION

From its inception, the term *corrective emotional experience* became synonymous with Alexander's (1950) manipulation of transference and suggestion. A psychoanalytic climate that approaches as binaries corrective experience and insight through interpretation has indeed changed, yielding to a view of each of these factors as contributing to therapeutic action across theoretical models. Jacobs (1990) stated that insight and corrective experience are synergetic forces in treatment, each contributing in essential ways to the therapeutic action of psychoanalysis. Similarly, Kohut (1968) argued for disentangling the concepts of corrective emotional experience from manipulation of transference and brief analysis when he wrote declaratively:

> This, in itself, legitimate concept has been relegated to a position of disrepute because Franz Alexander, who coined the expression, used

it in the context of what he considered to be "brief analysis," that is, the replacement of the working through of the transference with the patient's exposure to the analyst's playacting the opposite of the patient's transference expectations. Regretfully, then, a perfectly serviceable term became tainted by a seemingly irrevocable guilt by association. ... Still, by whatever name it may ultimately come to be known, the concept involved—independent of the adulterated meaning evoked by the term because of the circumstances of its origination—is a valuable one, and we should not shy away from its legitimate use. (p. 89)

I find myself sympathetic regarding the content of Kohut's argument, but like Wallerstein (1990), I question the value of using or retaining the actual term *corrective emotional experience* for any reason or context. The term *corrective* itself is problematically embedded in a kind of presumptive analytic authority and antithetical to notions of epistemology and meaning-making for most contemporary analysts of all stripes. As Ferro (2005) and Britton and Steiner (1994) have noted, clinical facts are always temporary assignments of meaning made by the patient and analyst. Hoffman's (1998) notions of social constructivism have also offered a way of thinking about the transience of clinical facts.

Moreover the term *corrective* is at odds with a view of psychoanalysis as not necessarily removing conflict but instead helping patients to work more successfully with their conflicts, a view more compatible with my own experience of successful analytic work.

In contrast to the notion of manipulating experience, we have developed a series of ways of thinking about those elements of interpretation related to the holding aspects of analytic work (e.g., Modell, 1976; Slochower, 1996), which are sometimes associated with corrective experience and more nonspecific factors in analytic work. We have also become more aware of how interpretation naturally expresses the analyst's participation as some form of new object (Cooper & Levit, 1998; Greenberg, 1986; Loewald, 1960).

Some contemporary psychoanalysts use the term *corrective emotional experience* to describe naturally occurring elements of therapeutic action without intending anything related to manipulation of transference. Gill (1979) in particular tried to differentiate at least two components related to the therapeutic effects of the analysis of transference. He stated:

First, the clarification of the contribution of the analytic situation to the transference leads to the recognition that the way the patient has experienced the analytic situation is idiosyncratic. The patient must then perforce recognize his own contribution to this experience, that is, the contribution from the past. Second, barring impending countertransference, the examination of the transference inevitably involves an interpersonal experience with the analyst which is more beneficent than the transference experience. *This constitutes a "corrective emotional experience" not sought for as such but an essential byproduct of the work* [emphasis added]. (p. 179)

So, Gill highlights, like Alexander, that the contrast between the experience of the current analyst's position vis-à-vis the patient's neurosis and accompanying old objects will contribute to therapeutic action. He differs from Alexander in that, for Gill, this contrast grows out of a natural dimension of his interaction and participation with the patient in the process of analyzing the transference rather than as a devised and manipulated stance.

One way in which corrective emotional experience has been used in the literature is sometimes to equate the term with gratification. Both Gill and Kohut spoke to such concerns in criticisms of approaches to the frustration–gratification index in psychoanalysis. Kohut (1968) emphasized that frustration is as much a manipulation as is gratification of the transference. Similarly, Gill (1994) suggested that some analysts privilege frustration over gratification, and that any "witting" intervention that the analyst does not intend to analyze may be seen as a manipulation.

Thus, in different ways, Kohut and Gill imply that corrective emotional experience became a term that was far more likely to be invoked if it referred to the analyst's manipulation of interpretation in favor of gratification in contrast to manipulations that sided more with frustration and deprivation on the gratification–frustration index.

THE CORRECTIVE EMOTIONAL EXPERIENCE, BLANK SCREEN CONCEPT, AND NEUTRALITY

What a fascinating turn Alexander took in the theory of technique in terms of the blank screen concept. On the one hand, he argues strongly that there is no such thing as a blank screen. In fact, he argues that since analytic functions are not naturally what we do, the analyst should make a rational decision to adapt this technical position. Echoing remarks he made in his 1950 article, he stated: "The objective detachment of the psychoanalyst is itself an adopted, studied attitude and not a spontaneous reaction to the patient" (Alexander & French, 1956, p. 94). Alexander took the analytic stance a giant step away from any more familiar version of analytic neutrality or technique by pushing the analyst to adopt a stance that will be most likely to oppose the patient's original experiences that engendered the neurosis, a technically ambitious proposal if ever there was one.

In fact, Alexander's proposals for technique were almost at complete odds with the basic premises of interactionism, just as they were with classical technique. His was in fact a position that was remarkably presumptive about the analyst's capacity to "know" the patient's original experience, more so than is at least theoretically espoused by nearly any brand of analysis. It was also rather concrete in terms of drawing direct analogies between these "original" experiences and how they had been encoded and are now reported in the present by the patient. He did not take up how durable are transference formations and how they are refractory to the analyst's interpretations (e.g., Bird, 1972; Gill, 1979). Finally, the dimensions of transference as related not only to the patient's unconscious experience but also to the patient's allusions to the transference (Gill, 1979) are largely absent.

Alexander thought that our neutral position could be defined in strictly behavioral or descriptive terms and wholly through the intentions of the analyst. He called the analyst's unique contribution to the formation of transference "an impurity," a view not completely inconsistent with his classically oriented colleagues at the time. As Gill (1994) pointed out, Alexander focused more on how analysts are perceived as individuals "which is different than saying that they are individuals" (p. 108). This is a remarkably pithy way to summarize the contribution of the analyst's subjective participation as emphasized in much of contemporary analytic theory. Alexander stands in almost complete contrast and antipathy with interpersonal and relational analytic theories because interaction was conceptualized as something that could be controlled, not that grew out of spontaneous and inevitable forms of expression and participation between the personalities of analyst and patient within the ritualized asymmetry of the analytic situation.

Regarding neutrality, Alexander indirectly anticipated some changes from diverse corners of psychoanalysis. He regarded his neutral stance as something to be determined with each patient, as did some later theorists who considered neutrality a uniquely developed position in each analytic dyad. For example, Kris's (1990) discussion of functional neutrality emphasized that the analyst will adjust his interpretive position vis-à-vis the patient's harshest forms of self-criticism, a highly variable determination partly dictated by the unique intrapsychic structure of each patient. Greenberg (1986, 1995) suggested that neutrality is determined through interactive work with each patient–analyst dyad, eschewing static determinations of what is neutral. Instead, Greenberg focused on fluid tensions and balance related to poles of danger and safety and oldness and newness in the analytic situation. For Kris and Greenberg, interpretations are a far cry from the technical prescriptions espoused by Alexander. Yet I view Alexander's notion of corrective emotional experience as anticipatory of many theorists' willingness to consider the unique qualities of each patient and his or her capacity to benefit from analytic interpretation.

Mitchell (1997) used Alexander as a trope of sorts for his critique of the classical notion of neutrality. Decrying Alexander's position of manipulating transference as grandiose and contrived, Mitchell suggested that it was no more ambitious or oversimplified than the assumption that the analyst's attempted "neutral" stance will be achievable. Both positions fail to take into account Gill's emphasis on how what is analytic is not the intended stance of the analyst but the willingness to explore the impact of one's participation. Along these lines, Gill (1994) critiqued Brenner's (1969) technical suggestions as too oriented toward frustration as a solution to the frustration–gratification index rather than emphasizing the importance of analyzing one's participation and impact on the patient. It is interesting also that Alexander was no stranger to the use of frustration in terms of creating the necessary "optimal intensity" of transference in establishing the corrective emotional experience. Alexander's concept of corrective emotional experience was probably popularly conceived as usually involving gratification of the transference, when in fact this was not at all the case.

In a sense, both Gill (1994) and Mitchell (1997) were suggesting that there are aspects of manipulation of transference embedded in a variety of clinical stances. I think it would be interesting and distinctly possible to write a critique of each psychoanalytic theoretical model as having (and maybe even enacting) a mode of unanalyzed transference, a "valorized illusory construct" (Cooper, 2007b). It is perhaps in this valorization that each theory has elements of what might appear to be an overly selective focus, privileging some psychic phenomena particularly from the point of view of those whose perspective lies outside the specific theoretical orientation in question. Put another way, as I developed in Chapter 4 on the analyst's "countertransference to the method of psychoanalysis," each psychoanalytic theory promotes particular kinds of postures that allow the analyst to execute particular technical priorities emphasized within that approach.

CORRECTIVE EMOTIONAL EXPERIENCE AND THE EXPERIENCE OF NEWNESS IN PSYCHOANALYTIC THEORY

Alexander's notion of corrective emotional experience as defined by transference manipulation constitutes his version of how the analyst functions as a new object. In retrospect, it can be speculated that Alexander's notions of the manipulation of the transference in providing a corrective emotional experience were a kind of concrete, literal, and simplistic variant of a developing thread in psychoanalytic theory related to many ways in which the analyst functions as a new object, explicated especially by Blum (1971), Cooper (2004b), Cooper and Levit (1998), Gill (1982), Greenberg (1986), Loewald (1960), and Winnicott (1963).

The new object concept was elaborated by Strachey (1934) to describe how the analyst becomes an auxiliary superego to the patient through the interpretive detoxification of troublesome and harsh self-assessments. Loewald's (1960) descriptions of the analyst's new object function emphasized that the analyst's primary newness derived from the opportunity for rediscovering the early pathways and patterns of object relations, leading to "a new way of relating to objects and of being oneself" (p. 229). Newness includes the analyst's vision of the patient's future since he suggested that each interpretation simultaneously takes a patient one step into a regression and into a new psychic possibility. In discussing Loewald's emphasis on the analyst as a consistently new, more mature object, Blum (1986) spoke of the analyst as a "real new object rather than the object of transference" and that this newness should be considered as one of the factors in therapeutic change.

Loewald's (1960) descriptions of the analyst as a new object had the effect of legitimizing the new object function as an intrinsic analytic function and an accompaniment of therapeutic action. Unlike Alexander 10 years before, Loewald's discussion of the analyst's newness did not involve any explicit change in stance or manipulation. At the same time, Loewald's eloquent description of therapeutic action did not really explicitly address any matters of technique or address the central matter of importance for Alexander (1950), namely, "the question how to keep the analysis on a transference level of optimal intensity, particularly how to avoid a too intensive dependent relationship resulting in an interminable analysis" (p. 484). It was this concern that led Alexander to the "quantitative" aspects of psychoanalytic treatment. Thus, Alexander was trying at almost a descriptive level to prescribe technique for a special clinical problem: problems related to the overdependent patient and the amount of time spent in analytic work. At times, rereading this article, it was difficult to determine which idea was more heretical for psychoanalysts, the manipulation of transference or the idea that duration of analysis could be reduced at a time when ego psychology was promoting increased attention to defense analysis and, to some extent understandably, increasingly long analyses.

Winnicott (1963) also put forward a sophisticated view of corrective experience integrating the analyst's newness; while different from Loewald's (1960) view, Winnicott avoided the issue of manipulation. Winnicott (1963) suggested that the analyst's failures in understanding challenge the patient's psychic sense of omnipotent control and yield to new capacities to appraise externality in the object world. Alexander sought to redress these experiential failures by nipping them in the bud to prevent overly regressive experiences and lengthy periods of analysis.

The concept of the new object has been a focus for many contemporary theorists, who understand that both the technical and nontechnical, personal quality of their interventions will be experienced as interpersonally influential and sometimes new. Greenberg (1986) suggested that the analyst's attention to relative degrees of safety and danger in the patient's transferential experience contribute to the relative success of any analysis. Greenberg was not suggesting a manipulation of transference but instead was trying to draw attention to the fact that most analysts know that clinical choices related to interpretive activity levels are often influenced by our knowledge of the degree to which a patient experiences "too much" repetition that is painful, in fact, some of the clinical data that influenced Alexander's more frank manipulation of transference. Numerous analysts within the relational tradition (e.g., Aron, 1991; Bromberg, 1991) pointed to how elements of the subjectivity are revealed implicitly and explicitly through the analyst's interpretive direction and sometimes enter into experiences of the analyst as a new object. By adding an awareness of Fairbairn's understanding of our attachment to old objects that are threatened by the newness of the analyst, we can understand additional levels of complexity about how the analyst determines danger and safety for any particular patient. They argued that some of the ways in which analysts are experienced as new relates to how they help the patient to be aware of their attachment to old object experience of the analyst, sometimes the old object experiences that Alexander worried were too destructive to be analyzed.

Gill (1994) raised similar concerns about Freud's use of the term *unobjectionable transference*, which he suggested was Freud's own use of manipulation; Gill used the term *manipulation* in psychoanalysis to refer to decisions not to analyze something and instead view it as realistic and thus unnecessary to analyze.

It is fascinating that analysts have a tendency to equate newness with goodness. I believe that this is an unconscious piece of grandiosity within the analytic profession. Despite the fact that our field has vilified Alexander for trying to be a good object or others, this was not Alexander's fundamental failing. His failing was in believing that he could be any kind of new object that could, by design, counteract the irrational and unconscious experiences of his patients.

This tendency of equating the new object with the good object probably is also reflected in Freud's emphasis on the unobjectionable positive transference. For example, why did we not have an unobjectionable negative transference or an unobjectionable negative countertransference? There was a great deal of enactment of the paternal/maternal authority of the doctor that was a part of early psychoanalytic theory as well as in ego psychology. I think that also little attention was paid to the negative transference in general, a criticism frequently levied against ego psychology by Kleinian analysts. Thus, one way to characterize the tendency for analysts to equate the corrective emotional experience with good object experience was its own anxiety about its own enactment of trying to be a good object as intrinsic to the doctor–patient relationship. I see most branches of psychoanalytic theory except the Kleinians as guilty of the problem of minimizing negative experience and bad object experience in favor of good object experience.

It is quite interesting to think about this problem of equating new object with positive experience as related to unconsciously colonialist attitudes in psychoanalytic theory. Brickman (2003) suggested that in many ways Freud and psychoanalytic theorists in general have equated the patient with the savage who is to be tamed by the colonialist analyst. She argued quite persuasively that primitivity is located in the patient and the other in ways that can be illuminated by thinking about the history of colonialism. Brickman's ideas inform some of my concerns about Hoffman's (2009) article "Passion in the Countertransference." Hoffman made an extremely valuable point about the ways that sometimes analysts may inhibit themselves from more vivid and personal expressiveness about the patient's negative experience and introjects. Yet the analyst is always at risk to enact the very positivism that Hoffman's writing over the years has sought to redress. Despite my strong agreement with Hoffman in his many articles over the years about the intrinsic element of suggestion in any interpretation, we must also be aware of the risk of forceful suggestion that seeks to help but may unwittingly minimize the patient's responsibility for change. I strongly suspect that Hoffman would agree that the analyst has to safeguard the patient's opportunity to experience the analyst in a range of ways including "good" and "bad" object experience.

I would imagine that Hoffman's response to this concern would be to point out that of course we are always at risk to enact the analyst's authority by fighting the patient's introjects rather than helping the patient take the fight to the introjects. My concern, that Hoffman shares, is that the analyst's "passionate" fighting of these introjects might make it more complex for the patient to feel and express himself about the analyst as a disappointing figure.

ALEXANDER'S IMPACT ON CONTEMPORARY PSYCHOANALYSIS

It is interesting to consider whether Alexander's more concrete and explicit manipulation of the analyst's distinctness from the old object parents was symptomatic of a failure on the part of psychoanalysis to sufficiently recognize the degree to which elements of the analyst's newness were vital and intrinsic aspects of therapeutic action. Ironically enough, by 10 years after the publication of his corrective emotional article, many analysts were more fully appreciating this dimension of psychoanalytic practice.

For example, it is notable that in introducing the term *corrective emotional experience* (Alexander & French, 1946), Alexander was partly exploring ideas about the role of the analyst in the therapeutic action of psychoanalysis. In describing a depressed analytic patient, he referred to how "the analyst assumes a role different from that of the parents" (p. 66). Most analysts would contend that analytic conduct does involve assuming a different role from that of the parent, but that this distinctness is achieved through the usual efforts of understanding the patient's experience and examining defense and transference (e.g., Loewald, 1960). In contrast, Alexander's use of the maintenance of transference, "optimal intensity" or "optimal level" of transference, essentially asserted that standard technique was insufficient in some cases. What is quite interesting about the concept of optimal intensity is that many analysts modify technique in relation to the intensity of the patient's experience of transference phenomena. For example, many analysts are probably prone to clarification when patients develop very harsh, self-critical stances; negative, paranoid-laden transference psychotic transferences; or quasi-psychotic erotic transferences. Sometimes, consultations are sought in the regressive circumstances about which Alexander warned us. Other analysts try to evaluate whether patients prone to such transference intensity should undergo analysis at all. Alexander's positivistic and ambitious effort in manipulating the transference sought to address these possibilities by nipping them in the bud through a particular kind of analytic behavior he saw as most likely to titrate the level of transference intensity.

I view Alexander's notion of corrective emotional experience as a concrete and overly simplistic solution to the notion of malignant transference intensity in the conduct of analytic work. In one sense, these suggestions were anticipatory of many subsequent theorists' willingness to consider the unique qualities of each patient and analyst and their patients' capacities to benefit from analytic technique. It is ironic that most of the general acceptance of nonspecific factors in therapeutic action, such as holding, internalization, or willingness on the part of the analyst to modify his or her technique, are at complete odds with Alexander's original use of the term *corrective emotional experience*. Instead, what has been minimized in his ambitious effort to modify analytic technique was an increased role for the analyst's authority and capacities as a rational tactician in the conduct of analytic work. At this point in the history of psychoanalysis, I see little value for retaining the term.

So, why has a term like corrective emotional experience been retained for so long? At one level, the notion of corrective emotional experience is utterly banal. If someone has had an analysis that has not provided an emotional and helpful experience, then I would suggest that they have had something other than analysis. Yet, *corrective* as a word suggests that we as analysts know in advance or after the fact how something will be helpful. We have had a quite difficult time reconciling the notion of being helpful with analytic work. Early on, Freud (1910a) described the problems intrinsic to the analyst's reaction formations. Freud elaborated the necessity for the analyst's modesty; in his "Recommendations to Physicians Practicing Psychoanalysis" (1912), Freud admonished psychoanalysts to "model themselves during psycho-analytic treatment on a surgeon of earlier times who took as his motto the words: '*Je le pansai, Dieu le guérit*'" (p. 115), which translates as "I dress the wound, God heals it."

If he or she fails to adopt this attitude, Freud warned, the analyst will compromise his or her ability to analyze certain resistances of the patient, whose recovery, as we know, depends on the interplay of forces in him or her. Freud was cautioning his colleagues against a belief that psychoanalysis can, or should, heal the patient.

Caper (1992) suggested that, far from being the call for indifference to the patient's pain that it has often been misunderstood to be, Freud's analogy between the psychoanalyst and the surgeon was based on a realistic modesty that aimed to put the analyst into a state of mind that is very important, if not essential, for the practice of psychoanalysis. In some way, I believe that Alexander's primitive attempts to "help" his patients became equated with the negative elements of helping. We have not really addressed whether there are elements of the analyst's wishes to help that do not have to be at odds with the aims that Freud and Caper have highlighted. This is the very valuable idea that Hoffman (2009) sought to explore. I am not convinced that he has successfully bridged the gap between our wishes and needs to help and the fact that we will always be incorporated by the patient into unconscious scenarios that are valuably pointed out by the analyst. If he or she is too engaged in combating critical others, then the extraordinarily complex and powerful tool of analysis for understanding the patient's internal saboteur and hostile introjects may be compromised.

Psychoanalysts have been struggling for many decades about our limitations in discussing the change process. Verbal reports of analysis lend themselves to those moments in which we can express the way dreams or a version of parapraxis conveys unconscious conflict. But, there is so much indeterminacy about how analysis works and how it is helpful. Perhaps we have clung to a general and, at that, notoriously problematic expression, the corrective emotional experience, to address factors other than analysis of unconscious conflict. I wonder if it has unwittingly involved the degradation of so-called relational factors and their contribution to analytic outcome and process.

Despite its banality, the notion of something being "corrective" is, it seems to me, a bizarre way to think about analysis. As many analysts have suggested over the years, the goal of analysis is hardly the removal of conflict but instead facilitating our patient's ability to work with his or her conflicts in new and more productive ways. As Gill (1954) put it, "And there is no doubt that we can still recognize our friends and colleagues even after they have been analysed" (p. 786). The term *corrective* is already embedded in a framework involving the grandiose notion of the analysts as rational objectivists and technicians that Alexander proposed. So, I would suggest that the corrective term is problematic in that the word itself is embedded in a positivistic language. Why can't we say that we hope that analysis will be helpful or useful? "Corrective" evokes for me either "correctional facility" or a perspective that presumes that an analyst knows how change should occur.

I do think that Alexander's attempt implicitly recognized something about the potentially problematic length of analysis. In my view, psychoanalysts have not taken enough responsibility for the inordinately lengthy analyses that are being conducted, at least in the United States. Yet, Alexander sought to shorten analysis by dispensing with the notion of listening to his patient's allusions to unconscious conflict or to transference. Unfortunately, his attempt at shortening became equated with circumvention of embedded unconscious conflict. His work does raise the question of whether there are ways for psychoanalysts to take more responsibility for the length of analytic work.

It has seemed to me that Freud really held a great deal more modesty about the results of analytic work than many of us who have followed. It is quite easy to become overly ambitious as an analyst given the openness of the canvas. There are also frank financial benefits that relate to the elongation of analytic work that we as analysts must try to find a way to discuss in our journals. If anything, Freudian theory would suggest that the problem of the analyst's self-interest must become a problem in the conduct of analytic work. This self-interest as it relates to the elongation of analytic work is by no means restricted to financial benefit. Analysts become mightily attached to their patients and have a great deal of motivation for their own relational needs to elongate the analytic relationship.

CONCLUSION

Alexander (1950) did begin to hint at the importance of the new object concept, however concretely and literally he defined this notion. He was writing immediately prior to Loewald's (1960) seminal article on therapeutic action that tried to elaborate the concept of the new object in a way that had not been attempted since Strachey's (1934) effort in this regard. From 1980 to the present, a number of analysts, such as Gill, Mitchell, Greenberg, and I, have tried to elaborate this concept in ways that are at great odds with Alexander but nevertheless attempt to describe ways in which the analyst's newness as an object factors into therapeutic action.

I see Alexander's attempt to manipulate the transference and to become an antitransference object as a kind of concrete, literal, manipulative, conscious, and naive attempt to be a new object as defined by the analyst. In contrast, all other definitions of newness starting with those of Strachey (1934) and Loewald (1960) and continuing to the present include the notion that newness need fundamentally relate, at least in part, to the patient's experience of the analyst. Alexander minimized the valuable contribution made by an analyst who can help a patient to see how new "badness" in the form of analytic interaction provides new opportunity for growth and insight, including relational depth related by the dyad "taking it on and working it out."

In the end, Alexander's term *corrective emotional experience* has been the verbal equivalent of a defense—a way for analysts to avoid finding ways to articulate factors related to relationship and extrainterpretive factors. We can all agree that Alexander partly became notorious because he was radically manipulative and idiosyncratically objectivist. Yet, I feel strongly that he became an easy target and mechanism for avoiding things that we do not understand and do not have a language for—the notion of therapeutic action that we now know is even more complex than we would ever have imagined. Let us retire Alexander and the term itself from villainy and accord him the status of another experimental analyst with perhaps Promethean ambition who allowed us to learn from his mistakes.

Chapter 10

Working through and working within

The continuity of enactment in the termination process

If we are committed to the notion that enactment in analysis is continuous and that interpretation is issued from within rather than outside enactment, then notions of working through are challenging to understand. I would suggest that just as patients who have a successful analysis continue to experience conflict after analysis—hopefully more resolved in their conflicts and free to make choices in the context of conflict—so too, these patients have a better capacity to understand and be curious about their predilections for patterns of enactment. Working through enactments with the analyst always will mean that the patient and analyst are working from within the context of enactment.

In this chapter I will explore a number of implications of the notion that termination occurs within the context of continuous enactment. I will suggest that a part of what the patient loses is not only his analyst but patterns of enactment between patient and analyst—some that have been useful to understand and develop curiosity about, some no doubt that are more refractory to change for each of us. I will also suggest that while regression, as it has been classically emphasized, is often a feature of termination stages of analytic work, it is sometimes better understood as the reemergence or development of patterns of enactment that endure throughout analytic process. I will suggest that the analyst is also prone toward regression during termination.

In analyses that have been going concerns, initial discussions of termination often stimulate shifts in the patient's perspectives regarding the therapeutic work and the relationship between patient and analyst. The illusory, more open-ended canvass for expanding curiosity engendered by the analysis will soon be temporally framed, even if patient and analyst know that this ending can always be renegotiated at a later date. The patient's growth during analysis may also move from foreground to background as the patient's and analyst's limitations in promoting growth may move from background to foreground. In this chapter, I am most interested in how the process of ending analytic work provides a context for exploring previously unworked-through and unexplored parts of interaction and experience.

Many analyses, including those that are highly productive, end at points at which the patient and analyst have run out of emotional and imaginative resources to take analysis to a further level of understanding. As Ferenczi (1927) put it: "The proper ending of an analysis is when neither the physician nor the patient puts an end to it, but when it dies of exhaustion" (p. 83). Some patients have been able to do enough productive work to place them in good stead in life, while others return to us or someone else for more analysis at a later date. For still another group of analytic dyads, the decision itself to terminate seems to facilitate renewed levels of work and commitment to resolve forms of impasse. In any relationship, there are multiple meanings when one person or both say that they are going to end the relationship. In the case of analysis, we hope that this is because the patient feels that he has been able to get what he or she wanted or close enough to what was wanted. There are also relationships in which when one person says, "let's stop," he is actually tendering an invitation not to stop but to try to be together in a different way: "Let's stop if we can't do something or understand something in a different way."

Keeping in mind the notion that analysis is a series of enactments, the concept of *exhaustion* takes on new meaning from what Ferenczi implied. Exhaustion might refer to a kind of deconstructive fatigue.

It is true that in some ways termination can be thought of as the beginning of an "infinite conversation" (Marshall, 2000) as the therapeutic relationship continues its dialogue through the individual's self-reflection. Yet, I am also struck that the initial talks about ending a therapeutic process can often mark a clearer process of discussing the nature of the very finite conversation that has already been taking place. This realization of the limited nature of the conversation can be invigorating and can potentially expand the patient's and analyst's fields of vision. Regarding the last type of endings, termination is a process by which analyst and patient resolve to try to get unstuck or move in different directions regarding a particular impasse, to try to grieve anew, and in a sense to push each other into both familiar but in some ways uncharted territory. In a sense, patient and analyst have an opportunity, once again, to be curious together about interpersonal patterns that we repeated during termination.

JAMES

I would like to mention a patient who was discussed earlier in the book with regard to some of the termination processes I described in this chapter. In Chapter 2, I discussed a patient, James, who struggled with feelings related to what I termed, "the grandiosity of self-loathing." James faced particular challenges in termination related to giving up patterns of enactment that had been a part of his analysis. Keep in mind that my focus here is quite selective in terms of wanting to discuss that element of James's termination that involved revisiting particular places of enactment between us.

It is always interesting to note whether a patient or I initiate discussion of termination. Not surprisingly James was the first of us to bring it up. Much in James's life had changed. He was feeling closer to his wife and she to him. His wife noted that he didn't withdraw as much when she felt that they were close. Mondays had often been dreadful for her prior to James's analysis. On Mondays James would often pull away without knowing it, and she had often felt left behind or even with a sense of loss.

At work James had become increasingly able to delegate responsibility and ask his partners for help when he needed it. He had been able to devote a few hours a week to his analysis without feeling that "it was the first thing to go," which had been his wont when he began analysis.

I have set the stage for something interesting that happened when James began to bring up termination with me. When he brought it up, it seemed to make sense to me. But what was striking, after the fact, was that this "make sense to me" was interestingly shallow and facile on my part. I seemed to have a kind of incuriosity about the whys and wherefores about James's sense that it was time to stop. I seemed to be going along with him in ways that were not unlike the earlier phases of his analysis that I described in Chapter 2.

If you recall, James and I had eventually discovered that his analysis was lodged in his mind as something for me. He had dreams in which he was trying to help me. He would focus on how much everyone around him needed him but his needs were absent. He had disavowed many of the actual needs that he came to experience over the course of analysis. He also discovered that he had held many angry feelings toward his parents, his mother in particular, about feeling that he was sort of left to fend for himself.

As we began to explore termination together over the first few weeks in which the topic was broached, I began to realize that once again I was leaving James to fend for himself. He was bringing up leaving (which actually did seem like a good idea and indeed was), and I seemed to reflexively cede him the authority to make up his mind and not really explore it. At one level I always cede the patient the authority to decide when they wish to leave since it is obviously the patient's decision. But at another level, I am also supposed to be dedicated to the notion of thinking about and reflecting on what things mean to my patients.

James began missing appointments in the immediate aftermath of talking about termination. The reasons were familiar to both of us since they had occasioned his earlier tendency to miss appointments—other people (usually those who worked for him) weren't able to complete work, and he was put in the position of having complete it. James, however, was acting in ways that we had spent a great deal of time examining in his analysis mostly revolving around failing to ask for the help he needed. If you recall, earlier in his analysis James seemed to describe his relationships with his employees and legal partner and his wife with the phrase, "they depend on me." We even discovered that I depended on him in the sense that he had unconsciously considered his analysis as "for me." We had explored why it was so that we all depended on him. His self-criticism in fact had resulted in an unconscious fantasy that he was responsible for everyone else, more responsible than anyone for everyone else.

One of the things that is interesting to consider in understanding James's behavior as we began to discuss ending our work is how much this behavior might be conceptualized as regression in the context of termination. This conceptualization is too simple on a few counts. One is that it leaves out an enormous piece of what was going on in James's analysis between us. Elements of an enactment either resumed or continued in ways that I hadn't previously been aware of once James brought up ending. Within this piece of enactment, James began to end his analysis (a decision that did in fact make sense to us both), and I unconsciously withdrew from my work task. I began to essentially treat him as though this was a decision that he had made and that I was facilitating. My incuriosity reinforced and enacted a sense that he had to fend for himself again, not depend on me to do what I had done fairly successfully with him—to examine and try to understand the complexity of his inner life.

I would describe what occurred in James's analysis as the beginning of the end, as it were, as related to both interpersonal elements of regression and recurrent forms of enactment between us. Once James broached the topic of termination I began to regress in terms of my analytic behavior and conduct in an interesting way. I had been able to successfully facilitate James's ability to look past and to look into elements of his self-sufficiency. I had helped him to experience and to view elements of his modesty as having a component involving "the grandiosity of self-loathing." Essentially I had shown him that his feeling of responsibility for everyone else was partly a way of adapting to an actual affliction regarding some of his own thwarted and now disavowed wishes and needs from his parents. What I refer to as "regressive" on my part was a tendency to leave him alone, as it were, to analytically fend for himself. By immediately acclimating to his statement about leaving without curiosity I was letting him down, acceding to his way of constructing the analytic situation as a place that was at least as much for my needs as his.

In our responsiveness to each other we enacted patterns of parent/child, analyst/patient implicit compacts—"Be grown up, take care of yourself, and don't think of yourself as needing too much. Don't ask too much of me. You will be better, more responsible and perhaps more powerful by going in this direction than feeling needy."

I have no way to know with certainty that what many analysts have referred to as the patient's regression in the context of termination includes elements of the analyst's regressive participation. I suspect that this is true and that many forms of regression are continuous with earlier forms of enactment between patient and analyst. In general, our enactment processes that have occurred during analysis are likely more continuous than discontinuous with what patient and analyst do during termination phases since we are learning about enactment as an ongoing process, not a process that is stopping once we shed light on these processes.

In James's analysis, his own forms of earlier behavior such as canceling sessions became a signal to me about some of the elements of enactment that were becoming more visible in our modes of relating to one another. I wasn't being curious about what he felt and how he thought about ending (mostly an inner experience that probably had some external manifestations that I wasn't aware of), and he was falling back on old patterns of acclimating to these messages from early caretakers.

It is my sense that even the ways that I had played my role in these enactments with James both during analysis and now in the beginning of his termination work involved "good enough" enactment or impingement. James had been able to open up and explore parts of his vulnerability and while he felt ashamed about needing things that he had earlier disavowed and sealed off, he had felt able over the course of time to feel new parts of himself. My tendencies to unwittingly communicate to him that he should take care of himself and be self-sufficient that I had unwittingly enacted in various ways during his analysis and now in termination had enough suppleness and enough permeability that they were different than what he had experienced with his parents. I was a new object in some ways even in the manner that I enacted earlier patterns as an old object. In Chapter 8 one of the things emphasized was the notion that old and new objects as a binary is a simplistic framework that minimizes both how much old objects may have elements of new experience in analytic work. Similarly, given the nature of continuous enactment, the analyst does well to regard so called newness as usually carrying forward many elements of old object experience.

The cues or signals that made me attuned to abandoning James to his old patterns of defense and adaptation became the leading edge of new forms of engagement during our termination work. I became more able to become curious about what termination meant to James and why he wanted to end our work at this point. I tried to work past the defensively held phrases that I held in my own mind about James's decision to terminate—phrases such as: "It makes sense. He's ready. Look how much he's changed. He has other things to do." All of these sentences in my own mind were true but stood as a kind of shield within my own mind protecting me from helping James to actually end and actually explore his feelings about this. I wondered in my own mind if these phrases might translate to the following statements from a parent: "He's grown up now."

One of the things that struck me about James in our ending was what he told me about how I had been with him that was helpful. He spoke in ways about me that seemed to resonate with some of my own experiences of myself with James and with some other patients who have struggled with defensive self-sufficiency. He told me that he thought that I might have some of the same problems in this regard that he did—that he felt that I wasn't a wimpy guy who wanted him to be a wimpy guy. He felt that maybe I empathized with him in trying to get more in touch with his feelings partly because he didn't think of me as a particularly sensitive guy (not exactly an advertisement for a good analyst). But I knew what he meant. I had maintained a very genuine and heartfelt appreciation for the parts of James that didn't want to have to know more about his needy self and I think that this helped him to not feel humiliated as much as he feared that he would.

James was actually quite anxious about losing me, more anxious than I was initially able to appreciate from my participation within our enactment together about his self-sufficiency. The more we explored his ending, the clearer it became to me just how much he was attached to me. We had enjoyed knowing each other, laughed a great deal together, and he had been able to cry in our work in ways that were quite new for him. James had been able to grieve not only what he had felt unable to get from his mother but, at least as important, what he had been unable to ask for.

It's my sense that James and I had developed many "good enough" ways of being together including "good enough" knowing, good enough impingement, and good enough enactments (mostly involving good enough ways of my not understanding him). What is a good enough way of not understanding a patient? It is a way of misunderstanding that usually yields to something productive about understanding and in the process the damage done, the failures in empathy or understanding, are bearable. Sometimes these failures and disruptions make it even more palatable for the patient in terms of opening new avenues of meaning. For example, I would speculate that a more "empathic", more sensitive analyst might have made James feel humiliated about getting more in touch with his needs. My clumsiness and the parts of me that James likened to himself (some of which I would agree with him about and some of which involved projections of himself onto me) provided a bridge to a less humiliating exposure of himself than he had feared in beginning analytic work.

Termination was threatening for James, not only because of the loss of me, his analyst, but also because our ways of being together, our stops and starts of understanding were gratifying to him. He would be losing me as a familiar partner in our ways of interpretively playing together with his inner life, including of course our modes of enacting conflict together. James's wife had an instinctual capacity to find James when he was unconsciously disappointing her and fleeing from intimacy. This is a part of what had allowed their marriage to endure and the marriage improved as James became more able to sustain rather than flee from intimacy. Nevertheless, a part of James feared that termination with me signified that he would lose the sense of other people being able to sort of get who he was and know how to deal with him. Our patterns of enactment themselves had become deeply reassuring to James because we had repeatedly found our way out of these patterns to eventually shed light on his many modes of titrating intimacy in a relationship. James feared losing me and losing our intricate and intimate ways of being together and being apart. I think it could be said that James was going to miss the ways that he had felt that I had interpreted as well as surrendered elements of his resilient core of self-sufficiency, a core that had vastly changed but that was still familiar to him and to some of our ways of working together.

INTERPERSONAL AND INTRAPSYCHIC ASPECTS OF REGRESSION RECONSIDERED

The essence of termination as it is classically conceived is about how the loss of analysis and the analyst trigger the reemergence of earlier symptoms, trauma, and unresolved grief. Within this view, over the course of analytic work the patient has been able to resolve conflicts in a good enough way to suggest ending. In some sense, the analyst does not have an interpersonal connection except as interpreter of the particular manifestations of transference expressed by the patient. The analyst is an auxiliary ego and superego, and in this sense, the analyst functions as a kind of container for a new homeostasis comprised of the patient's reconfigured symptoms (e.g., Loewald, 1960).

This view obviously does not emphasize how the dyad has worked with the patient's conflicts within the interactive context of analysis. Bollas (1989) put it well in saying that we as analysts "imagine" our patient's symptoms in a variety of ways over time. Symptoms within this view are seen within both an intrapsychic and an dyadic/interactive context. In my view, this imagining includes both how the analyst thinks and feels about the patient's difficulties over time and how we think about both the patient's and analyst's experience of how trauma, conflict, and particular affects are embedded in the interpersonal context of analytic work. My patient's flying phobia, for example, takes on different meanings for the patient over time as we realize that his unconscious fantasies involve the pilot being unreliable like his preoccupied mother, whom he has vowed never to trust again. I can experience his unconscious anxiety about trusting me despite his very conscious participation and his appreciation of me and what we do. Over time, his symptoms will seem understandable, saddening, or exasperating to me as we look into this in both his external life and within the analysis. It is one thing to be a passenger *with* my patient, but another to be the pilot.

While I recognize that sometimes a patient's struggles with painful affects, identity, and conflict may reappear during termination, and that some patients do indeed regress during termination, my attention is usually focused more on how self-other configurations related to conflict reappear and offer a new opportunity for examination. I am particularly interested in how the analyst is implicated in the patient's struggles by both patient and analyst. So, I would suggest that some instances of what some might call regression or a kind of psychic slippage involve renewed risks for change, new presentations of unsolved problems that the patient is more willing to take on in the context of ending. In fact, some clinical phenomena that look like regression are actually the exposure of unresolved conflicts within the patient and the dyad, more than actual retreat from previously consolidated gains.

I also wonder whether various versions of symptom regression in analytic work reflect a lack of sophistication about the idea that forms of impasse and stalemate are routine in every dyad and thus are likely to be revisited in termination. If we take it as a given that enactments are ubiquitous, then it makes sense that termination would stimulate new feelings and ideas about areas of enacted conflict and affect. I would take it even further and suggest that *termination brings up an experience not only of losing the analyst but also of losing the particular forms of enactment/play to which the patient has become accustomed.*

In a sense, I am suggesting that the patient and analyst not only are saying goodbye to each other as objects but also are saying good-bye to an experience of the relationship, the dyad, the "being together." This includes aspects of affective resonance, empathy, limitation, and various forms of enactment. When people lose someone, they also lose an experience of self with that someone. As I suggested earlier, for James there was something reassuring about the ways we both repeated and observed together. One of the most underestimated elements of therapeutic action and enactment may be the patient's observation of repetition itself. We usually focus more exclusively on repetition as stultification.

Regression in this context may relate to the patient's anticipation of what it will be like for him or her not to have the analyst, accommodations, adaptations, enactment, and all. The regression, in a sense, is related to an anticipated psychic future without these interpersonally enacted forms of conflict. Of course, the analyst need always consider the extent to which these feelings are also related to revived old object experience.

The notion of regression during termination has also been more strictly focused on the patient's behavior and experience as a sole player. This view fails to take into account the ways in which a psychoanalyst might "regress" in relation to the patient's changes during termination or, for that matter, to the loss of the patient. Klauber's (1977) examination of the analyst's regression in termination, dealing with particular patients who struggle with severe trauma related to object loss, is an exception to this general statement.

When James began to speak about termination, I became lulled into a more passive, unthoughtful stance toward the prospect of his termination. I became strikingly incurious. I believe that this incuriosity was embedded in a form of regression for me.

TERMINATION AND THE COUNTERTRANSFERENCE OF INDETERMINACY

In my experience, there are those rewarding treatments when things have gone so well that patient and analyst "know" when it is time to stop. At least as often, however, there are the more raggedly textured endings familiar to most analysts, including stops and starts about determining when termination will begin.

Clarity about good work coming to an end is not only a fictive occurrence. James and I were both really pleased with the progress he had made during our work together. However, to some extent the literature on termination has fallen victim to the allure of linearity in the narrative of analysis, focusing on a story of progress up to a certain point to be followed by a degree of regression during the termination phase. It is my sense that some of the most successful analyses end with less regression and instead feature a revisiting of some of the same points of entanglement that accompanied analysis or that even fueled the initial decision to stop.

Rarely is termination clear except in circumstances when external factors come into play. The most frequently discussed reason for this lack of clarity is the reality that analyst and patient could potentially work on matters at hand for a very long, perhaps even an interminable, amount of time (e.g., Bergman, 1997; Freud, 1937; Levenson, 1976). A less-frequently explored source for ambiguity about termination is the ubiquitous nature of enactment. If patient and analyst are always "in something or other," it can sometimes seem like they will not get out of that something or other. The patient and analyst may also hold illusions about their ability to get out of this something or other as well.

Among the many versions of uncertainty and ambiguity that the analyst must hold, the ambiguity about when to end analysis is quite demanding. I call it the *countertransference of indeterminacy*, not to reify one more psychoanalytic concept, but to name it so that we can in some sense expect it. There are after all many forms of indeterminacy in analysis with which the analyst struggles (a few versions of the countertransference of indeterminacy), including the array of technical and theoretical choices about how to best help the patient. But, the indeterminacy about how and when to end brings many issues to the fore regarding how ambitious patient and analyst should or want to be, whether they are giving up prematurely, or whether they are avoiding in some way saying good-bye.

This indeterminacy about ending is complicated by the fact that many contemporary analysts see enactment as ubiquitous. Just as conflict is never fully resolved, enactment of conflict never takes a time-out. The "unendingness" of psychoanalysis (another translation of Freud's word *unendliche*) was, in a sense, Freud's (1937) realistic and sobering statement about the unending task of self-understanding. It was also his way of noting the existential indeterminacy of self-knowledge. Contemporary psychoanalysts have more fully acknowledged their participation in and experience of this indeterminacy as they know and are known by their patients.

Levenson (1976) has suggested that ending is often more a matter of aesthetics than technique, likening the decision to end to that of the painter who decides when the work of art is complete. Many an artist is known to say that a work of art is never complete, only released. From the point of view of therapeutic accountability within a treatment situation, it can be disturbing to think about how vague and arbitrary these decisions may seem. Yet, these statements also capture something that feels familiar to me about how murky the decision to stop can be both when the analysis has gone very well and when there are still points of difficulty that might be further resolved. When things have gone well, there is often the sense of pleasure about successful work, accomplishment for the patient and analyst, and a sense of connection. But, it does not mean that the "when" takes on an easily discernible, concrete form, like the curtain drop for a play or the last out in a baseball game. When there is palpable and articulated uncertainty about whether the continued work will be helpful, often the ambiguity about the decision to stop feels rational and objective. Both Bass (2001) and Davies (2005) have articulated the denotations of finality associated with the word *termination* that fail to capture both the ways that endings and beginnings are less distinct and the enduring impact that both patient and analyst have had on each other.

Similarly, Levenson (1976) was probably implying that it may be more accurate to say that the very nature of termination is intrinsically ambiguous, and that some analyses may toil under the notion that there will be more clarity at some point. In some sense, ironically enough, any analytic perspective is most clear to the extent that it appreciates the intrinsic ambiguity of existence. Merleau-Ponty captured this when he said: "Ambiguity is of the essence of human existence. ... Thus there is in human existence a principle of indeterminacy ... and this indeterminacy does not only stem from some imperfection in our knowledge." Perhaps Levenson was implying that termination at its best, for patient and analyst, has incorporated an understanding and acceptance of this indeterminacy.

I have found that issues of ending come in and out of focus for both patient and analyst throughout analytic work (Bass, 2009). When issues of ending come into central focus, they may provide opportunities to work through a wide variety of forms of psychic conflict and accompanying elements of transference-countertransference engagement. Interestingly, analysts are often strikingly concrete about the ways that we listen to feelings and thoughts about termination. Sometimes, we may have a tendency to be overly literal or concrete when a patient expresses a desire to stop both because we want to honor these desires and because, in truth, it is always the patient's decision about when to stop. At other times, we may be too reflexively drawn to thinking about mention of termination as a form of resistance. The analyst's personal anxieties about loss, concern for the patient, narcissistic anxiety about treatment failure, or economic issues may also contribute to a relative collapse in the analyst's reflective capacities about termination.

This raises the question of why we are sometimes less likely to think about the multiplicity of meanings suggested by mention of termination. I am struck by just this type of correctness when James and I began to discuss termination. Even the words, *termination* and *interminable* are so different from a more literal translation of Freud's words as *endingness* and *unendingness*. Sometimes when I am surprised that a patient begins to speak of termination, I try to think about what we are not accomplishing or have not been able to accomplish that may be a source of unrest, sadness, or anger. In other words, the patient may be bringing up termination as a way of saying: "If I can't get more out of this or from you, I'd like to stop." Conversely, sometimes I try to think about what we are accomplishing that might be causing difficulty. For example, a patient might also be expressing something along the lines of the following: "I don't know if I can bear to talk about these feelings anymore."

One reason that we may be more concrete or literal about the meaning of termination than we are about other parts of analysis is because we have an ethical responsibility, as part of our accountability, to honor the decisions of our patients about when that process begins and ends. Psychoanalysis is a contractually arranged form of treatment. But, I suspect that this is the easy explanation. I think it is likely that analysts truncate the process of analytic play—the consideration of multiple meanings—in relation to termination of analysis because of its connection to death. As Hoffman

(1998) has suggested, death is always in the background of analytic work, but during termination it symbolically and affectively moves more into the foreground. Initial discussions of termination often open up how these experiences of ending and mortality are catalyzed.

CONCLUSION: TERMINATION AND THE PSYCHIC FUTURE

It is one thing to say that termination is not a temporally linear process, including as it does an intrinsically ambiguous indeterminacy about the nature of when and why we stop our work and whether we will resume at some point. It is another to say that regarding the patient's experience of time it is a particularly dense and "thick" (Tronick, 2003) period. The patient is coming to grips with a more explicit discussion and imagining of his or her psychic future. While every interpretation imagines a psychic future (e.g., Cooper, 1996; Loewald, 1960) for the patient, termination in a sense embodies this future. We are involved in helping patients to feel that future after analysis, including how the patient will hold the analyst in mind and how the patient imagines that the analyst will hold the patient in mind.

Density is also related to how termination includes many versions of good-bye involving multiple parts of both patient and analyst (e.g., Davies, 2005). It is hoped that some of the patient's identifications and counteridentifications that have been expressed during analysis are also familiar to the analyst during termination, although not always. It is also true that new parts of our patients sometimes emerge at this point. Seen in this light, part of termination is related to the ways in which both patient and analyst try again to move from enactment to self-reflection in the context of far more explicit limitations of both time and possibility.

Once termination has been discussed, the landscape of the patient's psychic future has changed, or often, the beginning of this discussion marks how the patient is already imagining his or her psychic future. Part of the ways that the patient now considers his or her future involve not only that the patient will lose the analyst—lose his or her person and that person's insights about his or her struggles, affects, and conflict—but the patient will also lose the particular forms of analytic accommodation that have become a feature over the course of their work together. A few questions emerge in considering the implications of the loss of the interactive patterns that the patient and analyst have developed together. Will there be and are there other relationships that provide the same opportunities for engagement even in the form of acclimation to particularly demanding parts of being with this patient? In essence, how much have the particular forms of adaptation from the analyst to the patient and, of course, the patient to the analyst left room for the patient to experience him- or herself and the other in a way that feels alive and "real."

Often, when things have gone well, the patient is aware that not everything is resolved, and that this is part of the grief that the patient will experience and explore during termination. In such instances, if aspects of idealization are mourned as well as reality about limitation within both the patient and the analyst, then the psychic future is opened in a way that can be invigorating. However, for patients who still feel a burr under the saddle as they leave analysis—something important that they have not been able to work out with their analyst—the psychic future can be dreadful, terrifying, or depressing. While it is hardly ideal to have an analyst who we feel is not able to help us understand or integrate some important matters, many patients are able to appreciate the ways in which the analyst has helped and struggles to help in new ways. Termination announces a farewell between two people, and ironically, it symbolizes the status of what has changed and not changed within the analytic work. This symbolization is ironic because even though the analytic change process actually continues after formal termination, the initiation of discussion about termination is often experienced as a kind of finality during parts of that process. In the best of circumstances, it catalyzes new attempts to find the burr under the saddle and new modes of understanding.

Naturally, termination is often discussed in terms that are more concretely related to the actual impeding loss of the analyst, and traditionally regression has been conceptualized as occurring in response to that loss. I have tried to suggest that termination also mobilizes an anticipation of the loss of the forms of enactment that have allowed the patient to grow during analysis, but that are not necessarily understood or resolved within the dyad. These enactments partially involve unconscious fantasies about the analyst; thus, termination can pose a threat to the loss of these fantasies as well.

This loss of enacted patterns between patient and analyst is only part of what might be termed a loss of the dyad. It is, of course, difficult to differentiate clearly between the patient's deeply personal experiences of losing the analyst versus a sense of losing the dyad, but I think it is worth trying to consider both. In addition to enacted patterns that comprise the patient's sense of the dyad are the many experiences of empathic resonance, intimacy, and limitation. There is a sense of losing the person of the analyst and, in terms of the loss of the dyad, "the way we were together."

Termination mobilizes the actual experienced discrepancy between habitually enacted relational patterns (interpersonal compromise formations if you will) and the needed, wished-for, and unresolved parts of therapeutic work as the patient begins to feel the loss of analysis and the analyst. When termination comes up as a subject in these circumstances, it is often an acknowledgment of these forms of impasse and marks a moment when analysis will either end in these less-than-optimal circumstances or become a kind of new beginning for the analytic pair.

Since to some extent these enactments are the stuff of all therapeutic work, termination provides another opportunity to revisit these enactments and to grieve the limitations of any analytic process.

References

Adorno, T. (1950). *The authoritarian personality.* New York: Norton, 1969.

Akhtar, S. (1996). Someday and if only fantasies: Pathological optimism and inordinate nostalgic relatedness. *Journal of the American Psychoanalytic Association, 44*, 723–753.

Alexander, F. (1950). Analysis of the therapeutic factors in psychoanalytic treatment. *Psychoanalytic Quarterly, 19*, 482–500.

Alexander, F., & French, T. (1956). *Psychoanalytic therapy: Principles and applications.* New York: Ronald Press.

Altman, N., & Davies, J. (2003). A plea for constructive dialogue. *Journal of the American Psychoanalytic Association, 51*(Suppl.), 145–161.

Anderson, P. (2002). *Punch Drunk Love.* Columbia Pictures.

Aron, L. (1991a). The patient's experience of the analyst's subjectivity. *Psychoanalytic Dialogues, 1*, 29–51.

Aron, L. (1992). Interpretation as expression of the analyst's subjectivity. *Psychoanalytic Dialogues, 2*, 475–507.

Aron, L. (2009a). *What is psychoanalytic process?* Paper presented at the Boston Psychoanalytic Society and Institute 75th Anniversary Conference, Boston, March 28, 2009.

Aron, L. (2009b). Day, night or dawn: Commentary on a paper by Steven Stern. *Psychoanalytic Dialogues, 19*, 656–668.

Aron, L., & Anderson, F. S. (1998). *Relational perspectives on the body.* Hillsdale, NJ: Analytic Press.

Bacal, H. (1993). Sharing femininity—An optimal responsiveness in the analysis of a woman by woman: Commentary on the Shane's case study of Kathy K. In A. Goldberg (Ed.), *The widening scope of self psychology: Progress in self psychology* (Vol. 9, pp. 81–86). Hillsdale, NJ: Analytic Press.

Balint, M. (1968). *The basic fault: Therapeutic aspects of regression.* London: Tavistock.

Bass, A. (1996). Holding, holding back, and holding on. *Psychoanalytic Dialogues, 6*, 361–378.

Bass, A. (2001). It takes one to know one: Or, whose unconscious is it anyway? *Psychoanalytic Dialogues, 11*, 683–703.

Bass, A. (2007). When the frame doesn't fit the picture. *Psychoanalytic Dialogues, 17*, 1–27.

Bass, A. (2009). "It ain't over 'till it's over." Infinite conversations, imperfect endings and the elusive nature of termination. *Psychoanalytic Dialogues, 19,* 744–758.

Beebe, B. (2000). Constructing mother–infant distress: The microsynchrony of maternal impingement and infant avoidance in the face-to-face encounter. *Psychoanalytic Inquiry, 20,* 421–440.

Beckett, S. (1953) *Waiting for Godot: A tragicomedy in two acts.* New York: Grove Press, 1993.

Benjamin, J. (2004). Beyond doer and done to: An intersubjective view of thirdness. *Psychoanalytic Quarterly, 73,* 5–46.

Bergman, M. S. (1997). Termination: The Achilles heel of psychoanalytic technique. *Psychoanalytic Psychology, 14,* 163–174.

Bion, W. R. (1959). Attacks on linking. *International Journal of Psychoanalysis, 40,* 308–315.

Bion, W. R. (1962). *Learning from experience.* London: Heinemann.

Bion, W. R. (1963). *Elements of psychoanalysis.* London: Heinemann.

Bion, W. R. (1967a). Notes on memory and desire. In E. B. Spillius (Ed.), *Melanie Klein today* (Vol. 2, pp. 15–18). London: Routledge.

Bion, W. R. (1967b). *Second thoughts.* New York: Aronson.

Bion, W. R. (1970). *Attention and interpretation.* London: Tavistock.

Bion, W. R. (1978). *Four discussions with W. R. Bion.* Pershire, UK: Clunie Press.

Bird, B. (1972). Notes on transference: Universal phenomenon and hardest part of analysis. *Journal of the American Psychoanalytic Association, 20,* 267–301.

Blechner, M. (2007). Approaches to panic attacks. *Neuro-Psychoanalysis, 9,* 93–102.

Blum, H. (1986). Countertransference and the theory of technique. *Journal of the American Psychoanalytic Association, 34,* 309–328.

Boesky, D. (1990). The psychoanalytic process and its components. *Psychoanalytic Quarterly, 64,* 282–305.

Bollas, C. (1989). *Forces of destiny.* London: Free Association Books.

Bonovitz, C. (2004). The co-creation of fantasy and the transformation of psychic structure. *Psychoanalytic Dialogues, 14,* 553–580.

Brenner, C. (1969). Some comments on technical precepts in psychoanalysis. *Journal of the American Psychoanalytic Association, 17,* 333–352.

Brenner, C. (1976). *Psychoanalytic technique and psychic conflict.* New York: International Universities Press.

Brenner, C. (1982). *The mind in conflict.* New York: International Universities Press.

Brenner, C. (1985). Countertransference as compromise formation. *Psychoanalytic Quarterly, 54,* 155–163.

Brickman, C. (2003). *Aboriginal populations in the mind: Race and primitivity in psychoanalysis.* New York: Columbia University Press.

Britton, R. (1998). *Belief and imagination.* London: Routledge.

Britton, R., & Steiner, J. (1994). Interpretation: Selected fact or overvalued idea? *International Journal of Psychoanalysis, 75,* 1069–1078.

Bromberg, P. (1979). Interpersonal psychoanalysis and regression. *Contemporary Psychoanalysis, 15,* 647–655.

Bromberg, P. (1991). On knowing one's patient inside and out: The aesthetics of unconscious communication. *Psychoanalytic Dialogues, 1,* 399–422.

Bromberg, P. (1995). Resistance, object usage, and human relatedness. *Contemporary Psychoanalysis, 31*, 163–192.

Bromberg, P. (1998). *Standing in the spaces: Essays on clinical process, trauma, and dissociation.* Hillsdale, NJ: Analytic Press

Bromberg, P. (2001). Treating patients with symptoms—and symptoms with patience: Reflections on shame, dissociation, and eating disorders. *Psychoanalytic Dialogues, 11*, 891–912.

Busch, F. (1993). "In the neighborhood": Aspects of a good interpretation and a "developmental lag" in ego psychology. *Journal of the American Psychoanalytic Association, 41*, 151–177.

Canestri, J. (2006). *Psychoanalysis: From practice to theory.* New York: John Wiley & Sons.

Caper, R. (1992). Does psychoanalysis heal? *International Journal of Psychoanalysis, 73*, 283–292.

Caper, R. (1997). A mind of one's own. *International Journal of Psychoanalysis, 78*, 265–278.

Cather, W. (20078). *O pioneers!* Oxford, MA: Oxford University Press.

Chasseguet-Smirgel, J. (1985). *The ego ideal: A psychoanalytic essay on the malady of the idea.* London: Free Association Books.

Coen, S. (2002). *Affect intolerance in patient and therapist.* Northvale, NJ: Aronson.

Coleridge, S. (1834). *S. T. Coleridge: Interviews and recollections* (S. Perry, Ed.). London: Palgrave Macmillan, 2005.

Compton, A. (1988, December). The idea of a psychoanalytic process. In *COPE-PAP*.

Cooper, S. (1989). Recent contributions to the theory of defense mechanisms: A comparative view. *Journal of the American Psychoanalytic Association, 37*, 865–891.

Cooper, S. (1993). Interpretive fallibility and the psychoanalytic dialogue. *Journal of the American Psychoanalytic Association, 41*, 95–126.

Cooper, S. (1996). Facts all come with a point of view. *International Journal of Psychoanalysis, 77*, 255–273.

Cooper, S. (1997). The future of interpretation. *International Journal of Psychoanalysis, 78*, 667–681.

Cooper, S. (1998a). Analyst-subjectivity, analyst-disclosure, and the aims of psycho-analysis. *Psychoanalytic Quarterly, 67*, 379–406.

Cooper, S. (1998b). Countertransference disclosure and the conceptualization of technique. *Psychoanalytic Quarterly, 67*, 128–154.

Cooper, S. (2000a). Mutual containment in the psychoanalytic process. *Psycho-analytic Dialogues, 10*, 166–189.

Cooper, S. (2000b). *Objects of hope: Exploring possibility and limit in psychoanaly-sis.* Hillsdale, NJ: Analytic Press.

Cooper, S. (2004a). Psychoanalysis preparatory to psychotherapy: The ambigu-ity of reflection when patients return to psychoanalysis. *Contemporary Psychoanalysis, 40*, 557–576.

Cooper, S. (2004b). State of the hope: The new bad object and the therapeutic action of psychoanalysis. *Psychoanalytic Dialogues, 14*, 527–553.

Cooper, S. (2007a). Alexander's corrective emotional experience: An objectivist turn in psychoanalytic authority and technique. *Psychoanalytic Quarterly, 76*, 1085–1102.

Cooper, S. (2007b). Begin the beguine: Relational theory and the pluralistic third. *Psychoanalytic Dialogues, 17*(2), 247–272.

Cooper, S. (2007c). The patient's and the analyst's victimization in the analytic process. *Contemporary Psychoanalysis, 43,* 621–637.

Cooper, S. (2008). Privacy, reverie, and the analyst's ethical imagination. *Psychoanalytic Quarterly, 77,* 1045–1073.

Cooper, S. (2009). What is psychoanalytic process? Paper presented at the Boston Psychoanalytic Society and Institute, 75th Anniversary Conference, Boston, March 28, 2009.

Cooper, S., & Levit, D. (1998). Old and new objects in Fairbairnian and American relational theory. *Psychoanalytic Dialogues, 8,* 603–624.

Curtis, H. (1990). The patient as existential victim: A classical view. *Psychoanalytic Inquiry, 10,* 498–508.

Davies, J. (1994). Love in the afternoon: A relational consideration of desire and dread in the countertransference. *Psychoanalytic Dialogues, 4,* 153–170.

Davies, J. (1998). Between the disclosure and foreclosure of erotic transference-countertransference: Can psychoanalysis find a place for adult sexuality? *Psychoanalytic Dialogues, 8,* 747–766.

Davies, J. (2004). Whose bad objects are we anyway? Repetition and our elusive love affair with evil. *Psychoanalytic Dialogues, 14,* 711–732.

Davies, J. (2005). Transformations of desire and despair: Reflections on the termination process from a relational perspective. *Psychoanalytic Dialogues, 15,* 779–805.

Didion, J. (2006). *The year of magical thinking.* New York: Random House.

Dostoyefsky, F. (1880). *The brothers Karamazov.* New York: Farrar, Strauss & Giroux, 2002.

Dylan, B. (1989). The man in the long black coat. In *Oh Mary,* New York: Sony.

Eggars, D. (2000). *A heartbreaking work of staggering genius.* New York: Simon and Schuster.

Ehrenberg, D. (1982). Psychoanalytic engagement: The transaction as primary data. *Contemporary Psychoanalysis, 18,* 535–555.

Ehrenberg, D. (1992). *The intimate edge: Extending the reach of psychoanalytic interaction.* New York: Norton.

Epstein, L., & Feiner, A. (1979). *Countertransference: The therapist's contribution to the therapeutic situation.* New York: Aronson.

Fairbairn, W. R. D. (1952). *Psychoanalytic studies of the personality.* London: Routledge.

Feldman, M. (1997). Projective identification: The analyst's involvement. *International Journal of Psychoanalysis, 78,* 227–241.

Ferenczi, S. (1909). Introjection and transference. In *Contributions to psychoanalysis* (pp. 35–93). New York: Basic Books.

Ferenczi, S. (1927). The problem of termination of the analysis. In M. Balint (Ed.) and E. Mosbacher (Trans.), *Final contributions to the problems and methods of psycho-analysis* (pp. 77–86). London: Hogarth Press, 1955.

Ferenczi, S. (1988). *The clinical diaries of Sándor Ferenczi* (J. Dupont, Ed. & Trans.). Cambridge, MA: Harvard University Press.

Ferro, A. (2005). *Seeds of illness, seeds of recovery: The genesis of suffering and the role of psychoanalysis* (P. Slotkin, Trans.). London: Routledge.

Foehl, J. (2008). Personal communication.

Fonagy, P. (2006). The failure of practice to inform theory and the role of implicit theory in bridging the transmission gap. In J. Canestri (Ed.), *Psychoanalysis: From practice to theory*. New York: John Wiley & Sons.

Freeman, W. (1994). *Societies of brains*. Hillsdale, NJ: Erlbaum.

Freud, S. (1907). Letter from Sigmund Freud to C. G. Jung, July 1, 1907. In W. McGuire (Ed.) and R. Hull (Trans.), *The Freud/Jung letters: The correspondence between Sigmund Freud and C. G. Jung* (pp. 68–71). Princeton, NJ: Princeton University Press, 1994.

Freud, S. (1909). Letter from Sigmund Freud to C. G. Jung, November 21, 1909. In W. McGuide (Ed.) and R. Hull (Trans.), *The Freud/Jung letters: The correspondence between Sigmund Freud and C. G. Jung* (pp. 265–267). Princeton, NJ: Princeton University Press, 1994.

Freud, S. (1910a). Five lectures on psycho-analysis. In J. Strachey (Ed. & Trans.), *The standard edition of the complete psychological works of Sigmund Freud* (Vol. 11, pp. 3–55). London: Hogarth Press.

Freud, S. (1910b). Leonardo da Vinci and a memory of his childhood. In J. Strachey (Ed. & Trans.), *The standard edition of the complete psychological works of Sigmund Freud* (Vol. 11, pp. 59–137). London: Hogarth Press.

Freud, S. (1910c). "Wild" psycho-analysis. In J. Strachey (Ed. & Trans.), *The standard edition of the complete psychological works of Sigmund Freud* (Vol. 11, pp. 221–233). London: Hogarth Press.

Freud, S. (1912). Recommendations to physicians practicing psychoanalysis. In J. Strachey (Ed. & Trans.), *The standard edition of the complete psychological works of Sigmund Freud* (Vol. 12, pp. 109–120). London: Hogarth Press.

Freud, S. (1914). *On narcissism*. In J. Strachey (Ed. & Trans.), *The standard edition of the complete psychological works of Sigmund Freud* (Vol. 14, pp. 67–102). London: Hogarth Press.

Freud, S. (1918). From the history of an infantile neurosis. In J. Strachey (Ed. & Trans.), *The standard edition of the complete psychological works of Sigmund Freud* (Vol. 17, pp. 3–124). London: Hogarth Press.

Freud, S. (1920). The ego and the id. In J. Strachey (Ed. & Trans.), *The standard edition of the complete psychological works of Sigmund Freud* (Vol. 19, pp. 3–68). London: Hogarth Press.

Freud, S. (1927). The question of lay analysis. In J. Strachey (Ed. & Trans.), *The standard edition of the complete psychological works of Sigmund Freud* (Vol. 20, pp. 183–199). London: Hogarth Press.

Freud, S. (1937). Analysis terminable and interminable. In J. Strachey (Ed. & Trans.), *The standard edition of the complete psychological works of Sigmund Freud* (Vol. 23, pp. 211–253). London: Hogarth Press.

Freud, S. (1954). The origins of psycho-analysis. In M. Bonaparte, A. Freud, & E. Kris (Eds.), *Letters to Wilhelm Fliess, drafts and notes, 1887–1902*. New York: Basic Books.

Ghent, E. (1990). Masochism, submission, surrender: Masochism as a perversion of surrender. *Contemporary Psychoanalysis, 26*, 108–136.

Gill, M. (1954) Psychoanalysis and psychoanalytic psychotherapy. *Journal of the American Psychoanalytical Association, 2*, 771–797.

Gill, M. (1979). The analysis of transference. *Journal of the American Psychoanalytic Association, 27*, 263–288.

Gill, M. (1982). *The analysis of transference, vol. 1: Theory and technique.* New York: International Universities Press.

Gill, M. (1983). The interpersonal paradigm and the degree of the therapist's involvement. *Contemporary Psychoanalysis, 19,* 200–237.

Gill, M. (1984) Psychoanalysis and psychotherapy: A revision. *The International Review of Psychoanalysis, 11,* 161–179.

Gill, M. (1994). *Psychoanalysis in transition.* Hillsdale, NJ: Analytic Press

Glover, E. (1937a). Report of the 14th International Psycho-Analytical Congress. *Bulletin of the International Psychoanalytic Association, 18,* 72–107.

Glover, E. (1937b). Symposium on the theory of the therapeutic results of psychoanalysis. *International Journal of Psychoanalysis, 18,* 125–132.

Goffman, E. (1961). *Asylums: Essays on the social situation of mental patients and other inmates.* New York: Random House.

Goldberg, S. H. (1991). Patients' theories of pathogenesis. *Psychoanalytic Quarterly, 60,* 245–275.

Gray, P. (1973). Psychoanalytic technique: The ego's capacity to view intrapsychic activity. *Journal of the American Psychoanalytic Association, 21,* 474–492.

Gray, P. (1990). The nature of therapeutic action in psychoanalysis. *Journal of the American Psychoanalytic Association, 38,* 1083–1099.

Greenberg, J. (1986). Theoretical models and the analyst's neutrality. *Contemporary Psychoanalysis, 6,* 87–106.

Greenberg, J. (1995). Psychoanalytic technique and the interactive matrix. *Psychoanalytic Quarterly, 64,* 1–22.

Greenson, R. (1974). Loving, hating and indifference toward the patient. *International Review of Psychoanalysis, 1,* 259–266.

Grotstein, J. (2005). Projective identification and projective transidentification: A reassessment and extension of the concept. *International Journal of Psychoanalysis, 86,* 1051–1069.

Guntrip, H. (1968). *Schizoid phenomena, object relations and the self.* New York: International Universities Press.

Guntrip, H. (1971). *Psychoanalytic theory, therapy and the self.* New York: Basic Books.

Harris, A. (2008). Self-care. *Psychoanalytic Dialogues.*

Herzog, J. (2004). Father hunger and narcissistic deformation. *Psychoanalytic Quarterly, 73,* 893–914.

Herzog, J. (2005). Triadic reality and the capacity to love. *Psychoanalytic Quarterly, 74,* 1029–1052.

Hoffman, I. (1983). The patient as interpreter of the analyst's experience. *Contemporary Psychoanalysis, 19,* 389–422.

Hoffman, I. (1991). Discussion: Toward a social-constructivist view of the psychoanalytic situation. *Psychoanalytic Dialogues, 1,* 74–105.

Hoffman, I. (1994). Dialectical thinking and therapeutic action in the psychoanalytic process. *Psychoanalytic Quarterly, 63,* 187–218.

Hoffman, I. (1996). The intimate and ironic authority of the psychoanalyst's presence. *Psychoanalytic Quarterly, 65,* 102–136.

Hoffman, I. (1998). *Ritual and spontaneity in psychoanalysis: A dialectical-constructivist view.* Hillsdale, NJ: Analytic Press.

Hoffman, I. (2006). The myths of free association and the potentials of the analytic relationship. *International Journal of Psychoanalysis, 87,* 43–61.

Hoffman, I. (2009). Therapeutic passion in the countertransference. *Psychoanalytic Dialogues, 19,* 617–637.

Hurston, Z. (1937). *Their eyes were watching God.* New York: Lippincott.

Jacobi, R. (1983). *The repression of psychoanalysis.* New York: Basic Books.

Jacobs, T. (1990). The corrective emotional experience. *Psychoanalytic Inquiry, 10,* 433–454.

Joseph, B. (1989). Transference: The total situation. In M. Feldman & E. B. Spillius (Eds.), *Psychic equilibrium and psychic change* (pp. 157–168). London: Routledge.

Josephs, L. (2003). Seduced by affluence: How material envy strains the analytic relationship. *Contemporary Psychoanalysis, 40,* 389–408.

Kernberg, O. (1975). *Borderline conditions and pathological narcissism.* New York: Aronson.

Kernberg, O. (1993). Convergences and divergences in contemporary psychoanalytic technique. *International Journal of Psychoanalysis, 74,* 659–673.

Kernberg, O. (1996). Thirty methods to destroy the creativity of psychoanalytic candidates. *International Journal of Psychoanalysis, 77,* 1031–1040.

Khan, M. (1970). Towards an epistemology of cure. In *The privacy of the self.* New York: International Universities Press.

Khan, M. (1973). The role of illusion in the analytic apace and process. *Annals of Psychoanalysis, 1,* 231–246.

Klauber, J. (1972). On the relationship of transference and interpretation in psychoanalytic therapy. *International Journal of Psychoanalysis, 53,* 385–391.

Klauber, J. (1977). Analyses that cannot be terminated. *International Journal of Psychoanalysis, 58,* 473–477.

Kohut, H. (1966). Forms and transformations of narcissism. *Journal of the American Psychoanalytic Association, 14,* 243–272.

Kohut, H. (1968). The psychoanalytic treatment of narcissistic personality disorder—Outline of a systematic approach. *Psychoanalytic Study of the Child, 23,* 86–113.

Kohut, H. (1969). *The analysis of the self.* New York: International Universities Press.

Kohut, H. (1984). *How does analysis cure?* (A. Goldberg & P. Stepansky, Eds.). Chicago: University of Chicago Press.

Kris, A. (1977). Either-or dilemmas. *Psychoanalytic Study of the Child, 32,* 91–117.

Kris, A. (1982). *Free association.* New Haven: Yale University Press.

Kris, A. (1990). Helping patients by analyzing self-criticism. *Journal of the American Psychoanalytic Association, 38,* 605–636.

Levenson, E. (1976). The aesthetics of termination. *Contemporary Psychoanalysis, 12,* 338–341.

Levenson, E. (1991). The purloined self. *Journal of the American Academy of Psychoanalysis and Dynamic Psychiatry, 15,* 481–490.

Loewald, H. (1960). On the therapeutic action of psychoanalysis. *International Journal of Psychoanalysis, 41,* 16–33.

Marks-Tarlow, T (1999). The self as a dynamical system. *Nonlinear Dynamics, Psychology and Life Sciences, 3*(4), 311–345.

Marks-Tarlow, T. (2009). Nonlinear science in the art of psychoanalysis. *Psychologist-Psychoanalyst.*

Marshall, K. (2000). Termination of an "infinite conversation": Reflections on the last days of an analysis. *Psychoanalytic Dialogues, 10,* 931–947.

McLaughlin, J. (1981). Transference, psychic reality, and countertransference. *Psychoanalytic Quarterly, 50,* 639–664.

Menand, L. (2001). *The metaphysical club: A story of ideas in America.* New York: Farrar, Straus & Giroux.

Mendelsohn, E. (2002). The analyst's bad-enough participation. *Psychoanalytic Dialogues, 12,* 331–358.

Merleau-Ponty, M. (1964). *The primacy of perception.* Evanston, IL: Northwestern University Press.

Mitchell, S. (1988). *Relational concepts in psychoanalysis.* Cambridge, MA: Harvard University Press.

Mitchell, S. (1991). Wishes, needs and interpersonal negotiations. *Psychoanalytic Inquiry, 11,* 147–171.

Mitchell, S. (1993). Reply to Bachant and Richards. *Psychoanalytic Dialogues, 3,* 461–480.

Mitchell, S. (1995). Interaction in the interpersonal and Kleinian models. *Contemporary Psychoanalysis, 31,* 65–91.

Mitchell, S. (1997). *Influence and autonomy in psychoanalysis.* Hillsdale, NJ: Analytic Press.

Mitchell, S. (2002). *Can love last? The fate of romance over time.* New York: Norton.

Modell, A. (1976). The holding environment and the therapeutic action of psychoanalysis. *Journal of the American Psychoanalytic Association, 24,* 285–307.

Morrison, A. (1994). The breadth and boundaries of a self-psychological immersion in shame: A one-and-a-half person perspective. *Psychoanalytic Dialogues, 4,* 19–35.

Nacht, S. (1963). The non-verbal relationship in psycho-analytic treatment. *International Journal of Psychoanalysis, 44,* 334–339.

Ogden, T. (1994a). The analytic third: Working with intersubjective clinical facts. *International Journal of Psychoanalysis, 75,* 3–20.

Ogden, T. (1994b). Psychoanalysis and interpretive action. *Psychoanalytic Quarterly, 63,* 219–245.

Ogden, T. (1996). Reconsidering three aspects of psychoanalytic technique. *International Journal of Psychoanalysis, 77,* 883–899.

Ogden, T. (1997a). Reverie and interpretation: Henry James (1884). *Psychoanalytic Quarterly, 66,* 567–595.

Ogden, T. (1997b). Reverie and metaphor. *International Journal of Psychoanalysis, 78,* 719–732.

Ogden, T. (1999). The music of what happens in poetry and psychoanalysis. *International Journal of Psychoanalysis, 80,* 979–994.

Ogden, T. (2004). The analytic third: Implications for psychoanalytic theory and technique. *Psychoanalytic Quarterly, 73,* 167–196.

Ornstein, A. (1995). The fate of the curative fantasy in the psychoanalytic treatment process. *Contemporary Psychoanalysis, 31,* 113.

Parsons, M. (2006). The analyst's countertransference to the psychoanalytic process. *International Journal of Psychoanalysis*, 87, 1183–1196.

Perrotta, T. (2006). *Little children*. New York: St. Martin's Press.

Pine, F. (2006). The psychoanalytic dictionary. *Journal of the American Psychoanalytic Association*, 54, 463–492.

Racker, H. (1968). *Transference and countertransference*. New York: International Universities Press.

Rafelson, B. (1970). *Five Easy Pieces*. Columbia Pictures.

Renik, O. (1993). Analytic interaction: Conceptualizing technique in light of the analyst's irreducible subjectivity. *Psychoanalytic Quarterly*, 62, 553–571.

Renik, O. (1995). The ideal of the anonymous analyst and the problem of self-disclosure. *Psychoanalytic Quarterly*, 64, 466–495.

Ricoeur, P. (1970). *Freud and philosophy: An essay on interpretation*. New Haven: Yale University Press.

Ringstrom, P. (2001, April). Panel discussion. First International Relational Association Conference Meeting, New York.

Robinson, J. G. (Producer), & Shadyac, T. (Director). (1994). *Ace Ventura: Pet Detective* [Motion picture]. United States: Morgan Creek Productions.

Rothstein, A. (2005). Compromise formation theory: An intersubjective dimension. *Psychoanalytic Dialogues*, 15, 415–431.

Russell, P. (1985). The negotiation of affect. Unpublished manuscript.

Rycroft, C. (1962). Beyond the reality principle. In C. Rycroft (Ed.), *Imagination and reality* (1968, pp. 102–113). London: Hogarth Press.

Sandel, M. (2004, April). The case against perfection: What's wrong with designer children, bionic athletes, and genetic engineering. *Atlantic Monthly*, 50–63.

Sandler, J. (1976). Countertransference and role-responsiveness. *International Journal of Psychoanalysis*, 3, 43–50.

Sandler, J., & Sandler, A. (1994). Theoretical and technical comments on regression and anti-regression. *International Journal of Psychoanalysis*, 75, 431–439.

Schafer, R. (1983). *The analytic attitude*. New York: Basic Books.

Schafer, R. (1990). The search for common ground. *International Journal of Psychoanalysis*, 71, 49–52.

Schwaber, E. (1992). The analyst's retreat from the patient's vantage point. *International Journal of Psychoanalysis*, 73, 349–361.

Searles, H. (1979). *Countertransference and related subjects*. Madison, CT: International Universities Press.

Seligman, S. (2005). Dynamic systems theories as a metaframework for psychoanalysis. *Psychoanalytic Dialogues*, 15, 285–319.

Shakespeare, W. (1963). *Othello*. New York: Signet Classics.

Slavin, M., & Kriegman, D. (1998). Why the analyst needs to change: Toward a theory of conflict, negotiation, and mutual influence in the therapeutic process. *Psychoanalytic Dialogues*, 8, 247–284.

Slochower, J. (1996). Holding the fate of the analyst's subjectivity. *Psychoanalytic Dialogues*, 6, 323–353.

Slochower, J. (2003). The analyst's secret delinquencies. *Psychoanalytic Dialogues*, 13, 451–470.

Smith, H. (1990). Cues: The perceptual edge of the transference. *International Journal of Psychoanalysis*, 71, 219–228.

Smith, H. (2000). Countertransference, conflictual listening, and the analytic object relationship. *Journal of the American Psychoanalytic Association, 48*, 95–128.

Smith, H. (2003). Can we integrate the diverse theories and practices of psycho-analysis? *Journal of the American Psychoanalytic Association, 51*(Suppl.), 145–161.

Smith, H. (2004). The analyst's fantasy of the ideal patient. *Psychoanalytic Quarterly, 73*, 627–658.

Spence, D. (1988). A discussion. In A. Rothstein (Ed.), *How does treatment help? On the modes of therapeutic action in psychoanalytic therapy*. Madison, CT: International Universities Press.

Steiner, J. (1993). *Psychic retreats*. London: Routledge.

Steiner, J. (2008). Transference to the analyst as an excluded observer. *International Journal of Psychoanalysis, 89*, 39–53.

Stern, D. (1983). Unformulated experience. *Contemporary Psychoanalysis, 19*, 71–99.

Stern, D. (1992). Commentary on constructivism in clinical psychoanalysis. *Contemporary Psychoanalysis, 28*, 331–363.

Stern, D. (1997). *Unformulated experience: From dissociation to imagination in psy-choanalysis*. Hillsdale, NJ: Analytic Press.

Stern, D. (2004). The eye sees itself: Dissociation, enactment, and the achievement of conflict. *Contemporary Psychoanalysis, 40*, 197–237.

Stern, D. (2009). *Partners in thought*. London: Routledge Press.

Stern, S. (2009). Session frequency and the definition of psychoanalysis. *Psychoanalytic Dialogues, 19*, 639–655.

Stone, L. (1961). *The psychoanalytic situation*. New York: International Universities Press.

Strachey, J. (1934). On the therapeutic action of psycho-analysis. *International Journal of Psychoanalysis, 50*, 275–292.

Strenger, C. (1989). The classic and romantic vision in psychoanalysis. *International Journal of Psychoanalysis, 70*, 593–602.

Summers, F. (2003). The future as intrinsic to the psyche and psychoanalytic therapy. *Contemporary Psychoanalysis, 39*, 135–153.

Symington, N. (1983). The analyst's act of freedom as agent of therapeutic change. *International Review of Psychoanalysis, 10*, 283–291.

Tansey, M. J., & Burke, W. F. (1989). *Understanding countertransference: From pro-jective identification to empathy*. Hillsdale, NJ: Analytic Press.

Teicholz, J. (2006). Qualities of engagement and the analyst's theory. *International Journal of Psychoanalytic Self Psychology, 1*, 47–77.

The thousand and one nights: The portable Arabian nights (J. Payne, Trans.). (1952). New York: Viking.

Todd, S., Moore, D., Todd, J., & Myers, M. (Producers), & Roach, J. (Director). (2001). *Austin Powers: International Man of Mystery* [Motion picture]. United States: New Line Cinema.

Tronick, E. (2001). Emotional connections and dyadic consciousness in infant-mother and patient-therapist interactions. *Psychoanalytic Dialogues, 11*, 187–194.

Tronick, E. (2003). "Of course all relationships are unique": How co-creative processes generate unique mother-infant and patient-therapist relationships and change other relationships. *Psychoanalytic Inquiry, 23*, 473–491.

Valenstein, A. (1972). On attachment to painful feelings and the negative therapeutic reaction. *The Psychoanalytic Study of the Child, 28*, 365–394.

Verdi, G. (1887) *Otello*. Italian libretto by Arrigo Biota.

Vogler, C. (1992). *The writer's journey: Mythic structure for storytellers and screenwriters*. New York: Michael Wiese Film Productions.

Volkan, V. (1973). Transitional fantasies in the analysis of a narcissistic person. *Journal of the American Psychoanalytic Association, 21*, 351–376.

Wallerstein, R. (1989). Psychoanalysis and psychotherapy: An historical perspective. *International Journal of Psychoanalysis, 70*, 563–591.

Wallerstein, R. (1990). The corrective emotional experience: Is reconsideration due? *Psychoanalytic Inquiry, 10*, 288–324.

Weinshel, E. (1984). Some observation on the psychoanalytic process. *Psychoanalytic Quarterly, 53*, 63–92.

Weinshel, E. (1990). Further observations on the psychoanalytic process. *Psychoanalytic Quarterly, 59*, 629–649.

Winnicott, D. (1951). Transitional objects and transitional phenomena. In *Collected papers* (pp. 229–242). New York: Basic Books, 1958.

Winnicott, D. (1958). The capacity to be alone. In *The maturational processes and the facilitating environment*. New York: International Universities Press.

Winnicott, D. (1962). Ego integration in child development. In *The maturational process and the facilitating environment* (pp. 37–55). New York: International Universities Press, 1965.

Winnicott, D. (1963). Communicating and not communicating leading to study of certain opposites. In *The maturational process and the facilitating environment*. New York: International Universities Press.

Winnicott, D. (1965). Child analysis in the latency period. Republished in D. W. Winnicott (1965). *The maturational processes and the facilitating environment* (pp. 115–123). New York: International University Press.

Winnicott, D. (1969). The use of an object and relating through identifications. In *Playing and reality*. New York: Basic Books, 1971.

Winnicott, D. (1974). Fear of breakdown. *International Review of Psychoanalysis, 1*, 103–107.

Wolff-Bernstein, J. (1999). Countertransference: Our new royal road to the unconscious? *Psychoanalytic Dialogues, 9*, 275–299.

Index